Karl Marx,
Romantic Irony, and the Proletariat

Karl Marx Romantic Irony and the Proletariat

THE MYTHOPOETIC ORIGINS

OF MARXISM

Leonard P. Wessell, Jr.

Louisiana State University Press
Baton Rouge and London

Design: Robert L. Nance
Typeface: VIP Bembo
Composition: LSU Press

Library of Congress Cataloging in Publication Data
Wessell, Leonard P, Jr 1939–
    Karl Marx, romantic irony, and the proletariat.

    Includes 19 poems by K. Marx, translated into English by L. P. Wessell.
    Bibliography: p.
    Includes index
    1. Marx, Karl, 1818–1883.   2. Proletariat.   3. Irony.   4. Romanticism—
Germany.   I. Title.
HX39.5.W46   335.4′092′4   79–12386
ISBN 0–8071–0587–2

The author wishes to thank the National Endowment for the Humanities and the Council on Research and Creative Work of the University of Colorado for support which made the research and preparation of this investigation possible.

Published with the assistance of a grant from the National Endowment for the Humanities.

To my father,
Commander Leonard P. Wessell, Sr.,
whose understanding of the
human soul has always
amazed me

CONTENTS

NOTE ON TRANSLATION

*A*ll translations from the German or French, unless otherwise noted, are my own. As much as possible I have checked my translations against those given in *Writings of the Young Marx on Philosophy and Society,* ed. and trans. Loyd D. Easton and Kurt H. Guddat (Garden City: Anchor Books, 1967), and *Karl Marx–Friedrich Engels: Collected Works* (New York: International Publishers, 1975). Often I have found myself in substantial agreement with one or the other translation. However, both sets of translations appear to have sought to render Marx's often lengthy and contorted German into a more flowing, lucid English. I have translated literally, however, even to the extent of offering translations that are lengthy, awkward, and sometimes dense. My intent in this has been to reflect more faithfully Marx's diffuse and billowy style than do more flowing renderings.

Karl Marx,
Romantic Irony, and the Proletariat

I
Introduction:
Marx as Romantic Poet

Karl Marx a poet? A *romantic* poet? What a contradiction! What has poetry to do with the founder of "scientific socialism"? I would venture to reply: a great deal! Indeed, it is my contention that Marx's version of "scientific socialism" is essentially a metamorphized poetry, that his "discovery" of the proletariat—a key element in the edifice of scientific socialism—had its impetus in Marx's early poetic interests of 1836 and 1837. The proletariat, in my judgment, constitutes the incarnation of one of German Romanticism's most important concepts, namely irony. The proletariat is irony made flesh, and this alone grounds its emancipatory powers. In short, the proletariat is the "actual" form that poetry must assume if it is to be realized within society.

The image of Marx deserves pondering. It is disconcerting enough to learn that Marx wrote poetry, let alone flirted with the idea of becoming a poet. These facts do not fit our image of Marx as a hardheaded thinker, as author of the dry though brilliant economic critique *Das Kapital*. Yet it is also consoling to acknowledge that Marx was not just a thinking machine, that he was quite human. The mature and "scientific" Marx was a stylist of no mean ability. Like most great thinkers, Marx exhibited some degree of artistic creativity. Even in *Kapital* we frequently encounter startling metaphors. One could, therefore, like Franz Mehring (Marx's Marxist biographer), simply view the poems as an early if not immature manifestation of Marx's predictable artistic capacity.[1] Accordingly,

1. Cf. Mehring's introduction to *Aus dem literarischen Nachlass von Karl Marx und Friedrich Engels 1841–1850*, ed. Franz Mehring (3rd ed., 4 vols.; Stuttgart, 1920), I, 25–28.

the poems would not be worthy of more than momentary consideration (which was precisely the extent of Mehring's comments) and would play no essential role in Marx's "scientific" ratiocinations.

It may seem quite a leap to argue from the fact that Marx wrote some romantic poems that his scientific socialism and the proletariat are transformed poetry. But most serious readers would surely agree that poetry is a great deal more than words organized according to rhyme, rhythm, and meter. It can denote something more fundamental, something grounded in the nature of man. Pulitzer prize-winning cultural anthropologist Ernest Becker begins his comprehensive science of man from the position that man is, before all else, a *Homo poeta*, that he has an inherent urge to create meaning, to dramatize his existence. "This thesis . . . answers the fundamental question about what man is doing in his world, the activity that differentiates him from other animals in the most characteristic way."[2]

The process of creating value is simultaneously the process of objectifying it. Man comes to possess meaning by *perceiving* it as it is embodied in his surroundings, be they material or social. If this is true, then human culture itself (and culture is perhaps man's most ambitious creation of value) is a system of objectified values. An individual who feels meaningfully integrated with his culture, with the cosmos, is one who can, so to speak, "read" the objective world as "words" of a meaning-system. Speaking broadly, reality *becomes* a poem. The objective world becomes a symbolic universe that legitimizes the individual's existence.[3] An objectivity that can be read as signifying the validity of human existence is, indeed, poetry. It is that which *Homo poeta* strives to create and to perceive. Therefore, the poetic, in its deepest sense, is concerned not so much with language as with meaning.

The analogy between poetry and man's symbolic universe can be carried a step further. When meaning has been externalized or incarnated into a material medium, it becomes empirically perceivable.

2. Cf. Ernest Becker, *The Structure of Evil: An Essay on the Unification of the Science of Man* (New York, 1968), 174.

3. Cf. Peter Berger and Thomas Luckmann, *The Social Construction of Reality: A Treatise in the Sociology of Knowledge* (Garden City, 1967), 104.

A symbolic system cannot proclaim the reality of human meaning-fulness simply as an abstract idea in the mind of an individual. Meaning can be socially mediated only by means of an empirical vehicle.[4] This is, in the broadest sense, aesthetic mediation. Writing about the aesthetic object, G. W. F. Hegel asserts: "In art these sensuous shapes and tones are not offered as exclusively for themselves and their form to our direct vision. They are presented with the intent to secure in such shape satisfaction for higher and more spiritual interests. In this way the sensuous is spiritualized in art, or, in other words, the life of spirit comes to dwell in it under sensuous guise."[5] According to Hegel, then, the empirical, when spiritualized, enters human consciousness as an aesthetic experience. The embodiment of a meaning-system as a formative principle into a sensuous medium transforms this objectivity into an aesthetic object. This principle holds not only for art objects in the strict sense, but also for society or the cosmos in a more vital sense. A spiritualized cosmos exhibits aesthetic qualities. The poetic as an anthropological principle is extremely important for the comprehension of human creativity and human creations.

This general anthropological truth was not lost on German Romantics. For such poets as Friedrich Schlegel and Friedrich von Hardenburg (known best as Novalis), poetry "appears to be a certain faculty of the human mind belonging to man's very essence, like reason or imagination . . . [and] is [also] presented as a cosmic principle comparable to the world-soul that animates the whole universe."[6] Convinced that a poetic energy lies at the heart of reality, these Romantics argued that reality was poetry—a cosmic or divine force that objectifies itself as nature and thereby "talks," proclaims itself to man. Novalis put it thus: "Poetry is the genuinely, absolutely real. This is the heart of my philosophy. The more poetic, the more true" (S, II, 647). Friedrich Schlegel was even more terse: "No

---

4. Concerning the sociological ramifications of combining meaning with a vehicle, see Pitirim A. Sorokin, *Social and Cultural Dynamics* (4 vols.; New York, 1962), IV, 3–44.

5. G. W. F. Hegel, *The Philosophy of Fine Art*, trans. F. P. B. Osmatson (4 vols.; London, 1920), I, 53.

6. Cf. Ernst Behler, "Introduction" to *Friedrich Schlegel: Dialogue on Poetry and Literary Aphorisms*, trans. Ernst Behler and Roman Struc (University Park / London, 1968), 15.

poetry, no reality" (KA, II, 227). The real is poetic, and the poetic is real. This is the underlying premise of German Romanticism.

Poetry for German Romanticism was both an anthropological and a cosmic principle. In Novalis' words, "Poets and priests were one in the beginning—only later times have separated them. The genuine poet is always a priest, just as the genuine priest has always remained a poet—and should not the future bring back again the old condition of things" (S, II, 444, 446). The poet has the essentially priestly task of making himself and others aware of the poetic nature of reality. The poet-priest accomplishes this by means of his poetic work. It is not too farfetched to say that the poetic creation is something like the Bible. As God reveals himself for the Christian through the Bible, so the cosmic poet reveals himself through the poem of the romantic poet. For German Romanticism, thus, the poem—as verse or prose— has the essentially religious task of uncovering the meaningful heart of reality for man.

Franz Mehring rather cavalierly referred to Marx's poems as "romantische Harfenklänge" (romantic harp-tones).[7] Mehring correctly contends that Marx's ballads, or songs about elves, maidens, knights, sirens were lacking in "romantischer Zauber" (romantic charm or magic). What Mehring failed to see was that this lack reflects not a dearth of talent so much as the ominous crisis evident in late Romanticism. It is indeed an irony of history that Marxism, which has its roots in a poetic vision, so often renders its adherents insensitive to the function of the poetic in human psychology. But this only testifies to the creative genius of Marx, who embedded a poetic vision so deeply within "scientific" terminology that many of his followers were and are unaware of it. In my judgment, Marx too was a victim of his own creative magic.

The fact that Marx wrote "romantic harp-tones" cannot be overlooked automatically, or relegated to the realm of the incidental biography. If, as I have suggested, the poetic is a fundamental ingredient in man's nature, and if poetry explicitly possessed cosmic and salvational meaning for German Romanticism, the student of Marx must hesitate before deciding that Marx's poetic endeavors were

7. Cf. Mehring (ed.), *Aus dem literarischen Nachlass*, I, 26.

nothing but the momentary exuberances of a somewhat love-sick youth. It is of course possible that Marx's poems are only superficial manifestations of the fleeting emotions of a young man, in which case they would be quite secondary concerns. It is also possible, though, that the poems are significant statements about the nature of reality for the young Marx—in which case, the poems would be crucial to one's comprehension of Marx's evolving thought. The ensuing investigation of Marx's poems can be viewed as a sustained reflection upon this latter possibility. It is my contention that Marx's romantic phase contributed significantly to the formulation of the basic problem he sought to solve throughout his life. Indeed, I will argue that for Marx the proletariat is essentially a poetic force. If my thesis is valid, then comprehension of the poems is essential to understanding Marx's philosophy.

Romantic Poetry

Ontologically, Romanticism begins with the oneness of all things. This all-pervasive oneness expresses itself in the multiplicity of nature, flowing through all things as spirit—divine Spirit. For the Romantic, the principle of life-animating Spirit is love, which seeks always to express and communicate itself. The expressive activity of love is a form of language. Aesthetic feeling, not conceptual ratiocination, lies at the heart of this language, and the linguistic form of love is musical in nature. As Romantic poet Ludwig Tieck wrote in a poem entitled "Liebe":

> "Love thinks in sweet tones,
> For thought stands too distant,
> Only in tones does [love] gladly
> Adorn everything it wants to.
> Thus is eternally present to us,
> Whenever music speaks with resonance,
>
> . . . .
> Pure love in all paths."[8]

8. Cf. DR, I, 686.

Here is another expression of Novalis' assertion that poetry is the genuinely real. What is ultimately real must be experienced as the musicality of cosmic love. Indeed, musical tonality is the heart of poetry, the poesy of poesy. Verse, then, is but an attempt to capture the musical mood of love by means of words.

The manifold of the empirical world, the "things" of nature, are but so many expressions, so many "words" of the World-Spirit. A song slumbers in all things, and the task of the romantic poet is to unlock the infinite musicality in things and thereby to transform reality. The poet's language does not copy nature; nor does it merely relate individual feelings. Rather it redeems spirit, be it divine or human, from the domination of the profane, by transforming things into the song of spirit, into spirit itself. Thus nature begins to sing. The poetic words are magical, because they enable man to intuit the underlying musicality of poeticized things. Thus, an image does not present itself as an object to be contemplated. Rather it annihilates, ironicizes, itself in order to liberate spirit from its enchantment, its imprisonment, in things. The final object of the Romantics' psychic energies is not poetic words but the breath of God uttering such words. Romantic poets did not wish to remain within the empirical confines of things; they sought to penetrate empirical appearance to the underlying structure—the life of God—that is, to transform the empirical world into a poem, into a dream. But, for them, dream is reality, for it is the voice of the spirit; indeed, it is spirit itself.

The inner musicality slumbering in all things is experienced as *mood*—the most common feature of romantic poetry. This poetry ultimately does not seek to present man with Apollonian plasticity, but with Dionysian emotion. Mood is experienced as feeling—not just the individual's private feelings, of course, but the divine feeling, or spiritual music, pulsating in all beings. Here also is the origin of the lyrical quality of so much romantic poetry. In the poem the word is made fluid, tonal. Romantic poetry is often a play of tonality permeated by mood. And since mood is the most immediate expression of a living subjectivity, romantic poetry is difficult to "explain." There is, of course, the surface layer of things—the objects and features mentioned by the words of the poem. To be sure, these objects have a conceptual content. The surface imagery offers a certain plasticity, clarity, structure, "explainable" meaning. But the heart of the poem does not lie in its surface so much as in the fluid energy of life beneath the surface. The contents of the surface are but hieroglyphics, evocative suggestions of an underlying mood. The import of the romantic poem, thus, is not what is empirically described, but the suggested inner mood pulsating in the form of what is said. Together content and form create an imaginative suggestion, rather than communicating a direct statement.

Likewise, romantic imagery is not *only* what it may seem on the surface. The romantic poet's metaphor is more than his attempt to express analogously his subjective reaction to nature, to objectivity. The romantic poet neither restricts himself to comparing his beloved with nature (her eyes with the glistening stars) nor does he merely read his subjective mood into nature. He does not want to say that an external though analogous relationship pertains between eyes and stars. The appearance of similarity is instead viewed as truth. All "things" are but expressions of the same underlying spirit. The life of the individual is a microcosmic repetition of the life of the whole. Nature itself possesses mind and soul, understanding and love, indeed even fantasy. Thus the universe, as Novalis once noted, is but the elongation of his beloved, and his beloved is but the abbreviation of the universe. Ego and nature "magically" correspond; they are the mirror of each other, the words and tones of the same ontological song. The love in a maiden's eye is the *same* love mirrored in nature's eyes. Thus, the emotional life of the individual poet is not an isolated occurrence, but a reflection *in micro* of the universal *macrocosmos*.[9] Should moods of fear, terror, insanity, suffering, or hatred be experienced, they also become significant for nature, for the universe. If the mood of despair is the last word of a romantic artist, then reality as a whole is despairing, and a theodicy crisis can easily arise. A *Weltschmerz* can (and did) replace the effusions of love experienced and communicated by the Romantics. As we study Marx's

9. For a further development of this thesis see H. Hillmann, "Schläft ein Lied in allen Dingen? Zur Bildlichkeit der deutschen Romantik," in *Deutsche Philologie*, ed. Hugo Moser and Benno von Wiese (Berlin, 1970), Bd. 88, pp. 150–61.

poems, we must not forget that his moods have cosmic significance; they indicate something about his interpretation of life and death—the question of questions. Marx's romantic poems have far more than the biographical significance suggested by Franz Mehring. They are cosmic statements, revealing the drama of existence.

Romantic poets generally sought to crystallize their moods in specific objects, characteristics, situations, or motifs. The realities used are generally not presented in their empirical objectivity so much as they are used to create an atmosphere, a texture of emotions. The "objective" words become a means whereby the poet (and his listener) become aware of the life of feeling. The immediate reality expressed by the poetic word is of less importance than the ethereal, evasive mood of the poet and his universe. The objective environment as elongated spirit becomes abbreviated into the dynamics of cosmic subjectivity.

Seeking a medium that would manifest the spontaneity of mood, of life, Romantics often turned to the genre of the *Volkslied* (folk-poem) in the belief that it represented an authentic expression of the life of the heart. Romantic poets sought to imitate the rhythmic simplicity and spontaneity of the folk-song. Sometimes the effect—and this is especially true of Marx's poems—was destructively ironic, as when the poem conveyed a *contrived* spontaneity, a mechanical exercise in naturalness. Marx often followed the romantic tendency to combine lyrical mood with ballad form. The narrative (objective) form of his ballads is often lyricized by being transformed into a *Rollengedicht* (role-poem) or a dialogue. A variety of techniques—questions, interjections, reflections, different speakers, or concluding formulae—is used to effect an apparently personal presentation. With the exception of some epigrammatic poems—diatribes against Hegel, philistines, and the times (all in the romantic vein)—Marx's poems are all lyrical ballad-like effusions of mood.

Marx's Poems

I have selected seventeen poems for translation and arranged them into three groups. From over 140 poems by Marx, I have chosen those that mediate an overview of Marx's poetic world. These poems appear *en face* on pages 226–81, herein.

Until 1975 the available corpus of Marx's poems was quite limited. In 1903 the only poems published were one poem in Mehring's edition of Marx's *Nachlass*[10] and two poems that Marx himself submitted to the Berlin literary magazine *Athenaeum* in 1841. In 1929, David Rjazanov, who directed the Marx-Engels Institute in Moscow, printed a collection of poems that Marx had sent to his father as a birthday gift in 1837.[11] This collection contained thirty-nine poems, some epigrams, the first act of a tragedy entitled *Oulanem*, and chapters from a novel called *Scorpion und Felix*. In 1975, the Institut für Marxismus-Leninismus of the Soviet Union and a similar institute in East Germany jointly brought out new collections of Marx's poems, some of which were thought to be lost.[12] In the fall of 1836 Marx had sent three collections of poems to his fiancée, Jenny von Westphalen: *Buch der Lieder* (*Book of Songs*) contained twenty-three poems, and *Buch der Liebe* (*Book of Love*), parts one and two, contained thirty-four poems. Another thirty-nine poems in the handwriting of Sophie Marx (Karl's sister) were found in a notebook for the years 1833–1837.[13] Thus, the total number of poems now available has tripled. The new edition offers a much clearer insight into Marx's poetic endeavors. To date, however, all interpretations of the poems have been limited to the poems in the Ryazanov edition.

Many of Marx's poems are explicitly directed to Jenny, and others indirectly reflect the difficult situation Jenny and Marx were facing. They had intended to marry, but had not yet obtained permission from Jenny's father. Moreover, Jenny was reluctant to marry until Marx had completed his studies and secured a position. Marx was obviously disturbed and angered by his separation from Jenny. But the poems reveal much more than these biographical facts. Although

10. Mehring (ed.), *Aus dem literarischen Nachlass*, I, 25–28.
11. D. Rjaznov and V. Adoratski (eds.), *Karl Marx–Friedrich Engels: Historisch-kritische Gesamtausgabe* (Berlin, 1929), *Erste Abteilung: Bd. I, Zweiter Halbband*, 1–89.
12. Günter Heyden and Anatoli Jegarow (eds.), *Karl Marx–Friedrich Engels Gesamtausgabe (MEGA) Text* (Berlin, 1975), *Erste Abteilung*, Bd. I, pp. 483–769.
13. Concerning the bibliographical background to the poem, see the lengthy *Apparat* to the new *Gesamtausgabe. Ibid.*, 1220–73. In the poems selected I have occasionally presented slight variants, given in the *Apparat*, to the poems given in *MEGA* I'. Such variants represent slight revisions made by Marx himself.

many of the poems are directed to Jenny or reflect upon the separation of the lovers, they paint almost no portrait of Jenny herself. From the poems alone, no one could say what Jenny looked like. Indeed, if we did not know who Jenny was and if the name "Jenny" were not a feminine appellation, it would be impossible even to designate the sex of the addressee, since it was not unusual in the eighteenth century for a man to address sentimentalities to another man. In short, the content of the poems does not focus upon the concrete.

The frustrated love of Jenny and Karl does, to be sure, function as the impulse or inspiration for many of the poems. But that is all. Marx's struggles are elongated into cosmic terms, into a cosmic struggle, and Marx's frustration in love becomes an abbreviation of cosmic frustration—recalling Novalis' comparison of the universe with the beloved. The purely personal aspects of Marx's frustration either fade or assume demonic proportions. Marx's heart beats at a "demonic" rate. Indeed, Heinrich Marx, Karl's father, asks about Marx's heart in a letter dated March 2, 1837. "Does [your heart] have room for softer feelings which in this vale of sorrow are so essentially consoling for a man of feeling? And since that [heart] is apparently animated and ruled by a demon not granted to all men, is this demon of a heavenly or Faustian nature? . . . Will you ever be receptive to truly human, domestic happiness?" (E, I, 626). Careful readings of Marx's poems, I contend, offer an invaluable source for comprehending the young Marx's "demonic" interpretation of the cosmos.

We know from Marx's May 10, 1837, letter to his father that Marx had by then rejected his romantic poetry and his romanticism. He had been seduced, he notes, by the Hegelian siren and had dived once again "into the sea" of Hegelian philosophy, eventually surrendering himself "into the arms of the enemy [Hegel]"(E, I, 9). In describing the features of the romantic poetry he has rejected, Marx notes that the poems evince "broad and formless feelings . . . the complete opposition of what is and what ought to be . . . [and] a breath of longing which sees no boundaries" (E, I, 4). This clearly connects Marx with the traditions of romantic poetry.

As we know, romantic poetry reflects a wide variety of feelings and moods. Underlying many such emotions, though, is a fundamental structure—frustration and angry reaction. H. A. Korff has succinctly summarized the essence of romantic longing: "The essence of romantic longing is its insatiety, as the essence of romantic wandering goal-lessness. What is the source of this insatiety? Because the romantic—one must grasp this—, although his longing fundamentally aims at something *super-earthly* . . . seems to seek satiety of his longing in the *earthly*. . . . The romantic seeks paradoxically [the heavenly] on earth. And with the consequence: he does not find it there."[14] Here is the origin of the disparity between what is and what ought to be, of the boundless and hence insatiable longing of Romanticism. Marx, too, sought the super-earthly in the earthy—both in his love and in the universe.

Longing—that willful desire to experience the heavenly in the earthly or universal oneness in "things"—is a common feature in all of Marx's poems translated herein. The modality of this longing and the accompanying and derivative moods of it differ. Marx's subjective reaction to the fulfillment or nonfulfillment of such longing varies. The variations in the tonality of the moods are the basis for arranging the poems into three groups. I've called the first group "Poems of Oneness." In these verses Marx constructs a romantic cosmogony and feels one with the cosmos. For the most part it is only in poems directed to his father that Marx achieves this feeling of oneness. In some of these poems, he seems absorbed, Dionysian-like, into the universe. The second grouping is entitled "Poems of Alienation." In this group the romantic longing is frustrated, apparently by the cosmos itself. The result is a growing sense of alienation. The opposition between what is and what ought to be has become an oppressive antinomy. Suffering and despair follow. The third grouping is called "Poems of Revolt." In these selections, the reaction to the antinomy of longing shifts from frustration and pain to hatred, defiance, and finally to inchoate revolt, to an ontological revolution. Although oneness, alienation, and revolt are three modalities of romantic longing in Marx's poetry, I do not mean to im-

14. H. A. Korff, *Geist der Goethezeit* (6th ed., 5 vols.; Leipzig, 1964), IV, 242.

ply that his poetic imagination chronologically evinces such a threefold evolution. On the contrary, it does not. Marx's attitude toward longing vacillated many times between 1833 and 1837. However, the mood of revolt and anger ultimately triumphed. Regarding his talent, the young poet's father cautioned Marx in a letter of December 28, 1836: "I beg and beseech you . . . calm, temper these storms, do not stir them up either in the bosom of the one who deserves and needs repose."[15] Marx's titanism—about which Fritz J. Raddatz has written illuminatingly[16]—is perhaps the most prominent mood in the poems. And thus it is the final triumph of revolt that grounds my ordering of them. It is justifiable, I believe, to group Marx's poems so that his titanic commitment to, frustration with, and revolt against Romanticism becomes clearly visible.

15. Rjaznov (ed.), *Karl Marx–Friedrich Engels*, Bd. I, p. 198.
16. Fritz J. Raddatz, *Karl Marx: Eine politische Biographie* (Hamburg, 1975), 35–36.

II
Romantic Irony and the Crisis of Romantic Lyricism

As noted, Marx, the young collegiate, wrote and sent many poems to his betrothed, Jenny von Westphalen, and to his father. And judging from the complaints of his father in letters dating from 1836 to 1838, Marx continued his flirtations with poetic dreams. Biographical evidence indicates that he maintained a lively interest in aesthetic and literary matters throughout his life. Indeed, according to Paul Lafarge, Marx's son-in-law, Marx "knew Heine and Goethe by heart . . . [and] every year he read Aeschylus in the Greek original. . . . His respect for Shakespeare was boundless: he made a detailed study of his works and knew even the least important of his characters."[1]

Despite Marx's abiding interest in aesthetic matters and his intense youthful flirtation with poetry, there have been very few if any attempts to discuss systematically the relationship between aesthetics and Marx's Marxism.[2] For the most part, the poems of the young

1. Cf. "Reminiscences of Marx" printed in Erich Fromm, *Marx's Concept of Man* (New York, 1961), 224. Concerning Marx's lifelong affair with aesthetic and literary matters, see S. S. Prawer, *Karl Marx and World Literature* (Oxford, 1976), and Julius Smulksyts, *Karl Marx* (New York, 1974), 75–100. Marx's certificate of release from the Bonn University (1836) showed that four of the ten courses Marx took for credit dealt with aesthetic matter: courses on (1) Roman and Greek mythology, (2) Homer, (3) history of modern art, and (4) the elegiacs of Propertius. Indeed, A. W. Schlegel, perhaps the most polished spokesman of romantic theory, was Marx's teacher for two of the courses. In both cases Schlegel evaluated Marx as "diligent and attentive."

2. There have been, of course, several attempts to construct a "marxist" aesthetics in terms of which Marx is "fused" with Engels, Lenin, and others. For two good presentations of Marx's aesthetics (though the early poems are not mentioned), see I. Meszaros, *Marx's Theory of Alienation* (London, 1970), 190–216, and Adolfo Sánchez Vásquez, *Art and Society:*

Marx have been left to the literarily untrained hands of his biographers.[3] With few exceptions,[4] little more is asserted than that Marx's poems are romantic, as can be adduced easily with some sample pieces. The result of such cursory review of the poems is that the relationship of Romanticism to Marx's emerging theorizing remains obscure.

Marx was a thinker for whom the careful formulation of a question was of prime importance; indeed, in a sense the question has priority over the answer, for the answer can only be ascertained via properly formulated questions. In 1842 Marx wrote: "True criticism, therefore, does not analyse the answer, rather the questions. Just as the solution of an algebraic equation is given once the task has been put in its simplest and sharpest form, so every question is answered as soon as it has become a *real* question. World history itself has no other method of answering and disposing of old questions

Essays in Marxist Aesthetics, trans. Maro Riofrancos (New York/London, 1973). Michail Lifschitz has, however, made some attempt to show the interrelationship of Marx's aesthetic and "scientific" theorizing. Cf. *Karl Marx und die Ästhetik* (Dresden, n.d.). Ernst Kux has briefly sought to illuminate the close relationship between aesthetics and economics in Marx's thought. Cf. *Karl Marx: Die revolutionäre Konfession* (Erlenbach–Zürich / Stuttgart, 1967), 72–80. Kux has, indeed, sought to interpret Marx as a romantic theorizer, but he has not developed a detailed analysis of the young Marx that would fully substantiate his claim. The study is, nevertheless, an important, though relatively isolated, step toward a more adequate understanding of Marx.

3. The list of authors who have, in dealing with the "young" Marx, not even mentioned Marx's romantic poems is too long to note here. For some typical biographical treatments of the poems, see David McLellan, *Marx Before Marxism* (New York, 1970), 41–46; Leopold Schwartzchild, *Karl Marx: The Red Prussian* (New York, 1947), 16–30; Robert Payne, *Marx* (New York, 1968), 59–74; Franz Mehring, *Karl Marx: The Story of His Life*, trans. Edward Fitzgerald (London, 1956), 10–11; and Boris Nicolaievsky and Otto Maenchen-Helfen, *Karl Marx: Man and Fighter*, trans. G. David and E. Mosbacker (London, 1973), 30. See also Raddatz, *Karl Marx: Eine politische Biographie*, 30–36. Raddatz is an exception to the rule in that he is highly trained in literature. However, he sees little in the poems except for a certain titanism.

4. Relative to Hillmann's most welcome exception, see his *Marx und Hegel: Von der Spekulation zur Dialektik* (Mannheim, 1966), 49–72. Cf. also August Cornu, *Karl Marx: L'homme et l'oeuvre* (Paris, 1934), 38–42 and 55–61; also Peter Demetz, *Marx, Engels und die Dichter* (Stuttgart, 1959), 75–86; William M. Johnston, "Karl Marx's Verse of 1836–1837 as a Forshadowing of His Early Philosophy," *Journal of the History of Ideas*, XXVIII (1967), 259–68; Kux, *Karl Marx: Die revolutionäre Konfession*, 31–41; Lifschitz, *Karl Marx und die Ästhetik*, 43–46; and Prawer, *Karl Marx and World Literature*, 1–22. The analyses of Cornu, Demetz, and Johnston are very limited in scope and offer little insight into Marx's poems. Kux, Lifschitz, and Prawer all (and quite correctly) stress the Promethean titanism in the poems. Prawer also lists various similarities between romantic poetry and Marx's poems.

than by means of new ones" (E, I, 379). In this investigation, I am concerned with the origins of the world-historical question, Marx's answer to which was the proletariat.

Addressing first not how Marx answered the question but how he formulated it, I will argue that the question has its roots in Marx's poetic assimilation and rejection of the idealism of German Romanticism. In specific, I will contend that the Marx of 1836 and 1837, like many other German literati of late Romanticism, maintained an ambivalent attitude toward romantic irony. Out of this ambivalence there evolved the formulation of the question, the answer to which led to his discovery of the proletariat. The doctrine of idealism in German Romanticism is grounded in the structural elements of romantic irony and the latent antinomy (and hence nihilism) implicit in the doctrine. It is this antinomy with which I am concerned—not with the history of the use of the term *irony*, which has already been told, and told several times.[5] It is the fate of this romantic antinomy —the heart of the doctrine of irony—that concerns us and that appears as both a destructive and a creative force in the poetry of Marx. Limiting my analysis to the philosophical and general poetological structure of irony, I will focus upon the ontopoetic theories of Friedrich Schlegel and Friedrich von Hardenburg (Novalis). Both thinkers are founders of romantic theory in Germany. I agree with H. A. Korff that Novalis' doctrine of "magical Idealism" and Schlegel's theory of romantic irony are two complementary sides of the same ontopoetic coin.[6] Each theory casts light upon the other. Since I am seeking to mediate an overall view of romantic philosophy and poetology, my approach must be composite and schematic. Concrete differences among thinkers must be neglected in order to exposit the general unity.

Definition of Romanticism

In seeking to ascertain Marx's relationship to Romanticism, the in-

5. Cf., for example, Ernst Behler, *Klassische Ironie, Romantische Ironie, Tragische Ironie: Zum Ursprung dieser Begriffe* (Darmstadt, 1972); Helmut Prang, *Die romantische Ironie* (Darmstadt, 1972); and Ingrid Strohschneider-Kohrs, *Die romantische Ironie in Theorie und Gestaltung* (Tübingen, 1960). See also Beda Allemann, *Ironie und Dichtung* (n.p., 1956), 9–98, 119–36.
6. Korff, *Geist der Goethezeit*. Bd. III. *Fruhromantik*, 252.

(continued)

vestigator immediately confronts the problem of definition. There appear to be almost as many approaches to the "essence" of Romanticism as there have been researchers. To date, no one theory for this multifaceted phenomenon has gained universal acceptance. However, Martin Henkel's thesis concerning the essence of Romanticism is useful to us in studying Marx's romanticism. Henkel writes: "The romantic generation suffers from the increasing profanation of the world, from its mere mechanistic interpretations, from the disappearance of the poetry of life. . . . Therefore, one can summarize romanticism . . . 'as the first self-critique of modernity.'"[7]

Henkel's thesis deserves some explanation, particularly when one recalls that Marx entitled some of his major works, including *Kapital*, "critiques." In a summary fashion, I hold that many eighteenth- and early nineteenth-century Germans (not only the Romantics) exhibited a profound dissatisfaction with their cultural and ultimately cosmological environment. The causes for this dissatisfaction are manifold, though interrelated. Chief among them are: 1) the rise of mathematical or quantitative thinking as the primary tool for interpreting reality; 2) the resulting "discovery" of the mechanical universe; 3) the technological transformation of human culture in the light of "scientific knowledge"; 4) the economic reflex of technology—industrialization; and finally 5) the ever-growing capitalistic (manufacturing) nature of production along with, to use Marxist terminology, accompanying ideologies. The general name for this complex of causes is the Enlightenment.

We must caution ourselves, though, against placing too much emphasis upon the industrial origins of Romanticism. Germany of 1795–1800 (the birth of German Romanticism) was anything but industrialized.[8] A revolution in thought produced the economic revo-

7. Cf. "Was ist eigentlich romantisch," in *Festschrift für Richard Alewyn,* ed. Benno von Wiese (Köln, 1967), 296. For other attempts to grasp the essence of Romanticism, see Martin Honecker, "Die Wesenszüge der deutschen Romantik in philosophischer Sicht," in *Begriffsbestimmung der Romantik,* ed. Helmut Prang (Darmstadt, 1968), 297–323; A. Grimme, *Vom Wesen der Romantik* (Braunschweig / Berlin, 1947); and Julius Petersen, *Die Wesenbestimmung der deutschen Romantik* (Leipzig, 1926).

8. For an introduction to the historical background to Romanticism, see W. M. Simon, "The Historical and Social Background," in *The Romantic Period in Germany,* ed. Siegbert Prawer (New York, 1970), 17–33.

lution in production. Such a "real" revolution was only in its inchoate stage. The "ideal" revolution—that is, the development of thought—was quite advanced. The human carriers of this ideal revolution were members of the intelligentsia and, as such, members of any class, so long as it was educated. The intelligentsia can be called "bourgeois" (*bürgerlich*) so long as an economic interpretation is not forced upon the designation. The bourgeois class consisted primarily of individuals who shared a common *Bildungsideal*, or "ideal of education." This class assumed sociological form during the Enlightenment (*ca.* 1680 on).[9]

To comprehend the nature of the spiritual crisis brought about by mathematical thinking, one must grasp what was at stake. Recalling Ernest Becker's thesis that the "poetical" constitutes a fundamental anthropological category, grounded in the human need for value, for a life-justifying meaning, we know that man must project into (or read out of) reality some vital meaning. Such an act reflects and structures the poetics of the human condition. Or, conversely, the human condition impels man to poetize reality.

The seriousness of man's poetical inclinations cannot be over-stressed. Man's needs for lasting value are ultimately confronted with the life-denying annihilation effected by death. I agree fully with Becker that "the idea of death, the fear of it, haunts the human animal like nothing else; it is a mainspring of human activity—activity designed largely to avoid the fatality of death, to overcome it by denying in some way that it is the final destiny of man. . . . [T]he fear of death is indeed a universal in the human condition."[10] In short, death threatens man with existential insignificance. His fundamental need to possess primary value, to have counted significantly in the scheme of things, is frustrated by death, which continually reminds him of the weakness and finitude of his power (or meaning) vis-à-vis the awesomeness of the cosmos.

The greatest task confronting man's poetical powers is the crea-

9. Concerning the sociological makeup of the *Bürgertum* in the eighteenth century, see W. H. Bruford, *Germany in the Eighteenth Century: The Social Background of the Literary Revival* (Cambridge, 1968).
10. Ernest Becker, *The Denial of Death* (New York, 1974), ix.

tion of a symbolic universe that protects him from the ravages of insignificance. Man must obtain for himself a sense of death-conquering and hence sacred power. "Thus it is easy to understand," writes Mircea Eliade, "that religious man deeply desires *to be*, to participate in *reality*, to be saturated with [*sacred*] power."[11] From this point of view it is also easy to comprehend that all culture (man's social objectification of himself) is essentially sacred because it enables man to immerse himself in an apparently durable value-objectivity, in "substantiality." Brilliantly penetrating the sacred foundation of culture, Otto Rank writes, "Culture is derived from 'cult,' not only linguistically, but also functionally, that is, as a continuous translation of supernatural conceptions [*i.e.* death-conquering power] into rational terms. Culture is conceived here as an expression of the irrational self seeking material immortalization in lasting achievements."[12] Traditionally, man has sought to legitimize his cultural creations by conceiving them as microcosmic reflections of the macrocosmos—or, to use Peter Berger's term, by "cosmization."[13]

The crisis that spawned German Romanticism has its theoretical roots in the raising of quantitative thinking to be the main source of cognition of the real. The qualitative aspects of existence (including spiritual ones) were relegated by many thinkers, from Galileo on, to the realm of subjective properties. "This astonishing change in outlook," writes J. W. N. Sullivan, " has been brought about by assuming that, of all the elements of our total experience, only those elements which acquaint us with quantitative aspects of material phenomena are concerned with the real world. . . . None of the other elements of our experience . . . [*e.g.*] our mystic communion with God, has an objective counterpart. All these things, which are ultimately products of motions of little particles, are illusory in the sense that they do not acquaint us with the nature of objective reality."[14]

11. Mircea Eliade, *The Sacred and the Profane: The Nature of Religion*, trans. Willard R. Task (New York, 1961), 13.

12. Cf. Otto Rank, *Beyond Psychology* (New York, 1958), 84.

13. Cf. Peter Berger, *The Sacred Canopy: Elements of a Sociological Theory of Religion* (Garden City, 1969), 27.

14. Cf. J. W. N. Sullivan, *The Limitations of Science* (New York, 1959), 135–36. For a

Under the influence of Newton, the concept of physical reality was reduced to a function of mathematical calculation. The essence of the physical, of *physis*, is inertia. It is *passive*, unless acted upon by another external force. As Harry Prosch writes about Newton's physics: " 'Being' and (active) 'force' were thus separated."[15] The essence of *physis* is not activity, life, or spirit (as it had been for the pre-Socratic philosophers); rather, it is *inertia*, or spiritual death. *Physis* (nature) lost its symbolic power to ground sacred power. The gods no longer spoke in and through nature—nature having become soulless atoms in motion. "The vivid world of the medievalist, a world shot through with beauty and instinct with purpose . . . is dismissed as an illusion. It has no objective existence. The real world, as revealed by science, is a world of material particles moving in accordance with mathematical laws, through space and time."[16] The cosmos, thus, was demythologized, made *entgöttert*.

Nature lost its spiritual primacy and, hence, its ability to ground a poeticized world. It was no longer to be contemplated, worshipped, or admired; rather it was to be transformed or made over by technology at the command of the human will. Enlightenment progressively turns to nature not as spiritual force, in order to merge into it, but as "stuff" for man's scientifically grounded will to power. Technology and industrialization became the means of human *making*, of the exercise of man's power. Functionally, nature became a desouled element to be technologically reshaped.

Industrialization, technology, manufacturing, early capitalism were to a large degree results of this transformation of social institutions to accord with the new theoretical relationship to nature as "matter-to-be-transformed." As Ehrenfried Muthesius notes: "The crisis aspect of this entire situation consists in the unwanted effects of such an enfolding of [technological] power. Despite all assurances there

---

penetrating discussion of eighteenth-century physics and the romantic reaction (the primary focus is British Romanticism) see Alfred North Whitehead, *Science and the Modern World* (New York, 1960), 56–89.

15. Cf. Harry Prosch, *The Genesis of Twentieth Century Philosophy: The Evolution of Thought from Copernicus to the Present* (Garden City, 1966), 52. Prosch's study presents clearly the theoretical crisis effected by the Copernican revolution in thought (see 3–82).

16. Cf. Sullivan, *The Limitations of Science*, 14.

dominates (*ca.* 1750–1830) a feeling of total insecurity, despite all outer enrichment man lives in an impoverished world because the reduced levels of being of the scientized and technologized world force aside the whole, sacred, full world-reality. The desouling of the world works desouling back upon man."[17] Here is the ultimate reason for the destruction of the cosmization of human existence. The German intelligentsia of the late eighteenth and early nineteenth century was faced with an unpoetical reality, with a reality that could not furnish a "sacred" justification of human existence. Reality seemed to have degenerated from poesy to the prosaic. There are abundant expressions of this feeling of crisis among German intellectuals.

For example, Friedrich Schiller, in his famous *Letters on the Aesthetic Education of Mankind* (1795), expressed the opinion that modern culture itself had given "wounds to modern humanity. The inner union of human nature was broken up."[18] As was often done, Schiller compared the fragmented life of modern man with the allegedly harmonious totality of Greek culture "which was an awakening of the powers of the mind, the senses and the spirit had no distinctly separated property. . . . Poetry had not yet become the adversary of wit [reason], nor had speculation abused itself by passing into quibbling."[19] Greek culture was poetical for Schiller. Modern society, by contrast, is typified by "the separation [of man's existence] into numberless parts, there results a mechanical life in the combination. There was a rupture between the state [culture] and the church [sacred power], between laws and customs; enjoyment was separated from labor, the means from the end, the effort from the reward. Man himself, eternally chained down to a little fragment of the while . . . never develops the harmony [poetry] of his being."[20] In short,

---

17. Ehrenfried Muthesius, *Ursprünge des modernen Krisenbewußtseins* (Munich, 1963), 22. Muthesius' study excellently portrays the crisis in German thought (*ca.* 1750–1830) caused by mathematical thinking and the technological will to power. In this respect see also Robert Heiss's delineation of the same problem in *Der Gang des Geistes: Eine Geschichte des neuzeitlichen Denkens* (2nd ed.; Bern / Munich, 1959), 124–243. Cf. also Otto Veit, *Die Flucht vor der Freiheit* (Frankfurt, 1947), 67–138. Veit focuses upon the increasing importance of economics in the nineteenth century.
18. See *The Works of Frederick Schiller* (7 vols.; New York, n.d.), IV, Pt. 2, p. 46.
19. *Ibid.*, 45
20. *Ibid.*, 47.

modern society has produced "a degraded humanity under its yoke. *Utility* is the great idol of the time, to which all powers do homage and all subjects are subservient."[21] Schiller concludes that "egotism has founded its system in the very bosom of a refined society."[22]

Similar dissatisfaction with contemporary society is expressed by Johann Gottlieb Fichte, the somewhat reluctant father of Romanticism: "My mind can accept no place in the present, nor rest even for a moment; it is irresistibly repulsed by the present; my whole being flows onward, incessantly toward a further and a better state of things" (SW, II, 266). Indeed, if things do not get better, if a state of things is not reached in which "the strife of evil against good is here done away with, for here no evil can occur" (SW, II, 277), then the world, Fichte asserts, will appear as a "monster continually devouring itself that it may again give birth to itself and giving birth to itself only that it may again devour itself" (SW, II, 266). If the world cannot be radically altered, spiritualized, "all human life [will] be transformed into a theatrical display for a malignant spirit, who has implanted in poor humanity this inextinguishable longing for the imperishable only to amuse itself with man's ceaseless pursuit of that which he can never overtake" (SW, II, 278). The early resonances of an incipient nihilism are clearly evident in Fichte's contempt for his "empirical" environment.

Likewise, Novalis perceived the alienated state of modern man as a loss of the divine presence. Characteristically, Novalis links the loss of the gods (or their retreat from nature) to the destructive force of quantity and loss of faith in poetic imagination. In his most romantic work, *Hymns to the Night* (*ca.* 1800), Novalis writes: "The gods disappeared together with their retinues. Alone and lifeless Nature stood. Withered number and strict measure [quantitative thinking] bound it in iron chains. As into dust and air, the immeasurable blossom of life disintegrated into dark worlds. Fled was conjuring faith, and the all-transforming, all-knitting heavenly companion, Phantasy" (S, I, 145).

Schlegel interpreted the contemporary loss of the gods as a loss of

21. *Ibid.*, 35.
22. *Ibid.*, 43–44.

mythology. "There is lacking, I maintain, in our poetry a middle point, as there was mythology for the ancients, and everything essential, relative to which modern literature is inferior to that of the ancients, can be summarized in the words: We have no mythology" (KA, II, 312). In other words, the "modern" poet has no collectively or socially accepted set of symbols—myths—that allow him to communicate the inner meaning of reality. The absence of mythology is not just an artistic problem; it is a problem of human existence per se (art being a reflection of it). The meaning of a mythology for man's sense of being at one with the cosmos and thereby transcending death is evidence in Schiller's famous poem "The Gods of Greece." Like so many Germans, Schiller sought (in vain) for a surrogate mythology in the Greek culture of antiquity—a surrogate, that is, for a lost faith in Christian myth. Concerning the beauteous and meaningful world of the Greeks, Schiller wrote,

> Ye in the age gone by,
> Who ruled the world—a world how lovely then!—
> And guided still the steps of happy men
> In the light leading-strings of careless joy!
>
> .   .   .   .
>
> And life's redundant and rejoicing streams
> Gave to the soul-less soul—whither they flowed
> Man gifted nature with divinity
>
> .   .   .   .
>
> All things betrayed to the initiate eye
> The track of gods above![23]

The finite world could give man joy, because he could perceive in it the "track of gods above." The empirical microcosmos is identified with the supraempirical macrocosmic source of meaning. But, alas, mourns Schiller, the gods are gone "now"—*i.e.*, in the eighteenth century.

---

23. *Ibid.*, Pt. I, p. 74.

> Art thou, fair world, no more?
> Return, thou virgin-bloom on Nature's face;
>
> . . . .
>
> The meadows mourn for the old hollowing life;
> Vainly we search the earth of gods bereft;
> Where once the warm and living shapes were ripe,
> Shadows alone are left!
>
> . . . .
>
> And through the woods I call, o'er the deeps,
> And—Echo answers me![24]

Man, for Schiller, longs to perceive lasting value, or meaning, incarnated in nature, in his life, in his culture—but he hears only the empty echo of his cries, not the poetry of the cosmos.

These few citations could be multiplied indefinitely to record the pervasive alienation felt by late eighteenth-century Germans. Henry H. H. Remak summarizes the role of Romanticism, European and German: "Romanticism is the attempt to heal the break in the universe, it is the painful awareness of dualism coupled with the urge to resolve it in organic monism, it is the confrontation with chaos followed by the will to reintegrate it into the order of the cosmos, it is the desire to reconcile a pair of opposites, to have synthesis follow antithesis."[25] Almost as if to certify Remak's thesis in advance, Schlegel writes: "The revolutionary wish to realize the Kingdom of God is the elastic point of progressive education [*Bildung*], and the beginning of modern history. Whatever has no relationship at all to the Kingdom of God is . . . only a secondary matter" (KA, II, 201). Similarly, Novalis, in his eschatological and revolutionary essay *Christendom or Europe* (1799), echoes Schlegel's call for the Kingdom of God on earth. "It [*i.e.*, a new Christendom viz. a new social order] must again pour out the cornucopia of blessing on all peoples. . . .

24. *Ibid.*, 76–77.
25. Cf. Henry H. H. Remak, "A Key to West European Romanticism," in *Colloquia Germanica* (1968), 1 / 2, 37–46.

When, and when all the sooner? One is not to ask about that. Patience only! It will, it must come, that holy time of eternal peace when the new Jerusalem will be the capital of the world: until then be cheerful and brave amongst the dangers of the time. Comrades of my faith, proclaim with word and deed the divine Gospel, and remain true unto death to the veritable and endless Faith" (S, III, 524). Unless the essentially eschatological and redemptory inspiration of Romanticism is kept in view, the investigator, I contend, will not be able to understand properly the nihilism and pessimism in which it ended. Romanticism was an attempt to erect the Kingdom of God on earth, to establish a new and sacred culture, to conquer death by the magic of poetry. Negative, bitter, sarcastic, and despondent feelings must arise in someone who has lost faith in the romantic "way" of redemption. I shall presently seek to interpret the young Marx as, so to speak, a "fallen-away" Romantic (like many Germans in the 1820s and 1830s). Marx's bitterness was not aimed at the desire for redemption (on the contrary that was his romantic heritage—a heritage he never surrendered); it was aimed rather at the failed gods of Romanticism. Marx's task became the creation of new gods, an efficacious savior, a sacred power—the Proletariat!

The Ontopoetics of German Romanticism

The world—culture or nature—appeared to discontented Germans as something alien to man's deepest needs. Metaphysically expressed, the human subject found itself faced with and oppressed by a world of objects. The problem was how to transform an estranged, objectified world into a manifestation of subjectivity, *i.e.*, how is the world to be poetized. It is in this connection that the philosophy of Fichte opens the door to a comprehension of the theoretical reflections of early Romantics such as Friedrich Schlegel, Novalis, Schleiermacher, and Schelling. Along with Goethe's *Lehrjahr* and the French Revolution, Schlegel mentions Fichte as one of the most important events of his time. Fichte "solved" the metaphysical problem of his day. In Fichte's opinion a philosopher seeks to explain the totality of reality either as a manifestation of subjectivity or of objectivity. The fundamental characteristic of Fichte's philosophy is that all reality is essentially a function of subjectivity. "Everything which is for the I is by means of the I" (SW, I, 455). This was Fichte's central legacy to Romanticism. It will be necessary to probe the nature of Fichte's legacy.[26]

The human condition, as Ernest Becker repeatedly reminds his readers, entails a creative poetics. Man is a being which can and does construct a symbolic universe wherein his life, individual or social, is staged as a dramatic event. Such a symbolic edifice grants man a sense of significant cosmic value. The motivation in man *to poetize* reality is "the utter anxiety of our finitude, our lifelong urge to drown our feelings of helplessness and inadequacy in some self-transcending source of sure power."[27] This is indeed the primordial anxiety of German Romantics, one they sought to assuage. Friedrich Schleiermacher, a friend of Schlegel and Novalis and the leading romantic theologian, speaks of a pious exultation of the mind in which "the whole soul is dissolved in the immediate feeling of the Infinite and the Eternal."[28] This feeling of the Dionysian connection between the finite self and the infinite whole is the awareness of cosmic meaning, of the poetry of existence. Thus Novalis could and did write: "Poetry is the genuinely absolutely real. This is the heart of my philosophy. The more poetic, the more true" (S, II, 647). Echoing Novalis, Schlegel avers: "No poetry, no reality. . . . To the magical wand of the mind everything opens itself up" (KA, II, 224).[29]

26. For a still unsurpassed interpretation of Fichte's philosophy in context with the romantic ontopoetics of Novalis and Schlegel see Korff, *Geist der Goethezeit*, III, 235–80. For two studies on the origin and nature of romantic philosophy (with reference to Fichte) see Arthur O. Lovejoy, *The Reason, the Understanding, and Time* (Baltimore, 1961), and Josiah Royce, *Lectures on Modern Idealism* (New Haven / London, 1964 [originally 1914]), 1–135. Of some interest is George Santayana's tendentious polemic. Cf. *The German Mind: A Philosophical Diagnosis* [originally entitled *Egotism in German Philosophy*] (New York, 1968). Still of use are Rudolf Eucken, *Die Träger des deutschen Idealismus* (Berlin, 1915), and M. Kronenberg, *Geschichte des Deutschen Idealismus* (2 vols.; Munich, 1909), II.

27. Cf. Ernest Becker, *Angel in Armor: A Post-Freudian Perspective on the Nature of Man* (New York, 1969), 134.

28. Cf. Friedrich Schleiermacher, *On Religion: Speeches to Its Cultural Despisers* (1799), trans. John Oman (New York, 1955), 12–13.

29. There is an enormous amount of literature on Novalis and Friedrich Schlegel. I have presented my basic thesis concerning the antinomic heart of each theorist's position in two articles which also refer to important secondary sources. See Leonard P. Wessell, Jr., "The

Romantic philosophy begins with the thesis that the poetic constitutes the essence of reality. "Poetry is the hero of philosophy," writes Novalis. "Philosophy raises poetry to a foundational proposition. [Philosophy] teaches us to know the worth of poetry. Philosophy is the theory of Poetry. It shows us what poetry is, that it is One and all" (S, II, 590–91). Since the real is poetic, the science of the real, namely philosophy, is in essence an ontopoetics, *i.e.* an ontological explanation of the real in poetic categories.

But what grounds the reality of the poetic? Here is where Fichte's legacy functions as the starting point of romantic philosophy. According to Fichte the real is ego, is I-ness. Reality is not an *it*, a non-I, or the inert matter of Newtonian mechanics. "I = non-I—highest thesis of all science and art" (S, II, 542), theorized Novalis. "Since we can assume no other reality than spiritual," wrote Schlegel, "then everything real is genial [*i.e.* mind-like]. Idealism [read Romanticism] observes nature as a work of art, as a poem. Man composes, so to speak, the world; only he does not know it right away" (KA, XII, 105). Mind, spirit, I-ness, or, in short, God underlies, generates, and penetrates nature, objectivity, or the apparent non-I. "The world," asserts Novalis, "is a *Universaltropos* of spirit [*Geist*]—a symbolic image of the same" (S, II, 600). All apparent exteriority, dead matter, or opaque objectivity is accordingly nothing but "congealed" or objectified subjectivity. "The External," writes Novalis, "is the Internal [*i.e.* the spiritual] raised to a secret condition" (S, III, 293). Friedrich Schleiermacher similarly writes: "To me the spirit [*Geist*] is the first and only being; for what I take to be the world is the fairest creation of spirit, a mirror in which it is reflected."[30]

It is obvious that when romantics speak of reality as "I" or as "spirit" they do not primarily mean their own limited, empirical egos. To do so would be to invite madness. Fichte himself wrote: "Reason, universal thinking, knowing per se is higher and more than the [finite] individual" (SW, II, 608). Schlegel referred to this absolute ego or God as the "Ur-Ich" (*i.e.* the Primordial-I). Schlegel

---

Antinomic Structure of Friedrich Schlegel's 'Romanticism,' " *Studies in Romanticism*, XII (1973), 648–69, and "Novalis' Revolutionary Religion of Death," *Studies in Romanticism*, XIV (1975), 425–52.

30. Cf. Friedrich Schleiermacher, *Soliloquies*, trans. Horace L. Friess (Chicago, 1946), 16.

writes: "This Primordial-I is the concept that grounds philosophy" (KA, XII, 337). Schlegel continues on to state: "The Primordial-I, the all-encompassing [factor] in the Primordial-I, is everything; outside of it there is nothing; we can assume nothing other than I-ness [*Ichheit*]" (KA, XII, 338). The *Ur-Ich* is the grounding principle of philosophy because it is the ground of reality. Schlegel writes: "The most essential thing of Idealism is the assumption of an absolute Intelligence which unites all reality in itself" (KA, XII, 96).

For reasons to be explained presently, the *Ur-Ich*—the One and All— transforms itself into the objective "things" of nature, into non-I. Not only does the *Ur-Ich* ground all objectivity, but it also grounds man's own finite or empirical ego. In other words, the ontological foundation for each single human ego, the "soul" of man, is the *Ur-Ich*. Conversely, man's conscious ego, his finite self, is only a part of his true divine self. For Romanticism, man's subconscious mind, so to speak, the collective unconscious, is ontologically *one* and *divine*. Schlegel writes: "Everything is in us; however, our I is only a piece of ourselves. The Primordial-I grounds our empirical I, which is in a certain sense this Primordial-I, only not from all sides" (KA, XII, 338). Novalis similarly states: "God is the super-sensate world in purity—we are an impure part of it. . . . Our so-called ego is not our true ego, rather only its reflection" (S, III, 469).

Because man's finite self is a "piece" of infinite subjectivity, the foundations for a dramatic dialogue between the human *Ich* and the cosmic *Ur-Ich* are established. Man can become aware of the *Ur-Ich* (the One) in the manifold of nature (the All). Schleiermacher himself sought "the immediate consciousness of the universal existence of all finite things, in and through the Infinite, and of all temporal things in and through the Eternal."[31] Indeed, man can raise himself to the level of divine consciousness—*i.e.*, to the level of the full potential of his unconscious mind. Novalis writes: "We are seeds of becoming I. We are supposed to transform everything into a Thou— into a second I—only thereby do we raise ourselves to the Great-I— which is *one* and *all* simultaneously" (S, III, 314).

31. Cf. Schleiermacher, *On Religion*, 28.

The problem facing Romanticism was how to *transform* the apparent opaqueness and oppressiveness of surrounding objectivity into the Thou of universal life. At any rate, "the mysterious linkage of the self to other selves and to the whole universe forms the central problem of philosophy."[32] Schlegel formulated this problem in the terms of the relationship between the infinite (*Ur-Ich*) and the finite. Schlegel queries: "The infinite and the finite appear to be separated and divided by an enormous abyss; from what source would a type of a unity, connection, or a transition [*Übergang*] from one to the other derive? This is the great question, the most difficult problem not only of ontology, but of entire philosophy" (KA, XIII, 275). This problem is religious and emancipatory in that Romantics sought to remove any discordance between the poetic and the empirical, the ideal and the real, or what ought to be and what is. We shall eventually see the proletariat was Marx's answer to this most romantic of questions. First let us look at the onotological dimensions of the problem and then examine some of its poetological aspects.

The Ontology of Romantic Poetics

In their pursuit of the infinite poetry of life Romantics developed a philosophical monism. All is One and One is All. Novalis expressed this monism in a religious manner. "If God could become man, He can also become stone, plant, animal, and element, and perhaps there is in this way a progressive redemption in nature" (S, III, 664). Similarly Schlegel writes: "It is a blasphemous error that there might be only one God; it is foolish that we only have *one* mediator" (KA, XVIII, 56). Schlegel was, of course, not pleading for polytheism. That would imply the existence of separate and isolated centers of divinity. What Schlegel was suggesting is that divinity is also all individual things. Just as Christ is the incarnation of God for Christianity, so too can a stone, plant, or any other element be an incarnation of the divine.

But does not this seem to imply a contradiction? Is not a stone just

---

32. Cf. Royce, *Lectures on Modern Idealism*, 69.

a stone and not a divinity? The law of contradiction seems to be applicable here. $A = A$ and $A \neq$ non-A. Normal or prosaic consciousness would, indeed, seem to have erected a "monstrous abyss" between God and things, or the infinite and the finite. Yet Novalis could write: "Stone is only in this world system *stone* and different from plants and animals" (S, III, 254). In other words, only from one *mental* point of view does being A *seem* to differ from another being non-A. Perceived from another, a poetic point of view, A and non-A merge. We shall presently examine this "magical" vision and how it can be generated according to romantic theory. For the moment the problem is how can a thinker find "a mediating principle between these so completely different and separated worlds" (KA, XIII, 275).

In order to solve this problem Schlegel first asked himself why thinkers came to believe that there are two separate realms in the first place. The prerequisite for separation entails that there must be at least two entities that are actually and ontologically distinct. In short, the principle of contradiction must not only be valid for the formal nature of thinking but also hold for the structure of reality itself. Another formulation of the principle of contradiction is the principle of identity. Insofar as the principle of identity has ontological validity for an entity *in time* it must, according to Schlegel, be conceived as a principle of permanence (*das Beharrliche*). It is an entity's (or a thing's) self-identity that isolates it ontologically from all other things. Another term for *das Beharrliche* is "substance," which in Aristotelian philosophy is essentially equivalent to being (*Sein*). Because the being of a thing is self-identical and perduring in isolation, finite being must of necessity exclude infinite being from its ontological structure. In other words, since infinitude and finitude are apparent contradictions, and since the law of contradiction has ontological value, finite substance must of necessity exclude infinite substance from its being and the reverse. Therefore, God and the world must constitute two distinct realms. Schlegel concludes: "Between an infinite and a finite being no connection is possible, nor too is a transition [*Übergang*] from one to the other thinkable, nor the transformation of one into the other possible" (KA, XIII, 275). Consequently Schlegel was of the opinion that any attempted synthesis of finite and infinite being must lead to a hopeless antinomy, to an insoluble contradiction. However, such a conclusion holds only on the assumption that being (and implicitly the principle of contradiction) is considered as the primary category of reality.

Schlegel's solution to the problem is as simple as it is ingenious. To be real for Schlegel is *to become*. Schlegel contends: "Let one make the attempt and remove from the antithesis of finitude and infinitude the concept of eternal being [*Seyn*] and posit in its place the opposing concept of eternal life and becoming [*des ewigen Lebens und Werdens*] and all difficulties disappear and it becomes evident that there is not only a connection between the finite and infinite, but that both are really one and the same and only different according to degree" (KA, XIII, 277).

Becoming is accepted by the idealistic Schlegel as "the mediating principle" between the infinite and finite because becoming is a type of contradiction. In the process whereby A becomes non-A there must be a period when it must be considered to be both A and non-A (therefore A = non-A in becoming). In the endless act of becoming, all is mediated and synthesized, all is one; yet this oneness does not annihilate the manifoldness of the many. In short, Schlegel sees both the finite and the infinite "as a living becoming activity at most only differentiated by degree, and the contradiction is only an appearance that arises when one fixes and kills life by making it into a thing" (KA, XII, 337). We must examine a bit closer the nature of becoming if we are to understand Schlegel's romantic solution to this fundamental problem of romantic ontology.

Becoming, because it is a type of contradiction, can possess both finitude and infinitude as properties. We must therefore determine the relationship of such properties to becoming and to each other. Infinitude is related to becoming as a *formal* property. Infinitude is the *form* of becoming. But precisely because reality is a becoming, the infinitude of becoming cannot be realized all at once. An actualized infinitude would negate the process of becoming. Therefore infinitude conceived only as the form of becoming is of necessity an empty unity, it lacks content. In other words, there can only *be* becoming if there is movement, *i.e.* if there are discrete "parts" that can change. Furthermore, there can only be "parts" ontologically if there are finite entities. Since reality is one and infinite, it must posit out of itself finite "things" which can be integrated into the process of becoming. Finitude is therefore a necessary ontological correlative to infinitude, it is the "content" or "stuff" utilized by infinitude to generate becoming. Furthermore, since finitude is posited out of infinite reality, it is in essence nothing but not-fully actualized infinitude, so to speak, congealed infinitude. Schlegel writes: "A becoming infinitude is, insofar as it has not yet reached its highest perfection, simultaneously finite, just as a becoming finitude contains, nevertheless, an infinite, inner fullness and manifoldness insofar as an eternally mobile, moving, self-changing, and transforming activity is efficacious" (KA, XIII, 277). Elsewhere Schlegel similarly remarks: "A becoming infinitude is an infinitude which is not yet finished and insofar finite. From this point of view of becoming, finitude and infinitude are consequently different by degree, not in essence" (KA, XII, 335). Consequently, finite things viewed in their essential structure have no real ontological autonomy. A finite being is only a momentary crystallization or phase of becoming. Schlegel writes: "*Being* is in and for itself nothing; it is only *appearance* [*Schein*], it is the boundary of becoming, of striving" (KA, XII, 336). Therefore, the oppressiveness of objectivity is *also* nothing but appearance. It occurs because of the failure of an individual to penetrate the torpid exteriority of being in order to perceive the underlying flowing core. Schlegel contends: "It is something endlessly fluid, dynamic which is supposed to be intuited here" (KA, XII, 330).

It is clear that infinitude and finitude are for Schlegel and Romanticism correlative modes of becoming. However, the description of reality merely in ontological terms is misleading. What is becoming, is, of course, the *Ur-Ich*. Therefore, becoming must also possess psychological properties. "We proceed with the assumption," writes Schlegel, "and maintain that everything in the infinite world-all is organized and animated, everywhere an infinite power [*Kraft*] and activity reveals itself, that even externally limited being is penetrated by the principle of life" (KA, XIII, 277). Becoming as a category of life assumes the form of striving, yearning, or longing. Longing is, of course, a type of mental movement, a going out toward a fuller existence. Concerning longing, Schlegel writes: "Longing in its original form is an indeterminate infinite impulse, an indeterminate activity which spreads itself out toward all sides and directions into the finite" (KA, XII, 430). Longing is a spiritual movement directed toward an infinite fullness of life. We have seen that infinitude as the form of becoming is an empty unity for Schlegel. Therefore, the *Ur-Ich* (or *Welt-Ich*) in its formal unity (*i.e.* in its self-identity) must be aware, however vaguely and unconsciously, of its existential emptiness. There arises consequently in the *Ur-Ich* a "tending" toward fullness, *i.e.* a becoming. Such a tending psychologically expressed is longing. "The highest, *last* goal of longing is infinite fullness" (KA, XII, 431). Longing is the product of the disparity between infinite fullness *de potentia* and infinite emptiness *in actu*. This contradiction or antinomy between essence and existence, between form and content is the mental category that the ontological contradiction underlying becoming assumes. In other words, longing derives from the merging of A and non-A, the need for fullness and the absence of such fullness. It is for this reason that Schlegel conceived longing as the mother of nature. "The first, primordial-source [*Urquelle*] of nature, the first step of the world's development, *longing* [*Sehnsucht*] is the mother of all things [*Dinge*], the primordial beginning of all becoming" (KA, XIII, 37). Longing is, in short, a cosmogonic principle. Spiritual life is, therefore, at the source of nature.

I shall not enter in any detail upon Schlegel's theory of physics and cosmogony (let alone the general romantic theory of nature). It will, I hope, suffice to note that *physis* assumed for Schlegel the general meaning it had for the pre-Socratic Greek philosophers: it is the spiritual "stuff" out of which nature is generated or, perhaps better, born. Schlegel asserts: "If you want to penetrate into the inner essence of physics, let yourself be initiated in poetry" (KA, II, 266). Physical things are, consequently, universal tropoi of spirit. "Space and time are members and parts of the World-I; they are real, living, spiritual beings and energies" (KA, XII, 480). Every finite objectivity can accordingly be defined as "das in ein Ding verwandeltes Ich"—"the I transformed into a thing" (KA, XII, 340). Nature is life—the life of the *Ur-Ich*. Furthermore, this life is a poetic one. Let us now examine the poetics of nature according to Romanticism.

The Poetics of Romantic Ontology

The source for the poetic structure of nature resides in cosmic longing. The volitional dynamics of this spiritual impulse is love. "Everyone will admit," claims Schlegel, "that longing is a type of love. . . . Therefore it is the fount of consciousness, the beginning of the *world*" (KA, XII, 373). "The purest form in which love occurs is, of course, longing" (KA, XII, 392). Novalis concurs: "Theosophy: God is love. Love is the highest *Real*—the primordial ground [*Ur-grund*]. Encyclopedic: Theory of love is the *highest* science" (S, III, 254). The world must, accordingly, be understood as an expression of a love-inspired *Ur-Ich*. Novalis describes the cosmogonic power of universal love in his *Astralis-Poem*:

> Upon one summer morning I became young;
> I felt then the pulse of my own life
> For the first time—and as love
> Lost itself in deeper ecstacies,
> I awoke ever more, and the longing
> For more inward, ardent intermingling
> Became more pressing with each moment.
> Voluptuousness is the creative power of my existence.
> I am the middle point, the holy fount,
> Out of which every longing flows stormily,
> To where every longing, manifoldly
> Broken, draws quietly together again.
> You do not know me and you saw me become.
> . . . .
> Totally absorbed I lay in honey-cups.
> I gave out scent, the flowers swayed quietly
> In morning's golden breeze. I was

An inner fount, a soft struggling, all flowed
Through me and over me and raised me lightly.

. . . .

I gushed back into my own flood—
There was a flash—now I could stir already
And move the tender fibers and calyx.
As I set about, my thoughts
Quickly turned into earthly ideas. (S, I, 317–18)

Novalis describes here poetically how the world-self crystallizes itself into the various "things" of nature. The morning breeze, the flowers are but so many outgrowths of longing for Novalis. The ultimate goal of this cosmic love is the externalization through the fullness (multiplicity) of things, of inner subjective potentiality, and then the reunification of multiplicity as a harmonious whole. Concerning a fully transformed nature Novalis has the World-Spirit say:

"One in all and all in One,
God's image on herbs and stones
God's spirit in men and animals,
One must take this to mind.

. . . .

The realm of love is opened up,
Fable begins to spin.
The primordial play of each nature begins,
Each thing contrives powerful words,
And so the great world-mind
Stirs everywhere and blooms endlessly.
Everything must reach over into each other,
One thing thrives and grows in the other;
Each represents itself in all things,
By intermingling itself with them
And falling avidly into their depths,
Refreshing its peculiar being,
And containing a thousand new thoughts. (S, I, 318–19)

Everything is part of the One because all things are stirrings of the great world-mind. That which generates the multiplicity or fullness of nature and then integrates such a manifold into oneness is *love*. Love is the world-mind's very stirrings and as such is the telos of becoming. Love is, as Novalis writes, "the *Unum* of the universe" (S, III, 248).

It is important to note that the "things" of nature conceived as the stirrings of the world-mind have a decidedly linguistic quality. "Everything which we experience is a communication," writes Novalis. "So the world is in fact a *communication*—revelation of spirit. . . . We have remained with the letter" (S, II, 594). Thus Novalis states in the *Astralis-Poem* that "everything contrives powerful words." Schlegel makes a similar claim: "The inner essence and nature of plants and animals are the words and language in which the distant locked-up Thou speaks to us" (KA, XII, 338–39).

Furthermore, such "powerful words" are woven together by Fable. "Fable begins to spin." Fable is the principle of poetic unity; it is the meaningful story to be communicated. In his famous *"Kling-sohr's Fairy-tale"* Novalis has Fable, personified as a being, spin the threads of the cosmos (S, I, 310). Fable is in effect the dramatic force that knits the "words" of nature into a poetic (meaningful) whole. In other words, a poetic principle underlies and structures the cosmic becoming of the *Ur-Ich*. Meaning constitutes the deeper essence of poetry. Romantics believed that they existed in a cosmic sea of meaning, in a cosmic poem, because Fable is a cosmic principle, the cosmogonic energy that crystallizes itself into the things of nature. Isolated, such things constitute a congery of incoherent "letters." United by the principle of Fable, such things become the coherent words of a cosmic poem, revelations of the inner life of the *Ur-Ich*.

Romantic metaphysics is, indeed, an ontopoetics. Romantic ontology is concerned with the fundamental category of reality. This category is, of course, becoming. Such an ontology is simultaneously a poetics because becoming is teleologically directed to the actualization of love. Insofar as the empirical realm of nature is conceived as objectified love, it becomes a poetical, indeed a lyrical, creation. We are now in the position to examine man's relationship to objectified poetry, or how the cosmic poem can be transformed into a redemptive experience for man.

The Ontopoetics of Redemption

Reality is infinite I-ness. Nature, on the other hand, consists of finite things, is objectivity, exteriority, in short, non-I. Nature is like a love poem written down on paper without anyone there to read it. Mathilde says to her beloved, Heinrich, in Novalis' *Heinrich von Ofterdingen*: "Let one but observe love. Nowhere is the necessity of poetry for the existence of mankind so clear as here. Love is mute; only poetry can speak for it. Or love itself is nothing but the highest nature poetry (S, I, 287). The words of love only become alive when they are communicating to a love-seeking consciousness. Without a listener there is no actualized poetry. Poetic expression in the form of objectivity is, to be sure, a prerequisite for a poem. However, correlative to poetized objectivity is a meaning-seeking consciousness. Moreover, consciousness is not just a *sine qua non* of poetry; it is the actualization, the coming-into-existence of poetry. The being of poetry is precisely its appearing-to-consciousness. In order to comprehend why the *Ur-Ich* had to objectify itself as nature and to explain man's role in the drama of reality, we must briefly consider the romantic conception of consciousness.

Reality is becoming. This becoming considered as a property of the *Ur-Ich, i.e.* viewed in its psychological dimensions, was designated as "activity." Once again it was Fichte who developed the model for romantic theorists. "For Idealism," writes Fichte, "intelligence [*i.e.* the *Ur-Ich*] is a doing [*Thun*] and absolutely nothing else; one should not even call it an active thing [*ein Thätiges*] (SW, I, 440). The primordial principle of reality is for Romanticism not a substance (as it was for Spinoza) but a function. Activity, to be sure, implies a *terminus ab quo* (subject) and a *terminus ad quem* (object). Nevertheless, the actor (subject) and the acted upon (object) are secondary and derivative categories. Activity or "doing" is, of course, that which the *Ur-Ich* seeks to become aware of. When the subject and the object coincide, self-consciousness is generated. Moreover, such activity was for Fichte (and for Romanticism) first and foremost a formative or creative energy. In other words, activity can only be *in actu* insofar as it exerts force. And as we have seen, creativity grounds the poetical power in spirit.

In order for the Primordial-I to become aware of its own activity, it must bend back upon itself. Consciousness can only rise for Fichte as an act of reflection, as an acting upon an acting. "The I has in itself," writes Fichte, "the law to reflect about itself as filling out infinity" (SW, I, 291). But the I can only act as it acts upon an object. Without there being a non-I which stands over against spiritual activity, activity has nothing upon which to exert its creative power and hence it cannot become. This meant for Fichte that the first act of the I is to posit itself as an object, as a non-I by limiting itself or transforming itself into finite objects. Fichte writes: "No, the I cannot reflect upon itself as anything whatsoever if that is not bound [*begrenzt*]. The fulfillment of . . . the satisfaction of the drive for reflection is, accordingly, conditioned [*bedingt*]. Since it cannot be satisfied without an object, it can be described as a drive toward an object" (SW, I, 291). Since objects have no original *an-sich* existence, no ontological autonomy, the I must first posit them, that is to say imagine them. Therefore, the *Ur-Ich* must divide itself or alienate itself by objectifying itself as an *alium*, as an-other-thing. The first act of the *Ur-Ich* is one of out-going, externalization, and limiting.

However, this original positing by the *Ur-Ich* must be an unconscious act. If I-activity results from an inner urge to overcome an opposing object, such an object must possess initially the appearance of being *an-sich*. Only a "real" non-I can oppose itself to the I. If the I knew initially that an object were nothing but I, there would be nothing, no opposition, to overcome. The *Ur-Ich* must, so to speak, place a spell upon itself as it posits itself as objective nature. Novalis suggests: "The greatest magician [*Zauberer*] would be the one who could bewitch [*bezaubert*] *himself* such that his spells [*Zaubereien*] would seem to him as alien, independent appearance. Could not that be our case? (NS, II, 202). "Nature is a petrified magical city [*Zauberstadt*]" (S, III, 564). Insofar as nature is objectified spirit and insofar as this objectification is not so recognized, it can indeed be said to be enchanted. Ontologically we have noted that becoming in its formal self-identity is empty. The psychological equivalent to this ontological state is unconsciousness. The *Ur-Ich* in its formal and infinite self-identity is empty of all content and therefore unconscious. Consequently, the *Ur-Ich* must posit (objectify itself in) nature as the non-I in order to have some *thing* to overcome. The overcoming of resistance causes "friction" that enables spirit to bend back reflectingly upon itself, to become aware of itself as acting. The ontological process of becoming is, therefore, simultaneously the coming to consciousness of the *Ur-Ich*. By reappropriating the manifoldness of objectivity, the *Ur-Ich* becomes aware of the fullness of its own subjectivity.

The first act of the *Ur-Ich* is to limit itself as objects. The second act is to return to itself by overcoming the limiting objects. The act of liberation from the spell of objectivity is what we call self-consciousness. The act whereby the I becomes aware that the essence of the non-I is I, is simultaneously the genesis of a poetic consciousness.

Just as spiritual activity must generate an objectivity to be overcome if self-consciousness is to arise, so too must it generate a subject (self) that overcomes and is aware of this. Consciousness is not possible without a subject. However, the very act of being posited constitutes a limitation on the primordial I-activity. The primordial positing activity is alone infinite. The result of positing, namely the posited, therefore, must be less than infinite. To be posited is to entail a negation and negation means limitation. Insofar as consciousness results from an interaction of I-activity with the finite objects of nature, it too must be finite. Fichte writes: "I posits in the I a divisible non-I [the things of nature] against a divisible [finite] I" (SW I, 110). The divisible I was called by Novalis the empirical or human ego. Schlegel, it will be recalled, spoke of the human *Ich* as a piece of the *Ur-Ich*. Human consciousness is, consequently, the means used by the universal *Ur-Ich* to become aware of itself, *i.e.* of its own spiritual activity. "The system of elements is in God himself. Then follow the gradations of stones, plants, animals; and humans finally are God's reflections upon and in himself. We are God's thoughts, his consciousness" (KA, XVIII, 152). Therefore, the drama of human existence is also the drama of God's own emancipation. The poet is, as Novalis said, truly a priest.

Romantics such as Novalis and Schlegel conceived man's destiny to realize the redemption of the divine. Novalis writes in *Heinrich von Ofterdingen*: "Nature herself [here absolute ego] wants to enjoy her great artfulness and therefore she has transformed herself into human beings so that she now delights in her own glory" (S, I, 209). Schlegel writes along a similar line: "All humans are simply so many expressions of power [*Kraftaüßerungen*] of the earthly for one and the same goal: the reestablishment of freedom, the return to the highest element" (KA, XIII, 11). "Man is the highest stage in the series of earthly productions whose purpose is the return to freedom" (KA, XIII, 15). "Man is a creative glance of nature back upon itself." (KA, II, 258). "One must seek *God* amongst humans," avers Novalis. "The spirit of heaven reveals itself most clearly in human affairs, in human thoughts and feelings" (S, III, 565).

The *Ur-Ich* dirempts itself into the plurality of human selves wherein and by means of which it comes to self-awareness. This thesis leads to the rather bizarre conclusion that it is man's destiny to become divine, to become God. This destiny, as we will see, was fully affirmed by Marx. Schlegel writes: "Every good human will become more and more God. To become God, to be man, to form oneself, are expressions which mean the same thing" (KA, II, 210). Novalis writes: "Every machine which lives now from the great *perpetuo mobili* shall itself become a *perpetuum mobile*—every human which lives now from and through God shall himself become God" (S, III, 297).

"When our intelligence and our world harmonize—we are *similar* [or equal] *to God*" (S, III, 253). We should not forget that the ontological root of every single human self is the divine Self. The *Ur-Ich* grounds each human *Ich*. Insofar as the *Ur-Ich* comes to self-consciousness in and through human selves, such selves must accordingly become divine as they become more fully aware. This implies that man contains the power to bring forth God. "Man is free," writes Schlegel, "when he brings forth God or makes Him visible, and he becomes immortal thereby" (KA, II, 258). It is not, however, the single, isolated individual that is the locus of the divine, but man as a species-being. Schlegel writes: "God has become man in the great person of mankind" (KA, II, 258). The redemption of man as well as the redemption of God resides in man's very being, in his poetic power. We must now examine this divine power if we are to understand the metaphysics of romantic poetology and the foundation of its poetic lyricism.

Magical Idealism

As noted above, the problem facing Romanticism was how to transform an opaque, oppressive, and prosaic objectivity into the loving, spiritual, and poetic subjectivity. How is a transition between the infinite and the finite to be effected? The solution to the problem is grounded in its very origins. As Novalis noted, the greatest magician was the one who could bewitch himself with his own spells. The "objective" world is the product of magic, *i.e.* the unconscious mental act of the *Ur-Ich*. Consequently only magic can undo what magic has done. "A science," writes Schlegel, " which would also be the art of producing the Divine, could be designated by no other name than *Magic*" (KA, XII, 105). "Such magic is the practical act and activity which is directed toward freeing nature from her chains and thereby producing the empirically visible Kingdom of God. In this respect, the Kingdom of God is the final goal of man, the highest ideal of all praxis. . . . Magic is nothing but praxis directed toward the infinite, which succeeds in presenting [the infinite]" (KA, XIII, 174–75). "One seeks," writes Novalis, "an omnipotent organ in philosophy: *Magical Idealism*" (S, III, 385). H. A. Korff has correctly stated: "Magical Idealism is in general the philosophically grounded faith in the *marvelous and magical power of the* [human] spirit."[33] Magical Idealism is the theoretical conviction that nature can be made divine, that objectivity can be transformed into subjectivity.

But why designate such an idealism as magical? Romantics did not believe that individuals could literally cast spells, etc. The essence of magic, as Jerome-Antoine Rony has noted, is the belief that we humans can "bend the whole universe to the rhythm of our desires" by an act of willing.[34] The causality underlying magic is essentially mental and derives from the power of the will.[35] Novalis believed

---

33. Cf. Korff, *Geist der Goethezeit,* III, 250.
34. Jerome-Antoine Rony, *A History of Magic,* trans. Bernard Denvir (New York, 1962), 35–38, 141–51.
35. *Ibid.,* 107.

in the absolute power of the human will. "I myself know as I will myself and I will myself as I know myself—because *I will my will*—because I will absolutely" (S, II, 552). "The world shall be as I will it. Originally the world is as I will—if I do not find it so, I must seek the error [in me]. . . . Whether the world is a degenerate world—or my contradicting will is not my true will—or both . . . ? Degenerate I—degenerate world. *Restoration*" (S, II, 554). "What I will, I can do. Nothing is impossible for man" (NS, II, 178). "A man can *ennoble* everything (make it worthy of himself) *by means of the fact that* he *wills to do it*" (S, III, 271). Thus the causal power which transforms the empirical world into the Kingdom of God can be designated as magical. "Magic is the art of using the empirical world voluntarily [*willkürlich*]" (S, II, 546).

The doctrine of Magical Idealism is, of course, grounded in the romantic assumption that the *Ur-Ich* lies at the foundation of the empirical realm. The human will, similar to that of the *Ur-Ich*, is causal by means of thinking, *i.e.* its acts are mental both in form and in content. The motive of such mental activity is love because love incites the will to act. "Love is the foundation of the possibility of magic. Love works causally in a magical manner" (S, III, 255). Novalis also writes: "The daily use of the sense organs is nothing other than the magical, marvelous capability of thinking or the voluntary use of the corporeal world; for the will is nothing other than the magical and powerful capability of thinking" (S, III, 466). Thinking is the manner in which willing is active, and willing is the causal energy of thinking. Therefore, to think is to bring into existence and such an act is "magic."

Because objectivity is "bewitched" thought, the oppressiveness of the objectivity resides not in the nature of the empirical object itself but in the fact that man has not yet understood (*i.e.* thought) the object correctly. Schlegel writes: "If everything outside of us is not a mere *non-I* [*Nicht-Ich*], but rather a living, counteracting *thou*, then every object can only be the shell of spirit. Every object must have an *inner meaning* [*i.e.* mental content] which must be perceived everywhere if we are correctly to understand the object. This meaning illuminates directly; the *thou* speaks in the moment when [the object's] essence is *understood in its entirety by the I*. [The *thou*] addresses [the I] and *reveals the essence of existence to it*" (KA, XII, 350). The transition or *Übergang* from the finite to the infinite occurs when man seeks to effect "a transformation of displeasure [caused by objectivity] into joy and with it time into eternity by means of a willful detachment and elevation of the mind" (S, II, 667). The "operation" whereby the human mind causally unlocks by means of its own mental powers the spiritual content congealed in the "things" was called "romanticizing" by Novalis.

The world must be romanticized. In this way one finds its original meaning again. Romanticizing is nothing else than a qualitative involution. The lower self [*i.e.* the empirical *Ich*] is identified with a better self [*i.e.* the *Ur-Ich*] in this operation. . . . Insofar as I give a lofty sense to the common, a mysterious appearance to the finite, I romanticize it. Contrariwise is the operation of the higher, unknown, mystical, infinite. These will be logarithmized by means of this nexus—they receive a familiar expression. *Lingua romana*. Reciprocal elevation and lowering. (S, II, 545)

The original sense of the world is the awareness of it as the expression of cosmic love. This is the mysterious, lofty, and mystical feeling that makes objects familiar. The world so romanticized will be experienced as a dream, as a fairy tale.

Irony as the Magic of Romanticism

The romantic belief in man's ability to transform the empirical world into the Kingdom of God on earth might at first appear simply to be megalomania. Nevertheless, the thesis is plausible, given the ontological premises of Romanticism. Man's very being is both finite and infinite, *Ich* and *Ur-Ich*. Schlegel notes: "We are capable of perceiving the music of the infinite cosmos, of understanding the beauty of this divine poem because we are a part of the cosmic Poet: a spark of His creative spirit lives in us and never ceases to flow with secret power under the ashes of self-made unreason" (KA, II, 285). There are, consequently, in man two basic impulses, one directing him to finite objects—a principle of individuation—the other directing him to infinite fluidity—a Dionysian principle. "In all poetic composing and thinking, as in all doing and acting of man, a double direction of his free activity occurs; either he raises himself to the divine, the infinite, or he sinks back into limitation or the imperfection of the dead, cold, earthly element" (KA, XIII, 14). Arising out of the two antithetical impulses is a third impulse, namely a longing for the unity of the two, for development toward psychological integration, for the reconciliation of subject and object. Man's tending after limited objects isolates and individuates him. He becomes aware of his essential emptiness *qua* his finite self. This emptiness can awaken in him the impulse to return to infinite oneness. "A yet higher [impulse] can nevertheless form itself whenever the earthly element has already developed; *the impulse to return to the free world, the longing for lost freedom.* . . . Only if [the impulse to individuation] is destroyed can the other one win room, develop itself" (KA, XIII, 4). Furthermore, this impulse to oneness "is the impulse of the earthly element to leave its form and to pass over into another. The earthly element can have no other task than to dissolve itself into a higher form. . . . Man is first of all an organ capable of longing for the transition [*Übergang*] into divine freedom [*i.e.* the oneness of love], of dissolution into the higher element. We must relate the final goal of man to this last impulse of the earthly element" (KA, XIII, 5). A dialectic arises out of the interaction of the two impulses in man.[36] Man perceives the finite world of objects. The object *qua* its empirical limitation cannot satisfy man's deepest need for infinite oneness though it "hints" at the infinitude objectified in it. This contradiction generates in man a longing for a Dionysian dissolution of the finite into the cosmic oneness. All boundaries, all separation between subject and object, all isolation must be sublated into the fluid *élan vital*. Such a longing is, of course, a movement of the will, of the spark of the cosmic Poet in man; it energizes the human will to romanticize the world. Human longing can romanticize the world because it is more than a finite force. It is the infinite energy of cosmic becoming congealed in the human self and seeking to return to itself. Man has the

36. Cf. Ernst Behler, "Ironie und Dialektik" in *Klassische Ironie, Romantische Ironie, Tragische Ironie*, 65–84.

power to tap his divine unconsciousness for the energy necessary to effect the transition to a higher unity by "annihilating" the autonomy of finitude. This power of creative annihilation is in essence romantic irony. "Romantic irony," writes Korff, "is nothing other than the lively feeling for the relativity of all finitude, which brings it about that the [human] spirit does not feel itself really bound to anything finite. It is the reverse side of Magical Idealism and its conviction of the absolute subjectivity of the world."[37]

Irony is the creative power of magic in that it can transform the objective into the subjective, it can release the spiritual imprisoned in material by enabling man to think the world correctly, *i.e.* poetically. Irony is the mental power of the human mind to destroy, to annihilate the spell of objectivity and thereby to negate the "enormous abyss" between the subject and the object. The objective world has *no* real being, it is only appearance. Nevertheless, in the state of alienation, of being enchanted, the objective appears to possess independent and nonspiritual reality. This is the source of suffering. Irony is the mental causality of the human will which annihilates the semblance of ontological independence on the part of objectivity. Irony is in short the "magic" of Magical Idealism.

In short, to romanticize is first of all to negate, or to annihilate the autonomy of the empirical realm. The annihilation of being in order to sublate it into becoming is a primal romantic attitude; it informs the romantic *ars dialectice cogitandi*. Novalis writes: "Whoever views life other than as a self-annihilating illusion is himself caught prisoner in life" (S, II, 563). "True anarchy is the creative element of religion. Out of the annihilation of everything positive, [religion] raises her glorious head as a new world creator" (S, III, 517). Schlegel similarly avers: "The appearance of finitude shall be annihilated; in order to do that all knowledge must be set into a revolutionary condition" (KA, XII, 11). "The earthly element [in man] is held back and hemmed in everywhere in its restless striving for dissolution and freedom from the chains of permanence [*Beharrlichkeit*]" (KA, XIII, 19). To be a romantic is to be a revolutionary in the most profound

---

37. Korff, *Geist der Goethezeit*, III, 248.

sense; it is to revolt against the permanence and eternality of being, of the given.[38] This revolt realizes itself as an annihilation of objectivity in order to re-create it as subjectivity. Objectivity must be sacrificed on the altar of irony. Schlegel writes: "The secret meaning of [religious] sacrifice is the annihilation of finitude because it is finite. . . . In the enthusiasm of annihilating, the meaning of divine creation is revealed. Only in the middle of death does the flame of eternal life ignite" (KA, II, 269). Sacrifice, destruction, and death constitute the door to life. The more objectivity loses autonomy, the more all becomes subjective. The oppressiveness of objectivity—designated as fate—is thereby transformed into the will of man. Novalis writes:

Fate, which oppresses us, is the inertia of our spirit. We will transform ourselves into fate by means of the expansion and education of our activity.

Everything appears to stream in upon us because we do not stream outwards. We are negative because we will to be—the more positive we become, that much more negative becomes the world around us—until in the end there will be no more negation—rather we will be all in All. *God wants gods.* (S, II, 583–84)

Irony is, in short, man's inkling that the world is his creation. Out of this knowledge a feeling of power grows which stimulates the human spirit to ever new acts of annihilation and creation.

Irony as annihilating creativity is not just an artistic force; it is a fundamental human power. This principle dramatizes human history, which is the "poetic" story of man's struggle to romanticize his existence and environment. Klingsohr, Heinrich's mentor in poetic matters, elaborates in *Heinrich von Ofterdingen* about the world-historical meaning of poetry.

"I do not," said Klingsohr "know why people take poetry in a common way when they speak of nature as a poet. She is not so at all times. There

38. For a general overview concerning the romantic attitude towards revolution, see Andreas Müller, "Die Auseinandersetzung der Romantik mit den Ideen der Revolution," in *Romantik-Forschunngen* (Halle / Salle, 1929), 243–333.

is in her, as in humans, a contrary essence, numb desire, a mute lack of feeling, and inertia which carry on a restless conflict with poetry. This conflict would be the fine matter of a poem, the mighty battle. Many lands and times, like most humans, appear to stand under the dominance of the enemy of poetry, while in others poetry is indigenous and visible everywhere. For the historian, the periods of battle are extremely interesting, their presentation a tantalizing and rewarding task. Those are generally the birth periods of poets." (S, I, 284)

The poetic is that which inspires man to wage war against oppression, as for example against other peoples. (It is the contention of this study that the proletariat was Marx's socioeconomic version of the romantic poet as a historical force. The proletariat triumphantly fights the battle for the emancipation or poetization of human existence.) War, then, is in its motivational essence a poetic act. Of all wars, maintains Novalis, a religious war is most poetical because it seeks absolute annihilation and re-creation. In a conversation with Klingsohr, Heinrich lyricizes about war:

"War in general," said Heinrich, "appears to me to be a poetic effect. People believe that they must fight each other for some miserable possessions and do not realize that the romantic spirit excites them in order to annihilate [*vernichten*] useless evils by means of themselves. They bear weapons for the cause of poetry, and both armies follow one invisible banner."

"In war," answered Klingsohr, "the primordial waters stir. New continents shall arise, new races shall step out of the great dissolution. The true war is the religious war; it aims at destruction, and the madness of people appears in its full form. Many wars, especially out of national hate, belong to this class and are genuine poetic creations. Here the true heroes are at home, heroes who, as the counterparts of poets, are nothing but world forces, involuntarily penetrated by poetry. A poet who would at the same time be a hero is a divine messenger, but our poetry is incapable of portraying him." (S, I, 285)

(It is my thesis that Marx was capable of such a redemptive poetry. Marx was able to portray the hero-poet, for him the proletariat. The proletariat was emancipatory for Marx because it combined in itself the power of ironic and magical creativity with real physical energy.) The drama of a romanticized history is the story of the war between poetic and antipoetic forces. Poetry will triumph because it is the ironic force of the divine in man.

Romantic Poetology: Lyricism

Perhaps there has never been a poetry as metaphysically lyrical as that of German Romanticism. In the lyrical mood inner and outer merge. The outer world reminds the lyrical "I" of its inner feelings, and the lyrical self seems to overflow into its surroundings, which in turn respond intimately to this self. In short, the lyrical entails a subjectivization of the objective environment.

> Does a song slumber in all things,
> Which dream on and onward?
> And the world begins to sing
> If you but strike the magic word.

This short poem by Josef von Eichendorff contains *in nuce* romantic poetology. First of all, there is the realm of "things," *i.e.* mere objectivity. Such a realm is, however, not something absolute. Spirit *does* slumber in the core of each thing. For instance, Schlegel writes: "Consciousness and spirit are, to be sure, existent in a stone, however *deeply locked away therein*, and because of the baseness and unfavorable nature of the outer form, the enclosed and bound spirit can only break forth after a long battle" (KA, XII, 441). The power that wins this "long battle" is, of course, the magic of the word. Poetry as the mode of the will's causality can unlock the spiritual heart imprisoned in objectivity. The poet is indeed a priest, *i.e.* he effects the transubstantiation of stone into the divine. The result of this redemptive magic is that the world begins to sing, to manifest its subjectivity through its empirical shell. The union of a sensate medium and a spiritual force is not only aesthetic but musical.

The poet becomes magical by "striking" the correct word. This means that the poet enables himself and others "to think" things in a different manner. Man's normal, everyday, and prosaic consciousness accepts the objective as irreducible. Prosaic consciousness is, however, only an illusion. "Only in appearance can anything finite boast to itself of a separate existence."[39] By means of the magical power of irony (the willful elevation of the mind) man as a poet can negate prosaic consciousness and raise himself to the viewpoint of the *Ur-Ich*, of the Whole. "Only when the free impulse of seeing and of living is directed toward the Infinite and goes into the Infinite is the mind set in unbounded liberty."[40] Insofar as the human mind "goes into the Infinite," it becomes divine and is thereby causally enabled "to see" the manifold of nature as a transformation of an infinite flow. In short: "Nature is an infinite animal; nature is an infinite plant; nature is an infinite stone" (KA, XVIII, 145).

Redemption or poetization of reality results from a new way of thinking (*i.e.* of becoming aware) because thinking is a creative activity. To think is to objectify the thinking self as the thought content. Novalis writes: "Thinking is speaking. Speaking and doing or making are one single modified operation. God said, let there be light and there it was" (S, III, 297). Language is generated by the need of the self to realize itself and thereby to free itself from the dominance of "things." Poetic language is, in short, an expression of the self and therefore a revelation of the self to itself. However, in this case the creative self is the *Ur-Ich*, man's collective unconscious, acting in and through the empirical *Ich*. Poetic language, as Novalis contends in his *Monologue* (the title itself is revealing), does not seek to mirror things, to correspond to the empirical reality of things. "Precisely the peculiar thing about language (and no one knows it) is that it is only concerned with itself. Therefore, language is such a wonderful and fruitful secret. For, when one merely speaks in order to speak, one speaks out precisely the most magnificient and original truths" (S, II, 672). Novalis continues on to compare language with mathematics. "[Mathematical formulas] constitute a world for themselves. They play with themselves, express nothing but their

39. Cf. Schleiermacher, *On Religion*, 57.
40. Cf. Schleiermacher, *Soliloquies*, 46.

own nature—just for that reason the rational play of things is reflected in them. Only by means of their freedom are they parts of nature and only in their free movements does the world-soul express itself and make itself into a tender measure and outline of things" (S, II, 672). This is also true for language. Because the poet's language is the thinking of the *Ur-Ich* in man, it expresses the structure of the Whole, of which all things are but emanations. Therefore, the creative subjectivity of the poet, not the objective world, should determine the language of poetry or the artistic treatment of any subject matter. Clemens Brentano, a lyrical poet of considerable talent, wrote: "The romantic is therefore a perspective or rather the color of glass and the determination of the object by means of the form of the glass."[41] The romantic painter Caspar David Friedrich suggested: "The painter should not merely paint what he sees in front of himself, rather also what he sees in himself. If he sees nothing in himself, let him cease painting what he sees in front of himself."[42] In short, the poetic subjectivity of the poet should be projected into the objective environment. This is, of course, the lyrical imperative! Furthermore, because the poet is creating out of the divine in himself, his subjectivization of things is, paradoxically, the revelation of the true universality *in* things.

The true universality found in all things is, of course, cosmic love. Love raised to a content of consciousness is experienced as feeling. The primary effect of romanticization of objects is the calling forth of feeling. As Schlegel writes: "Feeling is everything, the exact middle point of the inner life, the point from which philosophy proceeds and to which it always returns. . . . [Feeling] is the quintessence of consciousness" (KA, X, 459). This means that the language of romanticization must be that of feeling. G. H. Schubert notes: "The original language of man, as dreams, poetry and revelation teach us to know, is the language of love and, since the living middle point and soul of feeling is love, the language of love. . . . the only

---

41. Clemens Brentano, *Werke* (Munich, 1963), II, 258 as reprinted with other selections in Marianne Thalmann, *Romantiker als Poetologen* (Heidelberg, 1970), 84.
42. Cf. Casper David Friedrich, *Bekenntnisse* (Leipzig, 1924), 193–94 as reprinted in Thalmann, *Romantiker*, 92.

criterion of truth is the inward consciousness of that which we feel" (DR, I, 327–28). Feeling is the experience of love in things because it is the empirical appearance of meaning. But meaning experienced empirically is another description of aesthetic intuition. Therefore, the aesthetic consciousness itself is the redemptive experience of magic. "Beauty," writes Schlegel, "is the *spiritual meaning* of objects. . . . Beauty is something which comes out of the loving mind of the observer; it is the content of *feeling* or the content of the intuition raised by feeling to the spiritual. Insofar as a spiritual meaning is in all things, so beauty is applicable to all things" (KA, XII, 357). Feeling mediated by beauty "reminds" man of the spiritual essence of things. "Feeling, as the immediate perception of another I in the present world, [is] the reminder [*Erinnerung*] as a re-awakening and discovery of the complete I in the present, divided, and derived I" (KA, XII, 355).

The lyrical nature of romantic poetry should be clear. Poetry reminds man of the love in things. Another term for such a reminding is *mood*. Romantic poets use, of course, words that refer to concrete, conceptual objects, properties, relationships, etc. But such objectivity only constitutes the aesthetic surface of the poem. The poem's objectivity must be ironized in order to allow the "breath" of love to appear. Schlegel writes: "Love must hover everywhere invisibly visible in romantic poetry. . . . It is the holy breath which touches us in the tones of music. . . . The magical words of poetry too can be penetrated and animated by its powers" (KA, II, 333–34). Objectivity is lyricized insofar as it is enabled to hint "at the higher, infinite, hieroglyphic of the One eternal love" (KA, II, 334). The romantic is precisely mood. Mood is simply experience of the transformation of objective things into the life of spirit. Meaning and being merge in mood. Philipp Otto Runge writes: "The truth of feeling grabs all. We feel ourselves in this connection. All praise the one God who feel Him. . . . We place words, tones, or images in connection with our inner feeling, our inkling of God."[43] Poetic words communicate the "inkling of God." The liquification of objects, *i.e.* their transforma-

---

43. Philipp Otto Runge, *Hinterlassene Schriften* (Hamburg, 1840), I, 12.

tion into vehicles of mood, is precisely irony. As Korff writes: "The spiritual attitude which surrenders poetic objects in favor of the poetry in them, that is romantic irony."[44] The ironic relativization of objectivity, the annihilation of substance, is man's emancipation from the torpidity of empirical externality and the liberation of the bewitched poetry congealed in objects. One can well imagine the feelings of frustration and despair that a romantic would experience should he not be able to romanticize objects. This was indeed the fate of late romantics including Marx.

Primal Fluidity as Lyrical Imagery

If we are to understand the dynamics of romantic poetization, including the imagery used by Marx, we must focus upon the common element found ever-differentiated in romantic imagery. It will be recalled that the primary category of reality for Romanticism is becoming. Becoming can be conceived as a flowing. Both physically and metaphysically, the *élan vital* of the universe is experienced as a type of fluidity. Fluidity is the common feature behind and expressed in the concrete richness of romantic imagery. It is experienced subjectively as a feeling of intoxication, be it effected by "the seed of the poppy" (Novalis), alcohol, erotic stimulation, or the sublime appearance of nature. In his *Apprentices at Said*, Novalis has a youth "with sparkling eyes" reveal the secret of secrets:

Whose heart does not stir in skipping joy, whenever the innermost life of nature in its fullness enters into his mind, whenever that mighty feeling, for which language has no other name than love and voluptuousness, expands itself in him as a powerful, all dissolving mist and he sinks quiveringly in sweet fear into the dark, enticing lap of nature; his poor personality is consumed in the tumbling waves of desire, and nothing remains other than the focal point of the immeasurable creative force, a swallowing [ingesting] vortex in the ocean. What is this flame which appears everywhere? An inner embrace whose sweet fruit condenses in voluptuous drops. Water, the

---

44. Korff, *Geist der Goethezeit*, III, 266.

firstborn of joyous fusions, cannot deny its voluptuous origin, and reveals itself on earth with heavenly omnipotence as the element of love and merger. Not without truth have the wise men of old sought the origins of things in water, and truly they spoke of a higher water than sea or fountain water. In the latter the primordial fluidity [*das Urflüssige*], as it comes to appear in li-quified metal, is revealed, and for that reason men have always worshipped it as divine. How few have steeped themselves in the secrets of the fluid, and for many this inkling of the highest joy and life has never arisen in the in-toxicated soul. The World- Soul, this powerful longing for dissolving [*Zer-fließen*], reveals itself in thirst. Those who are intoxicated feel all too well this superearthly joy of the fluid, and in the end all pleasurable sensations in us are manifold dissolvings, stirrings of the primordial waters in us. (S, I, 104)

This quotation reveals the primal attitude of romantics towards *das Urflüssige*. It is a Dionysian longing for self-dissolution, absorbtion, and passing over into a higher force, into the eternally feminine. The result is an intensification of feeling, intoxication. Oceanic, erotic, and dynamic forces, as forms of the primordial waters, consume and ingest the finitude of man in enthusing ecstasy.

The opposite to fluidity is fixedness, torpidity, or hardness—*Star-rheit*. Nothing could horrify romantics more than the thought of being brought to a standstill, to be bound to the rigidity of things. Schlegel writes: "Being bound [*Bindung*] is the most bitter annihi-lation that there is for a spiritual being" (KA, XII, 439). In such a case a stone is a stone and, alas, nothing more. The All becomes cold, dead. Fixedness enters into human consciousness as horror. Schlegel writes: "The form of the earthly element is permanence, fixedness [*Beharrlichkeit, Starrheit*]. That feeling which quite prop-erly brings with itself the consciousness of the form of fixedness is horror [*Schrecken*]. Horror is *the growing stiff of spirit* [*Erstarren des Ge-istes*]. . . . One could explain this horror . . . as the *intuition of empti-ness* . . . as a glance into the dark, horrifying realm of death" (KA, XII, 441–42). This is the primal fear of Romanticism! Should horror, frustration, or stasis be the final mood produced by a romantic poet, it would indicate the collapse of his romantic universe. We shall find such images in Marx. At any rate, the great battle between poetry and anti-poetry, mentioned by Klingsohr, is the conflict between fluidity and fixedness, between becoming and being, between what ought to be and what is.

Irony and the Crisis of Romantic Lyricism

It has long been the custom of literary historians to view romantic thought and literature as essentially optimistic. What can be more positive than intuition of the divine in nature? Such a view of Romanticism is not false, only inadequate. In recent years investigators have found that romantic thought contains the seeds for a pessimistic if not outright nihilistic view of reality.[45] Signs of such a crisis are to be found in the efforts of such leading romantics as E. T. A. Hoffmann, Wilhelm Heinrich Wackenroder, Ludwig Tieck, Friedrich Schlegel, Jean Paul Richter, Novalis, Joseph von Eichendorff, Clemens Brentano, Johann Karl Wetzel, Friedrich von Baader and others. So-called late romantics or postromantics such as Nikolaus Lenau, August von Platen, Heinrich Heine, Christian Grabbe, Georg Büchner and others exhibit even more clearly this crisis.[46] Reality simply could not be poetized, however much the author sought to do so. A *Weltschmerz* developed. If the crisis in romantic creativity is to be grasped, it must be viewed as a product of romantic irony itself.

In my previous exposition irony has been treated formally, that is to say as the causal activity of poetization. The poet annihilates the autonomy of objectivity in order to transform it into a revelation of the inner life of the *Ur-Ich*. But, paradoxically, this life in its content

45. For a pioneering article on this matter see Werner Kohlschmidt, "Nihilismus der Romantik," in *Form und Innerlichkeit: Beiträge zur Geschichte und Wirkung der deutschen Klassik und Romantik* (Bern, 1955), 157–76.
46. For four brilliant studies on the romantic and / or postromantic crisis see Dieter Arendt, *Der poetische Nihilismus in der Romantik: Studien zum Verhältnis von Dichtung und Wirklichkeit in der Frühromantik* (2 vols.; Tübingen, 1972); Walter Hof, *Pessimistisch-nihilistische Strömungen in der deutschen Literatur vom Sturm und Drang bis zum Jungen Deutschland* (Tübingen, 1970); Christa Karoli, *Ideal und Krise enthusiastischen Künstlertums in der deutschen Romantik* (Bonn, 1968); and Walter Weiss, *Enttäuschter Pantheismus: Zur Weltgestaltung der Dichtung in der Restaurationszeit* (Dornbirn, 1962).

is also irony. Ontologically, the *Ur-Ich* is posited by romantic philosophy as becoming. Becoming is the synthesis of time and eternity, the infinite and the finite. However, this synthesis is of necessity asymptotic. The finite and infinite aspects of becoming "are both really one and the same thing and only different according to degree" (KA, XIII, 277). This "degree" of difference is, nevertheless, everlasting. The infinite can never fully be expressed in the finite if becoming is not to cease. Therefore, the realm of the finite must always become other than it is. This "always" is precisely the degree of difference between the infinite and the finite. Therefore, becoming as a process structurally entails a positing of a goal or an affirmation of a given objectivity, which is then followed by a negation of the achieved or affirmed in order to pass on, to transcend, to become. Psychologically expressed, becoming is longing or striving, about which Schlegel writes: "[Being as a goal] is only *appearance*; it is the boundary of becoming, or striving. Whenever striving arrives at a goal, that disappears and a new goal arises again. . . . As soon as [the goal] is obtained, appearance and what appears as being disappear in activity, a new endless Becoming becomes" (KA, XII, 336).

If the origins of the crisis in Romanticism are to become clear, it must be understood that the "goal" of romantic longing is not something complete, fully one, totally reconciled. Romantic longing does not seek the achievement of a goal, but the achieving process itself. In other words, the dynamics of movement is itself the goal. Novalis writes: "Genuine enjoyment is a *perpetuum mobile*" (S, III, 562). The destiny of the human self "would always be to be more and more" (S, II, 267). The psychological mode of becoming is longing. Therefore, the goal of longing is longing itself, the striving to be more and more. Longing is an urge toward unity, an aspiration to bridge all separation between subjectivity and objectivity. Romantic longing sought the Dionysian dissolution of the finite self in the infinite Self of the universe. Initially longing generates a sense of joy, fulfillment, and affirmation insofar as it propels the self toward its goal of unity. At the same time, however, longing can be maintained only if the gap between the goal and the striving is not closed. The duality of and distance between subject and object must be maintained. Psychologically, such a distance will generate a feeling of hunger, need, frustration, in short, negativity. Longing is a volitional contradiction raised to the level of consciousness. Longing is an antinomy of affirmation and negation, fulfillment and hunger, joy and sadness. In short, longing can be metaphysically defined as an activity of positing unity, annihilating all achieved unity, and transcending. This is also a definition of irony.

If the feeling of longing itself is the ultimate goal of longing, then any finite object *qua* being a goal of human striving is not and cannot be a final telos of human needs. The ironist must maintain distance between himself and objectivity, even a romanticized objectivity. As Schlegel wrote in his *On Goethe's "Meister"*: "We must raise ourselves above our own love and be able to annihilate in thought what [namely, objectivity] we worship; otherwise we lack, whatever capabilities we possess, the sense for the world-all" (KA, II, 131). However much any given objective contents of consciousness have been romanticized, they cannot, precisely because they are encased in a specific finite embodiment, constitute the ultimate unity in which man can totally dissolve himself. Any given unification of the absolute with the relative, the fluid with the rigid, becoming with being, is only momentary and therefore must be transcended. Indeed, only by means of such an abstraction (which Schlegel referred to as a hovering or soaring) can the human mind become aware of the absolute fluidity slumbering in all things. Romantic poetry, writes Schlegel, "can soar [*schweben*], on the wings of poetic reflection [*i.e.* abstraction], midway between the word and the artist [*i.e.* between created being and creating becoming]. . . . The romantic type of poetry is still becoming; indeed, its peculiar essence is that it is always becoming and that it can never be completed" (KA, II, 182–83). Similarly expressed, the human subject must "be able to abstract from every single thing [*i.e.* negate all finitude], to grasp hoveringly the general [*i.e.* infinitude flowing through finitude], to survey a mass, to seize the totality" (KA, II, 131). This power of abstraction is what is known as irony. K. W. F. Solger, who developed a theory of irony similar to Schlegel's, writes: "The artist must annihilate the real world. . . . This attitude of the artist whereby he posits the world as nothingness [*das Nichtige*], we call artistic irony."[47] Insofar as irony reduces objectivity to nothingness, it is related to comedy. Schlegel writes: "There are old and modern poems which breathe the breath of irony fully in the whole and everywhere. There lives in them a truly transcendental buffoonery" (KA, II, 152). Novalis writes: "What [Friedrich] Schlegel characterized so sharply as irony is, in my opinion, nothing but . . . the true presence of spirit. . . . Schlegel's irony appears to be genuine humor" (S, II, 428). Irony entails humor because it does not and cannot take objectivity too seriously, *i.e.* as the locus of its perfection. Humor implies that the object laughed at contains a lack of seriousness or, conversely, has been revealed to be nothing. Solger writes: "Without irony there is no art. If the Idea [*i.e.* Infinitude] is to transform itself into reality, then the consciousness must dwell in us that it is entering thereby simultaneously into nothingness [*Nichtigkeit*]."[48] This nothingness of finitude affects the human spirit as humorous because it is not absolute; it is rather that which enables the unconditioned to shine forth as spirit. The essence of spirit is, of course, longing or becoming. Accordingly Schlegel contends: "Irony is the consciousness of eternal agility [*i.e.* the dynamics of becoming], of the infinitely full chaos [*i.e.* the fountainhead of becoming]" (KA, II, 263).

But, as has been shown, the structural genesis of longing is an antinomy, the contradiction between the affirmed and the negated, between oneness and duality. This is the eternal gap that must remain if longing is to remain in motion. This gap is that which romantics wished to perceive. At one point Schlegel designated the romantic antinomy as Socratic irony. "Socratic irony . . . contains and incites a feeling of the insoluble conflict between the unconditioned and the conditioned, of the impossibility and necessity of total communication" (KA, II, 160). Solger too posits a contradiction as the essence of irony. "Genuine irony presupposes the highest consciousness by means of which the human spirit is fully clear about the contrast and unity of the Idea and reality."[49] Irony as its own goal requires a per-

47. Cf. K. W. F. Solger, *Vorlesungen über Aesthetik*, ed. K. W. L. Heyse (Leipzig, 1829), 125.
48. *Ibid.*, 199.
49. *Ibid.*, 247.

manent gap between the longing subject and the longed-for object. Infinite fullness will always transcend man's powers, recede from his longing. Novalis counsels: "Through voluntary renunciation of the absolute [*i.e.* of temporally achieved infinitude] there arises in us infinite and free activity—the only possible absolute which can be given to us and which we find through our incapacity to obtain and to know an absolute. This absolute given to us can only be negatively known insofar as we act and find that what we seek cannot be reached by any action" (S, II, 269–70). This negative absolute, this goal which can never be reached, this need that can never be fulfilled, this is experienced aesthetically by romantics as cosmic love. Concerning the secrets of love Novalis writes:

> Never does this sweet meal end,
> Love never satiates itself.
> Not intimately, not concretely enough
> Can love possess the beloved.
> By ever more tender lips
> What is enjoyed is transformed
> Inwardlier and closer.
> Burning voluptuousness
> Animates the soul.
> Thirstier and hungrier
> Becomes the heart:
> And thus endures the joy of love.
> From eternity unto eternity.
> Should those who are sober
> Ever have tasted,
> They would forsake everything
> And join us
> At the table of longing,
> Which never becomes empty.
> They would recognize love's
> Infinite fullness
> And would praise the nourishment
> Of body and blood. (S, I, 167–68)

The ironic act whereby Romantics sought to reconcile the finite and the infinite is essentially a dialectical process. The dynamics of this dialectic consist of creative negation or annihilation. Every goal, every empirical embodiment of spirit in nature, must be relativized and negated as a completed actuality so that the underlying flow of cosmic subjectivity can be emancipated. But this flow itself reveals itself to be nothing but the dialectics of irony writ large. All affirmation is followed by negation, all satiety by hunger. At one point Schlegel compared longing to a circle (cf. KA, XII, 10–11). At the center is a positive element—the unconditioned, infinite enthusiasm. Emanating from the center is a negative (and negating) radius—skepticism or abstraction from objectivity (*i.e.*, in effect, irony). Such a radius is ever growing. On the periphery there is to be found another positive factor, a point, namely man. This point contains within its very heart a longing to unite itself with the center. But the negative factor hinders the realization of such a unification. The resultant state of affairs is that the peripheral point—man—"is merely driven around the center in ever widening arcs." In short, all affirmation must end in an ever more encompassing negation. Negation, nothing, nothingness thereby shows itself to the dialectical secret of irony, the ultimate product conjured up by the magical word of romantic poetry. Whereas romantics had hoped to achieve *substantial* life (to borrow a term from Hegel) by means of irony, many often came to discover that such substantiality, too, had to be ironized. The result was endless hunger and suffering.

Arthur Schopenhauer, whose pessimistic philosophy is seen by H. A. Korff as the logical culmination of romantic philosophy, clearly grasped the vanity of eternal becoming.[50] Schopenhauer's "will to life" is a philosophical offspring of the dialectics of irony. Indeed, in my judgment, it is irony that has become aware of the hopelessness of its longing. Romantic longing, raised to an absolute by thinkers such as Schlegel and Novalis, was to reveal itself in the first decades

50. Cf. Korff's brilliant interpretation of Schopenhauer's philosophy as the culmination of romantic philosophy in *Geist der Goethezeit*, IV, 513–39. Charles I. Glicksberg interprets Schopenhauer's thought as the "implicit irony of pessimism." Cf. Charles I. Glicksberg, *The Ironic Vision in Modern Literature* (The Hague, 1969), 39–50.

of the nineteenth century as a blind, senseless, and insatiable will to life. This, indeed, is that into which Schopenhauer transformed the romantic antinomy at the heart of irony. The cosmogonic will active in man, the *Ur-Ich*, has no absolute goal; it is just a ravenous hunger. Pain, frustration, and meaninglessness are the trademarks of a world that is the representation or objectification of such an "ironic" will. "This vanity [called the world]," writes Schopenhauer, "finds expression in the way in which things exist . . . in continual Becoming without ever Being; in constant wishing and never being satisfied. . . . In a world where all is unstable, and naught can endure, but is swept onwards at once in the hurrying whirlpool of change . . . how can [man] dwell where, as Plato says, *continual Becoming and never Being* is the sole form of existence?" [51] Schlegel had done away with being, with permanence, in order to raise becoming, endless change, to the primacy of reality. This eternal becoming, the ontological source of romantic irony, is now viewed as the indelible mark of suffering. That which underlies nature, the lyrical mood of nature, is not rapturous joy, but suffering, a *Weltschmerz*.

Novalis had referred to nature as "an Aeolus-harp—She is a musical instrument—whose tones are the key to higher strings in us" (S, III, 452). "A *musical phantasy* [is] the harmonious consequence of an Aeolus-harp—*nature itself*" (S, III, 454). Nature is the joyous music of cosmic love. Justinus Kerner, a romantic poet of some talent, asks in his poem "Der Grundton der Natur" ("The Fundamental Tone of Nature"):

> When the woods roar in the wind,
> When leaf exchanges speech with leaf,
> I would like to ask the leaves:
> Do you entone joys?
> Do you entone complaints?

And the answer, Schopenhauerian in essence:

51. Cf. "The Vanity of Existence" from *Parerga* reprinted in *The Will to Live: Selected Writings of Arthur Schopenhauer*, ed. Richard Taylor (Garden City, 1962), 229–30.

Listen to the Aeolus-harp!
Pain is the fundamental tone of nature;
Pain is the roaring singing of the woods,
Pain is the whispering springing of the stream,
And for the most part out of human jokes
Pain resounds as the fundamental tone, only pain.
(DR, I, 772)

The ontological source of reality—God—causes pain, not joy. This led some romantics to toy with the idea that either God does not exist or that he is cruel.[52] A pessimistic atheism or a sadistic God, these are alternatives found in the horrifying visions of Jean Paul Richter. In his gruesome "Speech of the Dead Christ from the World-Edifice that There is No God" Jean Paul has Christ appear in a dream as a "noble form with everlasting pain." Christ is no longer a mediator of God, no longer an incarnation of the divine in the finite. Schlegel and Novalis could find God in everything—in plants, stones, animals, or a beloved. Christ, the symbol of such mediation, is no longer more than human. Responding to the inquiry about the existence of God, Christ plaintively says:

"I traveled through the world, I climbed into suns, and flew with the milky ways through the deserts of heaven; but there is no God. . . . I heard the eternal storm which no one governs, and the slumbering rainbow out of the west standing without a sun that created it, standing over the abyss and dripped down. And when I looked up into the immeasurable world toward the godly eye, the world stared at me with an empty and fathomless eye-socket; and eternity lay upon chaos and gnawed it and chewed itself.— Scream on, mistones, scream the shadows to pieces; for He does not exist!" (DR, II, 374)

The cosmos of Romanticism was conceived as musical because it

---

52. The theme of divine cruelty in romantic thought has been dealt with by Karl S. Guthke, "Der Mythos des Bösen in der westeuropäischen Romantik," *Colloquia Germanica*, 1 / 2 (1968), 1–36, and H. G. Schenk, *The Mind of the European Romantics* (Garden City, 1969), 49–80.

was the lyrics of cosmic love. In Jean Paul's vision there is no such locus of love. Consequently, the tones of the cosmos are mistones, disharmonies.

In the nightmarish vision, appropriately called "Annihilation" ("Vernichtung"), Jean Paul has Ottomar view the endless suffering of all living beings. Everything arises and is annihilated. Ottomar speaks with a "devilish form that does the destroying. Ottomar asks: 'Lying form, the [human] self still glows,—who is squashing the spark [of life in man]?'—The form answered: 'Horror! . . . I have drawn you out of my head—you are already dead,'—and he grabbed [Ottomar] quickly and cuttingly with his cold metal-like feelers and whispered: 'Be horrified and die; I am God'" (DR, II, 404).

Whether the ontological source of nature be chaos or an evil God— different expressions of the same romantic *Weltschmerz*—it all adds up to the same annihilating fate. Romantic man has not been able to overcome an alien and estranged objectivity. Despite all the mental magic of irony, man remains a prisoner of a cold and oppressive reality. The helplessness of nihilistic Romanticism can be seen in Georg Büchner's Danton, who pitifully wishes to become nothing and must experience his inability to do so. Danton avers: "[Peace is] in nothingness. Sink yourself into something more restful than nothingness, and if the greatest peace is God, is not God nothingness. However, I am an atheist. That accursed statement: Something cannot become nothing! And I am something, that is the pity! Creation has spread itself so far that there is nothing empty; everything is full of multitudes. Nothingness has murdered itself, creation is its wound, we are its drops of blood, and the world the grave in which it rots."[53] The "fullness of being," praised by Schlegel and Novalis, has metamorphized into Büchner's "multitudes." Infinitude and finitude are no longer dialectically correlative; they are antithetical and irreconcilable forces. Nature and Spirit cannot be reconciled. More terrifying yet, Danton cannot escape this diseased reality because

53. Cf. Georg Büchner, *Werke und Briefe* (Frankfurt, 1967), 50. The crisis in romantic theodicy led Büchner to a nihilistic atheism. Cf. Leonard P. Wessell, Jr., "Eighteenth-Century Theodicy and the Death of God in Büchner's *Dantons Tod*," *Seminar*, VIII (1972), 198–218.

the magic word of poetry is powerless to transform things. To be is to suffer; this is the ontology of goalless becoming.

The doctrine of irony arose out of the metaphysical problem concerning the relation of the absolute reality and the contingency or oppressiveness of finitude. Irony is the power of subjectivity to say no to an unredeemed objectivity, the power to destroy such objectivity. However, if irony itself is raised to the absolute, then the very negativity of irony becomes an ambiguous and eventually self-destructive ideal. Ironic subjectivity cannot immerse itself in a cosmic substantiality but must remain a prisoner of its own eternal negating. Søren Kierkegaard came to view irony as "thoroughly negative: in a theoretical dimension it establishes a disparity between Idea [*i.e.* absolute reality] and [empirical] actuality, actuality and Idea; and in a practical dimension between possibility and actuality, actuality and possibility."[54] Therefore, for any one who has been seized by irony, "everything spins around him, he becomes giddy, and all things lose their reality."[55] Hegel too viewed irony as a self-destructive subjectivity. The ironic self "can only live in the bliss of self-enjoyment."[56] But, encased in its limits, the ironic self "seeks to penetrate into truth and longs after objectivity [*i.e.* to become a part of a universal totality], yet . . . he is unable to overcome this unsatisfied and abstract soul-inwardness, and consequently is seized with a fit of sentimental yearning."[57] Indeed, the fit of sentimental yearning (Hegel) is correlative to the "ironic self" losing all sense of reality (Kierkegaard).

The ironic self can continue the pursuit of substantiality, but he can encounter no goal that will satisfy, no finitude fully manifesting infinitude. All such embodiments will divest themselves of any substantiality. Kerner, in his poem "The Pilgrim" ("Der Pilger"), has the pilgrim, as he sinks in exhaustion, look up to espy a castle high upon a mountain.

---

54. Cf. Søren Kierkegaard, *The Concept of Irony with Constant Reference to Socrates*, trans. Lee M. Capel (New York, 1965), 302.
55. *Ibid.*, 281.
56. Cf. Hegel, *The Philosophy of Fine Art*, I, 90.
57. *Ibid.*, 91.

"Oh, infirm one, take heart!
[The castle] will accept you as a guest."
[The pilgrim] pulls himself together,
He hastens up the mountain.

And when he reaches the heights—
He sees a castle no more,
He sees a cloud standing there,
Which soon will die away like himself.
(DR, I, 771)

Looking for spiritual repast, the pilgrim sees a goal where he hopes to find succor. However, when he approaches the castle (objective value), it reveals itself to be an illusion. There is no firm goal, no solid castle high above, only the ephemeral appearance suggested by the cloud mass. Furthermore, as quickly as a cloud will dissipate, so too will the pilgrim.

Poetry cannot catch, express, and transform the inner experience of man. Although genuine poetry arises out of the human heart,

Yet the highest poetries
Fall silent like the highest pain,
Only like ghostly shadows do they move
Mutely through the broken heart.
(DR, I, 770)

These words from Kerner's poem called "Poetry" ("Poesie"), illustrate well the *Weltschmerz* of the romantic lyricist who finds his art inadequate to transform human misery into the redeeming joy of poetic meaning.

Summary

Novalis called his idealism magical because he believed in the power of the poetic word to transform objectivity into cosmic subjectivity, and into a meaningful universality. The more the ideal of romantic longing became suspect, the more doubt arose concerning the causal efficacy of poetry to realize human emancipation. Poetry could, of course, cast a spell on things, but not truly transform them. Novalis had written: "In the *future* [*i.e.* romanticized] world everything is as [it is] in the *former* world—*and yet everything is quite other*" (S, III, 281). The romanticized world is other because it has been poetized by the magical powers of the human mind. It remains, however, the same in its empirical surface, in its empirical reality. Should man not possess such magical power, then poetic conjuration casts a spell only on the subject, not upon the object. Sooner or later, this spell will show itself to be an illusion and the world will return to the way it formerly was and never ceased to be. Objectivity appears, consequently, to possess an autonomous being not amenable to the magic power of the ideal, of the human mind and will. Early nineteenth-century Germans felt this antagonism very keenly. Indeed, as Richard Brinkmann has brilliantly shown, the parameters of what is called literary realism are defined 1) by the independence of empirical objectivity and 2) by the problematic relationship of human subjectivity to this objectivity.[58] This problem underlies Gaudenz Ruf's attempt to interpret late Romanticism (*ca.* 1810–1835) as typifying a crisis of lyricism.[59] Poets such as Heinrich Heine, August von Platen, Ludwig Uhland longed for a lyrical world, but found that objectivity could not be lyricized, that their attempts were ineffectual. The magic spell of poetry simply negates itself in falling victim to its own ironic powers. As a result nature and spirit cease to merge into lyrical oneness but disassociate into antithetical forces. The *ought* of Romanticism—*i.e.* the imperative to infuse nature with the breath of spirit—and the *is* of actuality—*i.e.* an autonomous and oppressive objectivity—show themselves to be irreconcilable. The task facing the generation of Germans living in the late 1830s was to resolve the antagonism between man and nature, essence and existence, objectification and self-realization, in short, between subject and object.

58. Cf. Richard Brinkmann, *Wirklichkeit und Illusion: Studien über Gehalt und Grenzen des Begriffs Realismus für die erzählende Dichtung des Neunzehnten Jahrhunderts* (Tübingen, 1966), 309–33.
59. Cf. Gaudenz Ruf, *Wege der Spätromantik: Dichterische Verhaltensweisen in der Krise des Lyrischen* (Bonn, 1969), 1–7.

This was the great riddle of history still to be solved. It became Karl Marx's life project. We shall see that the proletariat's mission is to ironize the *is* in order to realize the *ought*. Let us now turn to Marx's romantic poetry and observe the inchoate genesis of the question which found its answer in the proletariat.

III
Marx and the Crisis
of His Romanticism

In a letter dated November 10, 1837, Marx wrote to his father about his move to Berlin in the fall of 1836. Marx explained, since he was in a lyrical mood, how his previous life had come to an end and a new era was beginning (E, I, 3). That which Marx was leaving behind was a certain romantic mood—one inflamed by his love for Jenny von Westphalen. Furthermore, this love appeared to be beyond any hope for consummation. Marx described his love-inspired experience as "a hopeless love drunk with longing" (E, I, 4). This love had so taken possession of his soul that one can say that his subjectivity, his subject-being, appeared to be beyond the domination of any objective environment. This is reflected in the very journey to Berlin. Instead of contemplating nature, in itself, Marx, "quite out of humor," compared the rugged and indomitable rocks seen along the way with "my soul," the life of big towns with "my blood," etc. Lyricizing nature, Marx appeared to perceive only what his subjective attitude could see reflected in things, namely its own moods (cf. E, I, 4).

This subjective mood dominated Marx's poetic creations which were the first order of business upon his arrival in Berlin. In retrospect Marx designated this poetry as "purely idealistic" (E, I, 4). In order to grasp the meaning of Marx's conversion to Hegel, announced later in the letter, we must gain a clear idea of what Marx understood by "idealism." Idealism did not then mean for him what it does today in histories of philosophy, the position that reality or objectivity can only exist as an object for a perceiving subject. In the second paragraph of his letter Marx notes that "world history itself" occasionally must sit back "in order to understand itself and mentally to penetrate its own deed, that of the mind [or spirit]" (E, I, 3). Two paragraphs later he informs his father that he regards "life in general, as the expression of a spiritual [or mental] activity which works itself out in all directions, in science, art, and private matters" (E, I, 3–4). Both these contentions are perfectly consonnant with the idealistic philosophy of Hegel. Indeed, when speaking of his own "Hegelian" speculations, Marx relates that he wrote a "philosophical-dialectical development of divinity, as it manifests itself as the idea-in-itself, as religion, as nature, and as history" (E, I, 9).

It is evident that Marx, at least from a twentieth-century perspective, was very much an idealist at the time of the letter and during his "Hegelian" phase. If this is so, then what did Marx understand by idealism, particularly as typifying his poetic endeavors? Marx himself gives the answer by describing his poetry.

A very distant beyond, as removed as my love, became my heaven, my art. Everything real becomes hazy and what is hazy has no boundary. All the poems of the first three volumes that I sent Jenny are characterized by attacks on our times, diffuse and formless expressions of feeling, nothing natural, everything constructed out of moonshine, the complete opposition between what is and what ought to be, rhetorical reflections instead of poetic thoughts, perhaps also a certain warmth of feeling and struggling for vitality. The entire breath of a longing that sees no boundary expresses itself in many different forms and makes out of "poetic composition" a "diffusing." (E, I, 4)

The key point lies in Marx's opposing of "what ought to be" to "what is." Commenting upon a three-hundred-page attempt on his part to work out a philosophy of law, Marx complains that it exhibits "the same opposition between what is and what ought to be which is a feature of idealism" (E, I, 4–5). It is worth noting that Marx admits being "nourished with the idealism of Kant and Fichte" (E, I, 8). Both philosophers stressed the impossibility of the primordial self (Kant's transcendental unity of apperception and Fichte's

Absolute Ego) ever obtaining full harmony with the universe as a whole. Kant poignantly expressed this ideal particular to both philosophers when, in his *Critique of Practical Reason*, he wrote: "Only endless progress from lower to higher stages is possible to a rational but finite being."[1] We have seen in Chapter II that romantics such as Schlegel and Novalis metamorphized such an asymptotic progress into the doctrine of "longing," whose aesthetic mode is irony. We have also seen that the eternal gap between the ideal (subjectivity) and the real (objectivity) was a fundamental cause for the development of a romantic *Weltschmerz*, one, as we shall see, that is evident in Marx's own poetry. The fact that Hegel in 1837 was exempted from the stain of idealism is important. This was not so when Marx completed his dissertation (1840/41); indeed, Hegel's philosophy was then seen as idealistic and hence as a subjective ideal standing in an ironic opposition to the objective real. This opposition will be explained in the next chapter as it contains the seeds of Marx's Marxism. First we must return to Marx's youthful poetry.

Although Marx rejected his idealistic poems, particularly his farce, *Scorpion and Felix*, and his fantastic drama, *Oulanem*, he nevertheless had to admit "these poems are the only ones in which suddenly, as if by a magic stroke—oh, the stroke was in the beginning so shattering—the realm of true poetry like a distant fairy palace flashed toward me, and all my creations disintegrated into nothing" (E, I, 8). Here Marx touches upon all the themes essential to Romanticism. Poetry is "magical" and can accordingly affect an individual with a shattering force. The romantics in their positive hopes believed that the magic of the word would transform the world—oppressive objectivity—into a "real" fairy palace, *i.e.* into a realm of spirit. Novalis wrote: "It is because of the weakness of our organs and self-contact that we do not perceive ourselves in a fairy-world. All fairy tales are only dreams of that homeland which is everywhere and nowhere" (S, II, 564). But as for so many romantics the experienced fairy-world of poetry "disintegrated into nothing" for Marx. "A curtain had fallen; my holy of holies was ripped to pieces

1. Immanuel Kant, *Critique of Practical Reason*, trans. Lewis White Black (Indianapolis, 1956), 217.

and new gods had to be installed" (E, I, 8). These "new gods" are important for understanding the question that led Marx to reject idealism and attempt to find the answer in the real, in materialism.

For the moment, it suffices to note that the downfall of Marx's poetic heaven was a function of the antinomy between the ideal and the real. Such a contradiction is, I contend, related to the fact that the substance of Marx's poetry is characterized by "a longing that sees no boundary," yet seeks unity with the bounded, *viz.* the real. It is for this reason that all Marx's poems "are characterized by attacks upon our times." This is just another expression of the idealistic antinomy between the "ought" and the "is." This antagonistic relationship to "our times" shows that the malaise experienced by many later eighteenth-century Germans had not been overcome but had come to the fore in Marx. Marx's subjectivity (similar to Fichte's) could find no peace in the "is"; instead, it had to concoct a world "out of moonshine" (out of pure subjectivity). Therefore, it was faced with the inevitable collapse of the magically, but not really produced fairy palace of Romanticism. Whereas romantics had sought to combine infinity with finitude, satiety with hunger, Marx, like others of his day, experienced these contradictory attributes of God as antagonistic forces. Marx's boundless longing for union with the All had to confront objective nothingness. The story of this confrontation is the key to the unity of his poetry. The plot of this drama is structured around Marx's use of irony. Hegel's description of irony as a principle of art presents us with a fair picture of Marx's own poetry:

The ironical here . . . consists in the self-annihilation of what is noble, great, and excellent [as given in objectivity]. . . . In short it amounts to this, that irony contradicts and annihilates itself as manifested in individuals, characters, and actions, and consequently is an irony which overreaches itself. . . . Now if irony is made the keynote of the representation [of art], we have the extreme antithesis to art [in the Hegelian sense of a reconciliation between subjectivity and objectivity] accepted as the true principle of the work of art. For what we have here is in part insipid figures, in part figures that have neither content nor defined position. Seeing that what is of substance in them is proved to be an illusion. And, last of all, we have to bargain those yearning floods and unresolved contradictions of the soul. Compositions of this kind are not likely to arouse real interest.[2]

Hegel's thesis appears to be a description of Marx's own poetry. As poetry alone, Marx's endeavors do not arouse any real interest; however, as revelations of Marx's understanding of himself and his world, they are priceless.

Fluidity Symbolism and Irony

My contention has been that Marx's early poetry reflects the crisis of Romanticism, that is to say, the crisis of romantic irony. Although in the poems themselves Marx never uses the term irony, a large number—more than half—embody irony as the overriding attitude which constitutes their unity. Irony for the most part is present in Marx's poems under the guise of fluid-like symbols. Commenting upon Marx's poems, Arend van Leeuwen avers: "Reading this poetry with care, one is struck by one outstanding feature. It is the ever-recurrent use of the symbolism of an ocean, in most cases an ocean of water, but sometimes an ocean of fire and light. Closer investigation from a psychoanalytic viewpoint is likely to discover a strong inclination towards maternalistic symbols, arising out of a latent desire to return to the pre-natal and pre-conscious bliss of the womb. In terms of the phenomenology of religion, there is an evident tendency towards the symbols of a mother-religion."[3] Unfortunately van Leeuwen has made little attempt to pursue the water symbolism in Marx's poems, though he has made some enlightening suggestions. Above in dealing with Schlegel and particularly Novalis, we noted that a "primordial fluidity" plays an important role in their romantic philosophy. The real is *becoming*, eternal movement, a movement that manifests the musicality of the *Ur-Ich*. This *élan vital* is often referred to as something fluid, flowing, watery. It is, indeed, the dynamics immanent in divine creativity. The world of "only things" is but so many ever-changing "congelations" or con-

2. Hegel, *The Philosophy of Fine Art*, I, 91–93.
3. Arend van Leeuwen, *Critique of Heaven* (London, 1972), 48.

densations of the underlying ontological fluidity. The experience of such cosmogonic and cosmological energy—divine Eros—causes the romantic to turn with an ironic attitude toward "only things." This attitude was not without its internal dangers—dangers which, indeed, led to a *Weltschmerz* and Schopenhauer's hungry and aimless will to life. It is within this context that one can best grasp the constructive and generative role fluid symbolism plays within the collegiate Marx's romantic world. Fluidity represents Marx's "holy of holies" which had to be replaced by "new gods."

Feelings of Oneness

Marx did at one point intend to publish an essay *"de romanticis."*[4] However, as far as I know the manuscript has not survived. Besides his letter of November 10, 1837, to his father in which some reference to idealism (*viz.* Romanticism) is found, we do not possess any detailed reflections by Marx upon the romantic cosmos, Magical Idealism, irony, the poetic word, etc. Certainly there is nothing in Marx's writings comparable to the voluminous notes on romantic thought written by Schlegel or Novalis. Nevertheless, we do possess the poems themselves. If the poems are examined closely, it is possible, in my judgment, to find directly or indirectly the major themes of romantic philosophy.

In the poem "Creation" ("Schöpfung") Marx presents his readers with a cosmos conceived in a romantic manner. The opening stanza is centered upon the activity of an "uncreated creator-spirit." The flowing dynamics of such a spirit is presented in the first three stanzas. The spirit moves on "light waves," the world "billows" and life "gushes forth." Nothing is still, nothing inert, all is flowing. Such a movement can be viewed as the stirring of the world-mind. Even space and time do not constitute a "dead" geometrical continuum but are described in terms suggesting life. Indeed, space and time "pray" to the creator-spirit. This is, of course, a highly romantic conception. In short, the All is animated, all objects move, are active.

---

4. Cf. Marx's letters of March 20, April 27, and July 9, 1842, to Arnold Ruge.

Relative to the throbbing All, the creator-spirit "indicates approval," *i.e.* the creator-spirit experiences the cosmos as something that nourishes spiritual needs. The very approval, as an out-flowing of love, seems to clothe the cosmos in transfiguration. In short, Marx has created a cosmos that is "objectively" an extension of spirit, of love.

In the third stanza Marx more or less recapitulates. The eternal (or creator-spirit) moves ever on. The German word for this movement is *drängen*, which I have rendered as "to throng." *Drängen* implies that an inner impulse is pushing, striving for actualization. The ontological mode in which such striving exists is mental—the creator-spirit moves "reflectingly" (*"sinnend"*). The creative fount of reality is not inert matter moved by mechanistic causality but mental energy. This energy exists as "primordial thoughts" which, so to speak, condense themselves into "form and poetic word." Marx uses the verb *verhüllen* to refer to the activity of "primordial thoughts." The normal meaning of the term is "to cover up" or "to conceal." However, in this poem Marx intended another meaning. The verbal root *hüllen* means "to wrap," "to fold," or "to envelop." The prefix *ver* can indicate a concealing activity, but it can also mean a "causing to be." Alex Miller has translated the German as "holy thought primordial / Dons Forms, Words of Poetry."[5] This translation is not without ingenuity, although it is misleading. The English verb "to don" implies that that which is donned is different from the one who "dons." This misrepresents Marx's poetic intent. Marx was saying, I hold, that primordial thought, as the cosmogonic energy, was causing itself *to become* "form and poetic word," *i.e.* the concrete "objects" of the cosmos. Marx similarly in the first stanza refers to the "all-animating rule" of the creator-spirit's glance, which "burns itself with more firm magic into forms." Similarly, the primordial thoughts envelop themselves (*i.e.* congeal) and the result of their enveloping is precisely "form and poetic word." Therefore, the cosmos is not a creation *ex nihilo* as it is represented in Christian theology; rather it is an emanation emitted out of the mental energy that constitutes the reality of the creator-spirit. The "things" of the

5. *Karl Marx–Friedrich Engels: Collected Works*, ed. Institute of Marxism–Leninism, Moscow (New York, 1975), I, 534.

universe are not ontologically "other" than the creator-spirit's reality but congealizations of it. Consequently, Marx has in effect concocted a cosmos as the poetic expression of an *Ur-Ich*. The congealed forms of primordial thought, the concrete objects of the universe, are but so many poetic words. No wonder, the cosmos "resounds, as if afar from thunder-lyres." In other words, insofar as the things of the universe are poetic expressions of spiritual energy, and insofar as that energy is love, then the expression of such energy will be musical, will be lyrical. Indeed, the cosmos is a vocal "celebration of the creator."

The remainder of the poem, placed in quotation marks, constitutes the song of jubilation sung by the creator-spirit. The creator-spirit relates that "worlds rest in primordial mountain's weight." This image connotes, of course, a feeling of weightiness, solidity, or inertia. In my judgment, this image represents the empirical surface of finite things because, as often occurs in romantic thinking, congealed fluidity, taken merely in its empirical exteriority, assumes features of solidity, torpidity, bulkiness, or inertia. According to Schlegel the energy of the *Ur-Ich* assumes the form of *Starrheit, i.e.* permanence and fixedness. Such imagery occurs elsewhere in Marx's poems as we shall see. It is man's romantic mission, however, to penetrate the exteriority of things, or the fixedness of objects, in order to bring to consciousness the inner life and fluidity of creative energy. The power to realize this "magical" act is derived from love. In other words, only love can enable man to perceive the things of nature as "form and poetic word." This thesis is echoed in "The Singer's Love" ("Sängerliebe") in which Marx asserts: "Only love binds words / To the warm breath of the soul, / Draws spirit out of a higher place / Into the torrent and vapour of the [poetic] image" (MEGA, I^1, 503). Similarly, referring to the stars in "Creation," Marx states that they, as "holy images" of the creator-spirit, can only be appropriated by spirit. Spirit is grasped only by spirit. The creator-spirit has "poured" itself into the stars; therefore, the stars should reflect their "soul's light." The soul of the stars is, of course, the love-energy poured into them by the creator-spirit. In a similar manner in the poem "Two Heavens" ("Die Zwei Himmel") Marx equates love with the function of the sun in the universe. Indeed, the energy of the sun seems to be a form of love. "And through the entire mechanism [of the universe] / [The sun] flashes and is called: Love" (MEGA, I¹ , 484). Likewise the creator-spirit in "Creation," manifesting itself in the light of the stars (*i.e.* via objectivity), can only be "experienced" if the human spirit is inspired by love. Love is the causal energy of revelation; it is spirit grasping spirit. This act of revelation is, of course, the magic of irony. Indeed, it would appear that the human spirit is a necessary complement to the meaning of the stars. After all, if the stars are "poetic words," there must be a consciousness that can understand them. Only in that manner can the stars become actualized poetry. Once man has embraced the stars as poetic words, they vanish or flow into man, and reciprocally man vanishes into the creator-spirit. This vanishing is the return of spirit into itself, the generation of spiritual self-consciousness.

In the companion poem to "Creation," appropriately entitled "Poetry" ("Dichtung"), Marx shifts his perspective from the creator-spirit to that of man (or himself) who faces cosmic objectivity conceived as "form and poetic word." Man (or Marx) addresses the creator-spirit that streams out of the cosmos in upon him. He speaks to the cosmos as a "thou." The universe is not a dead "it" but a loving partner. Enveloped in rippling flame (*i.e.* liquified), man perceives the heavens which rise up, then sink down, only to fly up even higher. In other words, the cosmos begins to flow, to reveal its inner fluidity in its surface manifestations. The "primordial mountain's weight" has been dissolved; the heavens are now seen as "pain and joy condensed in song." Nature "reminds" man of love, of spirit. Marx's whole being begins to vibrate to this inner love and musicality of creation. The power of love is thereby set free in Marx (or in man). We must examine more closely the nature of this intoxicating experience of nature as "poetry."

It is clear from the poems just examined that Marx has created a romantic universe. Spirit, creativity, musicality, and fluidity are different aspects of the same cosmic reality. We have noted in the last chapter that the underlying attitude of romantics to creation is Dionysian. Inspired by cosmic poetry, man is impelled to dissolve himself in the ecstacy of "primordial thoughts." This Dionysian attitude, this passivity vis-à-vis nature, is adumbrated in Marx's poem "Awakening" ("Erwachen").

In this poem Marx presents man in his individuality. The first stanza reveals the individual in a state of ecstasy. The individual's eye, *i.e.* his consciousness, is "transported and trembling"; indeed, its emotional tension is compared to the "undulating tone" of musical strings. Moreover, these tones have slumbered in reflection bound to the lyre. The individual has, so to speak, been set into a fluid state. Such intoxication is simultaneously musical in nature. Music is therefore treated as a spiritual force that, once awakened, can penetrate the apparent opaqueness of reality, *i.e.* the "veil of primordial night." Correlative to the awakening of music's powers, is the reciprocal spiritual activity of the stars which flash "lovingly inwards."

Marx develops his theme more fully in the second stanza. The individual in fear and trembling perceives the immensity of the universe. The stars glide "in dance-like rows," that is they show themselves to be animated dynamically by poetry. The individual experiences his own individuation as being that of an atom. Such extreme individuation is surrendered, as the individual is absorbed into the cosmos. Marx uses the verb *versinken*, which means not only "to sink," but "to be immersed" or "to be absorbed." This absorption into the cosmos, as is clear from the third stanza, is precisely the individual's awakening.

This awakening has musical, magical, and even erotic aspects. If the soul as a "rippling flame" (fluidity) turns into its own breast, it will emerge "carried by a sweet smelling magical tone" toward a "daemonic abyss." In other words, the very activity of the human soul is shown to be a magical causality which propels man to pass over into the endless and awesome heart of the creator-spirit. The all-absorbing must indeed appear as a daemonic abyss. The merging into the divine abyss is felt erotically as the "flaming eternal lovekiss of divinity." The awareness of divinity, man's awakening, is, in short, the erotic feeling of progressive dissolving of human finitude in the *élan vital* of the cosmos. The result is, of course, the sense of cosmic oneness. Man as a finite "atom" has transcended the boundaries of this empirical finitude and has become one with spiritual universality.

Marx was very perceptive in his letter to his father when he referred to his poetic heaven as "a very distant beyond, as removed as [his] love. Everything real becomes hazy, and what is hazy has no boundary." Indeed, the haziness of things is precisely their liquefication or transformation into romanticized reality. Empirical things cannot intoxicate man as do poetic words unless they lose all "boundaries." Insofar as we may judge Marx himself to have been so intoxicated, his poems can be no more than "diffuse and formless expressions of feeling." This makes them lyrical to the extreme, even if they lack "composition" and instead exhibit "diffusion."

The tendency toward poetic diffusion involves more than a dearth of talent on Marx's part. Marx was correct in stating that the poems are marked by "nothing natural, everything constructed out of moonshine." Marx certainly lacked the poet's ability to concretize his emotions. Marx could not find adequate imagery to express the poetic universal he wished to mediate. In this sense one can speak of a "forced" talent. Marx's imagery often strikes the reader (particularly the historically informed reader) as all too conventional, contrived, and forced. Nevertheless, in my judgment, Marx's failure to individualize poetic abstractions, to give concrete form and naturalness to his poetic heaven, derives in part from the fact that the poems are marked by the "complete opposition between what is and what ought to be." Let us recall that romantics wished not only to experience the unconditioned (sacred power), but to experience the unconditioned in and by means of empirical objects. The creator-spirit shines upon man only indirectly through the heavenly stars. It is at this point that the crisis in romantic lyricism begins. "We *seek* everywhere the unconditioned [*das Unbedingte*]," wrote Novalis, "but always *find* only things [*nur Dinge*]" (S, II, 412). Insofar as Marx can experience his "heaven" (and he appears to have done so in the poems just examined), it must of necessity be remote, beyond, or hazy. That is, "only things" must recede into the background of consciousness. If one extrapolates from the Dionysian imperative, then "only things" must ultimately disappear. But let consciousness be focused upon "only things" and the absence of the unconditioned will become apparent. The more sharply "only things" are experienced in opposition to the unconditioned, the more empirical reality will produce in the romantic mind a sense of alienation. Nature will metamorphize from a loving "thou" into an oppressive *alium*, into a soulless "it." We find this mood of alienation in a large number of Marx's poems.

Feelings of Alienation

The opposition between nature and spirit is the theme of "Song to the Stars" ("Lied an die Sterne"). In the first stanza the stars are once again represented as moving, as swelling with plenitude. But, as the next stanzas indicate, the "most beautiful soul" fails to perceive the divine in them. The lyrical heart raises its eyes to the stars hoping "child-like to suck in hope and Eternity's substance." But the stars only glitter as an illusion because the gods have never injected spirituality into the stars. The stars have no soul! That is, they are indifferent to human longing. Insofar as the stars can be said to have a spiritual relation to man, it is that of "mocking" (cf. stanza five). The inner musicality of the human spirit—"the breast's song of fire"— shatters its longing against the stars (cf. stanza six). But man's suffering makes no difference to the cold stars, indeed, also to the earth. "We must from pain turn grey, / Desparingly go under, / And then look to the mockery / That earth and heaven remain." In other words, objectivity, despite man's obvious suffering, remains unaffected. Objectivity is indeed an alien force, an oppressive enemy. The primal fear of romantics that reality is soulless was assuming form for Marx.

However, as Marx indicates in the last three stanzas, if cosmic objectivity were to reflect man's inner suffering, it would, in effect, be destroyed. For example, the stars would cease to shine; eternal night would reign. Such an annihilation of the cosmos is, of course, ironic, although irony without creativity. If man's soul is robbed by the stars of its beauty, then so too should the stars lose their glitter. Reality must become nothing, pure negativity for the frustrated romantic. We shall see that this destructive, ironic attitude of revenge is an integral part of Marx's revolt against Romanticism and hence his search for the proletariat.

The opposition between subject and object or spirit and nature expressed in "Song to the Stars" has many ramifications. In one way or another the various aspects of Romanticism show themselves to be illusions. For instance, we noted in the previous chapter that the poet magically transforms "only things" into romanticized reality. The poet derives such power from his unconscious self, *i.e.* from the *Ur-Ich* grounding his individual *Ich*. From the point of the empirical *Ich*, the poetizing power of the *Ur-Ich*, the spark of the divine poet in the individual, can appear as a cosmic force that seizes the human soul, that inspires it. This is but one aspect of Dionysian absorption. This intoxicating power will appear as a supra-personal, *i.e.* non-individuated, force. The German language can combine the indefinite pronoun *es* ("it") with certain verbs to indicate an activity is taking place as opposed to the actor. For instance, *es spukt in diesem Haus* means not only that "this house is spooky" or "it is spooky in this house" (which are valid translations), but also that there is an inde-terminate force, an *es*, which is causally active in a frightening man-ner. Similarly, the sentence *es träumt mir* not only means that "I am dreaming," but can imply that dreaming is going on in me. In a few of Marx's poems such as "Zauberharfe" ("Magic Harp"), use is made of this grammatical and semantic peculiarity. Only in this case the *es* is identified with the causal power of music. It should be re-called that romantics identified the life of the *Ur-Ich* with musicality. The language of music in creating its own poetical world reveals the poetic universal of the cosmos. In other words, man transcends the finitude of his being by means of the revelatory power of the inner music of his own divine subjectivity. In the poem "Harmonie" (MEGA, I^1, 572–73), which I have not translated, Marx locates the power to produce the redemptive *Zauberbild* (magical image) in man's subjectivity:

> [The Magical image] is similar to the sound of a zither
>   Played upon an eternal lyre
>   In constant glowing, constant celebrating,

In an elevated, ardently longing impulse.
Oh, listen to the strings which echo in you,
Your feet will not surge to seek any further.

Longing itself is the source of the music that produces the magic image, that transforms nature into spirit. The instrument that produces such music is "an eternal lyre." This super-individual force, this spark of the divine musician in man, is redemptive. It can be compared with an *es* or universal (power) that works upon the human self, that animates man's creative powers. The poet comes to hear the music of his cosmic subjectivity and thereby the music of the cosmos.

In the "Magical Harp" Marx continually refers to an *es* which, similar to "the joys of harps" and to "the sound of strings," awakens a master singer, *i.e.* the musical and lyrical powers in man. But this musical *es* affects the singer as something "fearful." It seems as if the song is one of complaint, not of joy. The singer pursues this *es* "deep into the grave." The *es* draws the singer on; indeed, the lyre is "played by no one." In short, music is a power that appears to transcend and to overpower man. Yet, the singer discovers that his own heart (*Ur-Ich*) is playing the lyre. Indeed, the musical *es* is his own being, his very pain. In no place in the poem is there any mention made of a "thou" which answers the music of the human heart, which offers the human heart succor. The music of his being does not enable man to pass beyond his own finitude. "It grasps him so strangely fearful of melancholy, / He saw the light outside no more." The musical self, longing to merge in love with a "thou," finds itself instead caught prisoner in its own insatiable longing. Music does not transform objectivity but only reveals the inner suffering of the human heart. Music does not conjure up a "magical image," only reveals inner pain. The "outside" exists no more for the isolated and frustrated lyrical self. The whole tenor of the poem suggests that the musical *es* is an ominous, destructive, or annihilating power. In short, the *es* does not enable man to encounter a "thou" in the exteriority of objectivity.

The same suffering of an isolated self is evident in "Sehnsucht" ("Longing"). An interlocutor asks the lyrical self of the poem why it is all aglow. The lyrical self asks to be shown "an eye" where streams glow, where songs bubble. In other words, the lyrical self wants to encounter love ablaze in a beloved one, in an objectivity. The interlocutor seems puzzled at the lyrical self's frustration. For after all, "Here the tide rages, here profit surges, / Here it glows in bands of love." The "here" referred to is the here of the empirical environment. The lyrical self emphatically denies this assertion. "'Here it does not surge, here it does not glow.'" Desire burns within the lyrical self, but there is no answer, no beloved in the "here" to fulfill such longing. The lyrical self, its heart glowing, sinks down thunderstruck. The German term for thunderstruck is *entgeistert*. Literally this past participle means "despirited." If we take the term at face value, it implies that the lyrical self has become through the frustration of its passion *de-spirited, i.e.* inwardly annihilated. In short, spirit, caught in the confines of its subjectivity, must go to pieces. Spirit is condemned to an objectivity that can not be lyricized. Longing or *Sehnsucht* is not here the liberating force for Marx that it was for Novalis. Longing languishes in self-destruction.

It is fascinating that Marx makes direct use of fluidity imagery as a symbol for human alienation. In the "Old Man of the Water" ("Der Wassergreis") Marx represents the water as an ominous and oppressive power.

> Water rushes so strangely there.
> Circles on its waves.
> Believe well! It does not feel,
> As the wave breaks,
> It is cold in its heart, cold in its mind,
> Rush only, rush only onward!

Water does not feel—*i.e.* it is not a sign of redemptive love. Fluidity is no longer the fountain where man can be cleansed, no longer the womb in which man can be reborn. Just as the stars have revealed themselves to be soulless, indifferent, mocking, so also now water simply rushes on and on. This reminds one of Schopenhauer's will to life, that ceaseless and goal-less becoming. Worse even, water acts upon spirit as a destructive force. Van Leeuwen interprets the old man as God. I think that the old man represents mankind or, more specifically, that which is mortal in man and is in need of regeneration. The water would be the regenerative power. But the spiritual in Marx's old man is not transformed and regenerated by the water. On the contrary, the "waves are indeed his murderers, / They consume and gnaw the old one's bones." The water not only has no baptismal power, no power of renewal, it is simply lethal. It even annihilates man's very physicality. Marx closes his poem by repeating the first stanza given above. The opposition between subjectivity and objectivity is clearly evinced. A fluidity indifferent to man can no longer realize salvation; rather, as a soulless entity, it oppresses man.

Marx highlights the hopelessness of the romantic attitude in "Das bleiche Mädchen" ("The Pale Maiden"). The maiden, so pure, meets a knight who overwhelms her. Her love knows no bounds. Novalis, as we saw in the last chapter, conceived of the beloved as an abbreviation of God. In Marx's poem the pale maiden's love for the knight is so intense, so divine in its own right, that even God (*viz*. Chirst) is reduced to a secondary place. The maiden says: "How cold must heaven be, / Through which he was not sparkled, / A land full of pain and agony, / Inflamed with pain." Romantic love demands the absolute. But the knight does not return any love. Abstractly put, the empirical environment does not radiate a lyrical response to the maiden's longing. Since her heaven is frustrated, since she is left alone in her finitude, the maiden despairs. "And she hurls herself with force / Into the bubbling waves, And into the dark cold night / She is drawn away." Romantics such as Novalis had conceived death as a higher realm where loving souls can unite all the more intimately in the cosmic *élan vital*. Death is here treated by Marx as a blank end, at best as an escape from an oppressive reality. Death does not offer hopes of higher transformations. Death in the water does not even truly symbolize an escape, let alone a romanticization of life.

> And no withered foliage falls
> Down from the branches,

> Earth, heaven are deaf.
> They do not awaken again.
> And the wave rushes quietly on,
> Through valley and cliffs,
> On the hard, rocky place
> Her ribs smash to pieces.

In his poem "Menschenleben" ("Human Life") Marx approaches a metaphysical formulation of the opposition between subjectivity and objectivity or between inner life and outer (and repressive) fluidity. Romantic poets such as Novalis were keenly aware of the mutability of "only things." Because every thing flows or changes, everything is subject to the ultimate negation of death. As Novalis wrote: "Time originates with displeasure. Thus all displeasure is so long and all joy so short. . . . Displeasure is finite like time. Everything finite originates out of displeasure. So is our life" (S, I, 667). Romantics sought by means of the magic poetry to penetrate finitude, time, and displeasure and grasp the inner eternal love congealed in "only things." Time thereby becomes sublated into eternity, becomes an expression of absolute love. In "Menschenleben" Marx repeatedly underscores the transitoriness of things. "The moment / Flees stormily away; / Whatever it takes away / Does not return." Human life is, accordingly, not a reflection of eternal spirit but "death / An eternal death; / Distress dominates human striving." Man's wants, longings, and efforts—all are destined to frustration because all will pass. Life is simply "the play of breezes." Life is a contradiction; its last word is a self-mocking. This is simply irony turned against itself. In short, there is no eternity in "only things," in nature, or in objectivity. The flow of things is not redemptive but ironically destructive.

From the above poems it is clear that Marx has come to experience the cosmos as "only things." Objectivity simply annihilates human subjectivity, leaving man in a state of alienation. Marx further adumbrated this theme in his "humoristic" novel *Scorpion and Felix*. "Our life is . . . a circus; we run about, search in all directions until we fall upon the sand and the Gladiator, namely life, kills us. We must have a new savior [*Erlöser*]" (MEGA, I¹ , 694). A lyrical heart faced with an indifferent objectivity, with a heartless cosmos, must in its agony eventually come to experience reality, even eternity, as an oppressor. Oulanem cries out a curse:

> Soon I shall press Eternity to my heart and howl
> Humanity's gigantic curse into it.
> Ha, Eternity! That is an eternal pain,
> An inexpressible, immeasurable death!
> We are clockwork, blind-mechanically wound up
> To be the calendar-fool of time's space. . . .
>
> . . . .
>
> That all is blind discord and battle, to shake
> Itself out of itself, to wear itself out in quarrels,
> All that stands up now and has two legs
> And a breast to grasp life's curse!

The fundamental premise of romantic ontology was that the cosmos is nothing but the expression of loving subjectivity, of eternal life. Marx now conceives man in mechanistic terms, man is a "clockwork" that is the "fool of time's space." The "ought" of romantic lyricism is that objectivity must be lyricized. The "is" of late Romanticism is that this is impossible. Romantic man finds himself instead caught in the senseless and directionless becoming. "Ha! I must bind myself to the wheel of flame, / To dance with joy in the circle of eternity!" Eternity is a circle, not a progression. The "primordial mountain's weight" cannot in Oulanem's speech be transformed into an *élan vital*. Empirical exteriority, however dynamic, remains unchanged. Thus man finds himself the victim of an oppressive objectivity. He is not one with the flow of becoming but is riveted to the fixedness and hardness of indifferent being.

> Bound, eternally, fearfully, splintered, empty,
> Bound to the marble-rock of Being,
> Bound, eternally fastened, eternally!

. . . .
Now quickly!—the lot is cast—everything ready,
Destroy, what poetry's lie devised,
Finish with a curse what a curse began.

Lyricism had lied in promising redemption from objectivity, from
the "marble-rock of Being." The metaphysical realm of Romanticism is correctly called a curse. The romantic cosmos—at least on
romantic premises—is indifferent to man's deepest needs. It is heartless objectivity to which man is eternally bound—unless he can destroy it, unless he can find a new savior.

In summary, there appears to be no loving *Ur-Ich*, no unconditioned, in "only things." Or, if there is a God in the cosmos, then that
God must be an evil one. As Oulanem says: "And we, we are apes
of a cold God." God is, in short, a viper "that expands itself out to
universal form / From its peak to grin at us." God, if there is such a
being, is cold and evil because He takes no cognizance of man's poetic needs. Marx says in the "Spielmann" ("The Player"): "God
knows it not, honors not art." Romantic lyricism had obviously col-
lapsed for Marx. The universe, at least as it now is, is not a "poetic
word." It is certainly not the story of human salvation.

Symbols of Evil

Before proceeding to the next section I should first like momentarily to pause and undertake a brief excursus, developing a theme suggested by van Leeuwen. Van Leeuwen is the first scholar to see clearly
the importance of "the symbolism of an ocean" in Marx's poems.
Van Leeuwen goes on to suggest that such oceanic images indicate
a tendency in Marx's poems "towards symbols of a mother-religion."[6] I should like to expand speculatively upon this felicitous insight. However, I caution the reader that my reflections are only
offered tentatively and as suggestions. They are not meant to be
taken as dogmatic psychological theses. I hope only to cast light

6. Van Leeuwen, *Critique of Heaven*, 48.

upon the symbolic content of Marx's poetics. For after all, Marx was not thinking discursively in rational abstractions in his poems, rather symbolically and imaginatively. In other words, Marx was dealing with important problems such as that of evil within the structural dynamics of imaginative discourse. The "real" meaning of poetic symbols is for the most part not immediately evident in the surface content of the image. The transformation of a prosaic object, for example water, into a vehicle of meaning is precisely its symbolic function. In the case of symbolic or imaginative thinking psychology can offer deeper insight.

We have seen that the archetype of fluidity has many schematizations in Romanticism. The intoxicating allurement of fluidity was often associated with femininity, be it erotic or motherly. The feminine, particularly as symbol, is that which nurtures, absorbs, and enthuses the romantic self. The romantic desired to merge mystically with the feminine. From a psychoanalytical viewpoint, such a mystic merger "is a return to what some psychoanalysts call the 'oceanic reunion,' the world of the fed, satisfied baby on the delicious edge of sleep. . . . The mystic feels his absorption to be a happy helplessness in which a force that is greater than himself but includes himself handles him as a parent handles a little child."[7] And this parent is above all the mother.

However, there is another side to the Dionysian power of fluidity. As is so often the case in human psychology, there is ambivalence in the desire. The negative aspect to Dionysian absorption is being swallowed up, personally annihilated, or killed. Accordingly, the liquifying effects of femininity can present themselves as a hostile power, as waves which dash the individual self to pieces. The conflict between the need of the individual to achieve individuation, to become an independent center of power, to act autonomously, and the longing for a sustaining nourishment, for being cared for, or for absorption is, as Ernest Becker has recently shown, the real source of the Oedipus complex. Becker writes that "the Oedipus complex is . . . whether [the child] will be a passive object of fate, an appendage

---

7. Mortimer Ostow and Ben-Ami Scharfstein, *The Need to Believe: The Psychology of Religion* (New York, 1969), 122.

of others, a plaything of the world or whether he will be an active center within himself—whether he will control his own destiny with his own power or not."[8] We have already encountered the ambiguity contained in romantic longing—that urge to become one with a goal and yet to maintain distance. Otto Fenichel, a psychoanalyst, writes of the neurosis of compulsive wandering. "In a symbolic way, this pursuit of rest and protection at the mother's breast is expressed in the frequent yearning for the boundless ocean through which nostalgia is to be and yet never can be gratified ('Long voyage home'). The usual restlessness in wanderers is rooted in the fact that for the most part the protection they seek once more becomes a danger, because the violence of their longing is felt as a dangerous instinct. . . . When home, the seaman thinks his place will be at sea; when abroad, at home."[9]

What Marx has been doing in his poems cited in this section is to deal with the problem of evil, imaginatively constructing the problem within the conceptual and poetic viewpoint of German idealism. Paul Ricoeur, in a brilliant work examining various typologies of evil, shows one mythic explanation of the origins of evil to be "the drama of creation and the 'ritual' vision of the world." This vision, according to Ricoeur, anticipates typologically the most refined ontogenesis of modern philosophy, particularly that of German idealism.[10] Basing his explanation on Mesopotamian mythology, particularly as expressed in the epic *Enuma elish*, Ricoeur has described a typology of evil in which evil is identified with chaos—a fluidity which antedates all order, being, or cosmos. This chaotic fluidity is, however, a productive power. The chaotic origin of things, of the cosmos, is above all Tiamant, "the mother of them all." Tiamant exists as the vastness of the marine waters, the source out of which all things arise. But, such a chaos is not only a power of production but is a potentially hostile power that must be reckoned with, that, indeed, must be controlled. From this point of view, evil exists prior

8. Becker, *The Denial of Death*, 35–36.
9. Otto Fenichel, *The Psychoanalytical Theory of Neurosis* (New York, 1945), 370.
10. Paul Ricoeur, *The Symbolism of Evil*, trans. Emerson Buchanan (Boston, 1969), 175–210, 177.

to order, which is the good. Evil is, so to speak, the past of things and will triumph only if it becomes also the future of things.

The conquering of evil or chaos is indeed creation, the cosmogonic deed. It is also the ontogenesis of the divine. God is identified with the creation and maintenance of cosmic order; He is, in short, the future of being. In terms of the *Enuma elish*, the role of vanquishing disorder falls to Marduk, one of the younger gods. Marduk destroys the mother, Tiamant, and creates the cosmos that man inhabits. This deed is the original ritual that man, under the aegis of a king, will continually reenact with his own rituals. Through the ritual of sacrifice life is produced.

What is of interest for us in this ancient mythological explanation of evil and its overcoming is the attitude assumed by those who suffer from the hostile waters or mother. Tiamant wanted to destroy all the gods including Marduk. Marduk severed his dependence upon the "mother of things" and actively opposed his primordial parent. He resolved the Oedipal conflict as described above by killing his mother and making himself into the creator-god. "The essence of the Oedipal complex," writes Norman O. Brown, "is the project of becoming God—in Spinoza's formula, *causa sui*; in Sartre's, *être-en-soi-pour-soi*. By the same token it plainly exhibits infantile narcissism perverted by the flight from death."[11] And Marduk—or any self threatened by death—becomes God, becomes his own *causa sui*, by actively attacking that which oppresses him. Ricoeur writes: "Creation is a victory over an Enemy older than the creator. . . . This Violence is inscribed in the origins of things, in the principle that establishes [order] while it destroys [chaos]."[12] The genesis of the divine is concomitant with and the result of the annihilation of the primordial chaos. Therefore, resistance, violence, destruction, and even killing are essential ingredients of the creative act that vanquishes all evil. The creative act that brings about the cosmic order is consequently inseparable from the criminal act that destroys the "mother of all things." Evil destroys evil. This is creation!

11. Norman O. Brown, *Life Against Death: The Psychoanalytical Meaning of History* (New York, 1959), 118.
12. Ricoeur, *Symbolism of Evil*, 182–83.

Romantics in their absolutization of longing sought a Dionysian relationship vis-à-vis mother-nature. When the romantics experienced the frustration of longing by cosmic objectivity, they could do nothing else but languish and suffer. Pessimism, despair, or a *Weltschmerz* was an inevitable result of the romantic's helplessness in the face of evil. The crisis of romantic lyricism that perdured in so many poets is a reflex of the insoluble antinomy between longing and frustration, *ought* and *is*. We have seen that Marx, at least in his poems, suffered from the same lyrical contradiction. Given the premises of Romanticism, there could be no solution to the problem of evil—that is, so long as the Dionysian and passive attitude toward mother-nature retained the primacy of the ideal. Progress against evil is only possible if a new mood, a different attitude is assumed, namely that of Marduk. This mood can be described as one of revolt. If the passive attitude can be designated as Dionysian, the new attitude can be called Apollonian. By an "Apollonian" attitude I mean an urge in the self for individuation, for self-creation. Instead of seeking power as that which dissolves and absorbs the self, the Apollonian self will seek power as a creative manifestation of its own selfhood as the self comes to control and form its environment. The resolution of the Oedipal complex results in the mastery and possession of the world. Theologically expressed, if the Apollonian urge is absolutized as an ideal, it means that the self must become the creator, must, in effect, become its own God. Although Schlegel and Novalis conceived man's mission as that of becoming God, they conceived man in his anthropological being as essentially subsidiary to divine reality. Man's becoming God was accordingly the Dionysian absorption of man into God. But the romantic God had become the enemy in late Romanticism, certainly in some of Marx's poems. If this enemy is to be vanquished, then the divinity in man must be severed from God and reduced to a category of anthropology. In other words, divinity in man must become a predicate of man, an ideal that man realizes by becoming himself, *i.e.* by actively destroying and reconstituting his environment. It is not so much that man becomes God, rather that god becomes Man. But if man, in order to triumph over evil, must annihilate it, then his task is to ironize reality. In other words, irony is nothing but the power of creating by destroying. Marx in his theoretical speculations eventually came to disassociate irony from poetics and associate it with a revolution against a capitalistic society.

In the state of alienation, however, irony will first be experienced as an urge to revolt. We have already seen in two instances in Marx's poems that the frustrated self is impelled to destroy the universe or, at least, to wish the demise of the cosmos. Oulanem cries out: "Destroy, what poetry has devised, / Finish with a curse what a curse began." This attitude is one of revenge, that is, destruction with no thought of creation. In the next grouping of poems we will see this negative irony gradually emerge as a positive irony, *i.e.* become associated with creation. This feeling of revolt is, of course, the ironic mood directed to Apollonian goals. Eventually Marx will tentatively equate man with God or, at least, suggest a parity between the two. Such a "romantic" mood of revolt remained of necessity abstract. It was more of a wish than a program for fulfillment. Nevertheless, in my judgment, this ironic attitude determined Marx's subsequent reflections on the problem of evil and human emancipation.

Feelings of Revolt

In many poems (as shown above) the objective world, the cosmos, oppresses Marx. Objectivity does not manifest love but frustrates it. Despite the destructive power of objectivity, Marx never felt weak in his subjectivity. In the poem "My World" ("Meine Welt") Marx writes of his tireless energy. "Worlds cannot quench my longing, / Nor the magic power of a god, / Higher than they all is my will, / Which is stormily on guard in my bosom" (MEGA, I^1, 531). Marx's titanic will drives him on and on; he cannot rest. In "Feelings" ("Empfindungen") Marx writes: "Never can I carry out in peace, / What has seized my soul so intensely, / Never remain comfortably quiet, / And I storm without rest." This attitude of strength, activity cannot, of course, overlook the pain and suffering inflicted by objectivity. The indifference of the world to man cannot be denied. "Alas, the dead, mute [stars] gape / With scorn at our deed, / We and our activity decay, / And they wander in their course." Despite such indifference, Marx would not want to share the fate of the stars (objectivity). The stars are determined by the nonprogressive cycle of birth and death, creation and dissolution. "And so it reels on through the years, / From the void up to the all, / From the cradle to the bier, / Eternal ascension, eternal fall." This "eternal" cycle is, in effect, the goal-less and aimless dynamics of irony as a formal ideal. Man, at least, is willing to transverse the circle that God has imperiously laid upon man. Whatever the objective situation is like, man always can act, can resist.

> Therefore, let us dare everything,
>   Never rest, never cease;
> Only not dankly say nothing at all,
>   And want and do nothing at all.
>
> Only not having broodingly gone on,
>   Fearfully in the lower yoke,
> For yearning and longing
>   And deeds, they remain nevertheless for us.

Further signs of Marx's incipient mood of revolt are evident in his "Siren Song" ("Sirensang"). In the first four stanzas, music, femininity, divinity, and water intermingled to produce a tempting allurement. In the first stanza the waves are described as moving, hovering, trembling, rising and falling, etc. "That is the path of the siren." In other words the flowing undulation of the water is an external representation of the inner power of the sirens (femininity), who, of course, are seductive powers through their music (cf. stanza two). This music seems to be an "exalted heavenly celebration." The sirens by means of their music draw or attract "all distance, earth, stars into their song." This song affects the listener "so deeply, so exquisitely" that Marx even asserts that the tone of the song "breathes forth flames." Fire is, of course, a typical symbol for a consuming or dissolving power. The tones are even compared with "cosmic forms" which "hold fast the listener." The power of music, femininity, and fluidity to control the romantic mind, to render it passive, is evident. Marx then hints at a destruction that accompanies this fluidity. The tones enrapture the listener "until the flood submerges him." Death rather than rapture would appear to be the bard's fate. Marx recapitulates in the fourth stanza. A world flows out of the waves "as if in the water's depths / The gods all were sleeping / In the dark-blue sea." The emphasis in this stanza is upon "it seems." As we shall see, it is an illusion that the gods dwell in the sea. What dwells there is death! All the elements of the romantic or Dionysian temptation are present—femininity, musicality, fluidity, and death. To become one with the waters of nature man has but to submit to the attractive powers, to be passive.

At this point (stanza five) a young singer, blissfully approaching in a boat, is introduced. The naiads of the deep, where "the lyre rules," are awakened by the bard's song. And then, as if answering the bard, "there echoes like longing, / Like distant magic tones / From the songs of the sirens." The sirens or goddesses adorn themselves in order "to bedazzle the youth" and attempt to lure him into the depths of the sea.

> Come into our spirit's wreaths,
>   Your heart shall learn magic,
>   Hearken only to the dance of the waves,
>   It resounds like the pain of love.

The sirens claim that the heavens have entered into the waves and fill them with life. Finally the sirens conclude their song of seduction:

> It drives you to know the All,
>   To burn within the song,
> To burn in heaven's appearance,
>   The strings' sound touches you.
>
> Descend down to us,
>   Extend to us your hand,
> Your limbs will become spiritual,
>   When you see the deep land.

At first the youth appears to fall victim to the Dionysian temptation. "It seizes the youth like a delusion / . . . / He cannot tear his glance away, He is inflamed by them, / Perishes in hot desire." But then the youth begins to reflect and strives to gain composure. His heart "looks around in a proud attitude, / In a godly form, / And loudly it rings out to [the sirens'] ears." Here we have a description of an Apollonian attitude. Vis-à-vis the Dionysian temptation, one that will only reward him with death, the youth assumes an attitude of self-control which can only be called "godly." The youth answers the sirens by informing them that "there burns no eternal God" in the cold depths and that their intention is only to scorn him. The gods rule in his breast, not in the bosom of the sirens. Consequently the youth proclaims the independence of his own power. "You can never seize me, / Not my love, nor my hate, / Nor my longing's glow." The sirens are powerless before the youth's defiance. "And the sirens sink before his threats and glances." The sirens are finally engulfed by the waves. Instead of submitting passively to destruction at the hands of the waters, the youth has struck a note of active resistance. The very musical powers in man that have shown themselves too weak to unlock the spirituality in objectivity now show themselves strong enough to resist the need for such an unlocking.

Marx further develops this defiant attitude to water in "The Song of a Sailor at Sea" ("Lied eines Schiffers auf der See"). The sailor has lost his little brother to the sea. The sea gnaws at the little brother's bones as if it had the bones of the old man. The sailor, however, is not intimidated. Instead he has sworn "to revenge the pain on you [the sea], / To beat you without relent." Even if there is a hurricane, the sailor ventures fearlessly out upon the sea to do battle with it ("And I fight with wind and wave"). The sailor sings his song of defiance in the opening and closing stanzas:

> You [waves] may play, you may beat,
>   And skip about my skiff,
> You must carry it to the goal,
>   You are subject to me!

The sailor possesses the power not only to defy the chaotic destruction of the water, but also to subject it to his own goals.

In some of these poems one finds an intense mood of defiance and revolt. In "The Prayer of One Who Despairs" ("Des Verzweiflenden Gebet") Marx admits in the first stanza that God can damage man. Indeed, God can snatch everything away from man and thereby make him despair. Nevertheless, despite all, one power remains in man's control, namely revenge. The despairing one can avenge himself (cf. stanzas two and three), paradoxically, by building his own throne upon his very pain. Despair results from being continually frustrated—in this poem, by God. Instead of pining away in his weakness, the individual will actively oppose that which torments him; he will enjoy his defiance of God. This is revenge. Even if God should break down the walls of the despairing one's edifice of revenge, "Eternity defiantly will build them anew." In short, the despairing one feels that there is greater strength in his defiance and revolt than in God's ability to cause him despair via the vicissitudes of objectivity.

The ability of man to conquer a despairing and oppressive cosmos is, in effect, a function of his ability to create out of himself, to absolutize himself. Marx deals with this theme in "Sought" ("Gesucht"), which is addressed to Jenny in "Two Songs to Jenny" ("Zwei Lieder an Jenny"). The song is a dialogue. In the first stanza the "hero" is asked where he is going and answers: "To find a world." The partner in the dialogue then makes mention of the waves "here below" and the stars "there above." The partner is asking if the world does not already constitute a goal. Why should the "hero" be looking for another one? The "hero" rejects any pursuit of goals that lead "beyond." Here the stars are no magical images; rather they bind and chain man. No, man must find a new world and in himself.

> "The world shall arise out of myself,
> Incline itself out of itself to my breast,
>   Its well-springs are my life's glow,
>   My soul's breath, their ether-dome."

Marx has not abandoned the romantic imperative to create a world in the image of subjectivity. The wellsprings of this world are "life's glow," the "soul's breath," in short, man's subjectivity. Human subjectivity will ground the ether-dome of the new world. Let us recall that irony, according to Schlegel, is the divine breath that should be omnipresent in all parts of a poem. Similarly, the "soul's breath" will be evident in the worlds arisen out of man. How romantic in conception! There is, nevertheless, a significant difference. Anthropology has replaced theology, man has replaced God. Man creates his own world out of himself, not in harmony with the cosmic God, but in opposition to God. In short, man enlarges his Apollonian individuation until it becomes all. This is precisely the world that arises out of the human self.

This revolutionary defiance is romantic in structure and inspiration, *i.e.* it derives from man's subjectivity, particularly inspired by love. For instance, in the "Concluding Sonnet to Jenny" ("Schluß-Sonnet an Jenny") Marx, apparently expressing directly his own feelings, announces his dedication to perfection in Jenny (cf. stanza one). Marx, inspired by Jenny, describes himself in terms such as "boldly," "proudly," and "dominatingly." All such appellations suggest an Apollonian sense of independence and power. So inspired, Marx can say: "I walk a firm step through wide spaces, / Smash before your countenance pain, / And dreams flash out to the Tree of Life." According to Mircea Eliade, the "tree of life" is a traditional symbol for "sacred power" and its life giving capacity.[13] Marx, inspired by Jenny, assumes almost a violent attitude toward pain (or that which produces it). He is bent upon smashing pain. However, the dreams that lead him to such violence also aim at the "tree of life," *i.e.* Marx's negative destruction is undertaken with the hope and purpose of transforming things into sacred life. This mixture of defiant destruction and creativity is ironic in tone.

If Marx is willing to smash pain, if this act of destruction is not only revenge, but creation, and if Marx rejects any aid from a source outside man, then he must, in effect, ascribe to man God-like powers. The volitional heart of such defiant power is not the Dionysian

13. Mircea Eliade, *Patterns in Comparative Religion*, trans. Rosemary Sheed (New York, 1963), 380.

yearning to dissolve; rather it is pride. This conception is developed in "Human Pride" ("Menschenstolz"). In the first three stanzas, Marx (and Marx clearly intends himself) stands before the magnificence of the sky. Masses of clouds have piled up thereby lending a sense of awesomeness to the sky.[14] Standing before the marvel of cosmic objectivity, Marx asks himself if the waves should bear him into "the sea's flood," if he should stand "amazed before the masses,"—that is to say should he acknowledge the superior power of nature? A positive answer would imply that Marx (or man) feels his finitude, his essential weakness, and his helplessness vis-à-vis the infinite awesomeness of the universe. Such an attitude of humbleness is the antithesis of pride. Marx's answer is decisive: "No! You poor pigmy-giants, / And you cold, stone master, / See the glance, the one turned away, / The fury of the soul glows through it." Marx's soul simply refuses to acknowledge any power outside of itself and turns away from cosmic glory. This is Apollonian individuation potentialized to the extreme. Marx continues: "Nothing can stop us, / Nothing locks in our hoping, / Forms hasten away, / And the breast's joy and pain remains." Objectivity is soulless—the clouds "never feel the fire of love / Which creates them out of nothingness." This is not to say that the human soul cannot be injured by objectivity. But even in injury, man retains the power to destroy his enemy, a soulless cosmos. "Even still in its fall, / [The soul] drags suns into annihilation's flood." But the soul is like a phoenix, that is, "out of itself it rises victoriously / . . . / And in its eye the flash of thunder." Indeed, the soul's "own greatness is its lofty prayer." This greatness inspires the soul to "construct a throne for gigantic scorn" and "its proud disdaining is hero's reward."

In the fourth and fifth stanzas before the end Marx speaks of an

14. S. S. Prawer holds that Marx is evoking "huge buildings and the bewildering confluence of people characteristic of a modern city." See *Karl Marx and World Literature* (Oxford, 1976), 10. Marx thereby seems to be suggesting that the human soul can rise above such social oppression. This interpretation replaces a cosmic objectivity with an urban or social one. The same titanic rebelling remains. However, I think Prawer's interpretation is untenable. Under Prawer's thesis the poem would be *sui generis* relative to the other poems that are concerned with cosmic objectivity. There certainly occurs cosmic symbolization in the poem itself. Marx uses "halls" and "building" elsewhere with cosmic significance. Finally, Marx never explicitly mentions a "modern city" but seems in the end to revolt against "the world's broad countenance."

intermingling of souls, of the exchange of love between himself and Jenny. Love frees the soul from the lonesomeness in the All. Abstractly put, when humans are socially bonded through love, they are transformed into a self-sufficient force. Marx does not seek to transform Jenny into a shell manifesting God as did Novalis with Heinrich's treatment of Mathilde. Marx only seeks an inspiration in the exchange of love that will enable him to transform himself into a God-like creator. Similarly, in "The Singer's Last Song" ("Des Sängers letztes Lied") Marx writes of a singer inspired by love. "[The singer] feels himself so powerful, / Similar to a giant oak, / Stands there, God-like in form, / In his realm of marvels" (MEGA, I^1, 492). Returning to "Human Pride," Marx directly addresses Jenny:

> Jenny! May I boldly say it,
>   That we, our souls, have lovingly exchanged,
> That they beat glowingly as one,
>   That a storm roars through their waves.
>
> Then I'll throw the glove scornfully
>   Into the world's broad countenance,
> And let the gigantic she-dwarf plunge with groans,
>   Her debris will not crush my glow.
>
> Similar to God I dare to roam,
>   March triumphantly through the realm of ruins,
> Every word is flame and acting,
>   My breast equal to the creator's bosom.

In these last three stanzas we see clearly what "human pride" means. It is man's belief in the divinity or at least God-like strength of his own being. The "opposition between what is and what ought to be" has been accepted by Marx as a challenge to his pride. Marx is willing, so to speak, to take on the entire cosmos, to destroy "the she-dwarf" (*i.e.* nature conceived as a feminine sustainer). The destruction of the universe "will not crush [Marx's] glow." Every word of Marx's is a flame and deed, *i.e.* a destructive and annihilating power, a revolutionary force. Marx is, of course, not thinking in terms of a social or political revolution where real physical force is used. The word (*i.e.* thought) itself is still the revolutionary or ironic force. This is indeed a romantic concept of irony.

It is obvious that a profound alteration has occured in Marx's thinking. "Pride" can be viewed as a type of longing and as such it is the volitional origin for man's ironic activity. Pride, however, differs from romantic longing, which is essentially Dionysian. Pride implies that the proud self not only refuses to allow itself to be determined heterogeneously, but insists on the experience of its own strength as the source for value. Insofar as Marx has raised pride to an ideal, he has also committed himself to the *causa sui* project, to man's creation of himself as divine. Marx resolves his cosmological version of the Oedipus conflict in favor of the revolting child. The primordial parent, be it God or mother-nature, must be destroyed so that man can make his own powers into the breath, ether-dome, and wellsprings of a new man-made world. Man thereby becomes his own parent, his own creator. This is human pride, *i.e.* man's parity with God.

Summary

Marx's poems evince a momentous ontological revolt. God is ironized or annihilated only to be reconstituted as man's own powers. God is functionally that power which overcomes the threat of death and insignificance. The term *God* is a theological symbol for "sacred power." Marx had written in his letter to his father that "new gods had to be installed" in place of the dead romantic gods. Marx, at least in some of his poems, has shifted the locus of sacred power from a subject "beyond" to man conceived as a divine subject. Man will create a world out of himself and this world will give him meaning. Human power must, in short, become sacred power. But any world that man creates is a cultural world. Thus Marx is saying, in effect, that man must make himself into the poet of his own redemption and his man-made world into the words of this salvational poem. Man needs culture as that which can embody his dreams of conquering death and insignificance.

If salvation is to come through the man-made, then the whole problem of emancipation must be rethought. Emancipation will, to be sure, still be achieved through irony, *i.e.* by creation through destruction. But this irony can no longer work according to the causality suggested in the doctrine of Magical Idealism. The magical world of poetry has failed. Marx had indeed caught sight of "the realm of true poetry like a distant palace" in his poems. But the romantic way had "disintegrated into nothing." Marx had spoken in *Scorpion* of the need for "a new savior." Such a savior would have to do away with the opposition between what ought to be and what is. This is a momentous task. Marx rethought this problem in the notes and introduction to his Ph.D. dissertation (1840).

IV
Irony, Prometheus, and the Problem of Philosophy

"The Key" to Marx's Thought

Marx's underlying thesis persists—from his first works to his last struggles. It is the key to his philosophy, to his economics, to his politics: It is to make of each man a man, that is to say, a creator. The young Marx, heir of Fichte and Hegel, evoked this creative power to oppose all forms of alienation. Creation is the opposite of alienation. . . . This profound humanism . . . endows[s] each man with the possibility of being a man, a creator, a "poet," in the deepest sense of the word, in that full sense that made Maxim Gorki say: "Esthetics is the ethics of the future."[1]

Marx was not only the heir of Fichte and Hegel, but of Romanticism. Schlegel, Novalis, and Schleiermacher, as Hegel noted in his history of philosophy, were some of Fichte's most important followers. It is more proper simply to say that Marx was the heir to German Idealism. I have purposely cited Roger Garaudy because he is an "orthodox" Marxist, one of the leading theoreticians of contemporary France. It is to Garaudy's credit that he has been able to look beyond the scientism of "historical materialism" and to grasp the poetic core underlying Marx's thinking. The key to Marx's "philosophy, to his economics, to his politics" is indeed the romantic imperative to make man into a cosmic poet, *viz.* creator. In the opening chapter of this work I suggested that poetry in its deepest anthropological sense is concerned with meaning, with sacred power. Aesthetics is the ethics of the future for a Marxist such as Garaudy in the

---

1. Roger Garaudy, *Karl Marx: The Evolution of His Thought*, trans. Nan Apotheker (New York, 1967), 203.

sense that the Marxist seeks to create by means of human power a cultural cosmos, an objectivity, that will immortalize value in social and material form. In this context the individual will have a permanent "substance" in which he can submerge the finitude of his being. Economics, politics, philosophy are but so many "cultural" and "aesthetic" forms that are to mediate to man the sacred power to triumph over death and insignificance.

But the power to create, the power to effect immortality, is traditionally an attribute of the gods. It would seem to follow that man must be a god, even if he is but thinking "matter" in a materialistic universe. Garaudy himself gives away the secret of Marxism. "Marxist materialism, faithful to its Fichtean and Faustian early inspiration, is the creator of a world inhabited by untroubled gods, whose creation inaugurates a dialectic opening on infinity."[2] "Marxist materialism" has indeed a theological telos. Only it is not God who is divine, but *man*. Marxist man will transform himself into an "untroubled god." The magico-poetic dreams of Marxists are clearly evident. I shall comment more on this theme in the next chapter and in the Epilogue. At any rate, on Garaudy's own premises, it is clear that Marx's program was poetic in the general anthropological sense defined in Chapter I. The question immediately presents itself: How is man to transform an oppressive objectivity into a cultural poem? What will enable man, the creator-poet, to affect empirical reality? Before such questions can be answered, they of course must be "correctly" formulated. In this chapter we will be concerned with Marx's formulation of this question of questions.

In the last chapter we saw that Marx's attitude toward objectivity shifted from Dionysian passivity to Apollonian activity. Insofar as it is man's mission to create a "world inhabited by untroubled [human] gods," man must expand without limits his "narcissism"[3] or

2. *Ibid.*, 109.
3. According to the psychoanalyst Erich Fromm—a Marxist of sorts—narcissism is a state in which the individual is filled with himself: "he has become 'god and the world' to himself." See *The Heart of Man: Its Genius for Good and Evil* (New York, 1964), 71–116. This is an adequate synopsis of the "key" to Marx's theories, although Fromm would not admit this of Marxism. Indeed, Fromm himself indulges in narcissism when he writes: "God is I, inasmuch as I am human." Cf. *The Art of Loving* (New York, 1962), 70.

actualize his "pride."[4] Given an oppressive environment, man's initial attitude toward this objectivity must be antagonistic, destructive, or ironic. This we saw was the "romantic" attitude displayed in some of Marx's poems. This mood connects Marx's romantic phase with his developing thought. The romantic in Marx sought emancipation, salvation, in short, "a new savior." Such an attitude remained with Marx throughout his life and was, in my judgment and apparently also in Garaudy's, the inspiration directing his critical reflections. The task facing the postromantic Marx was how to recast this problem in terms that would allow for a solution. Such a question must proceed from the imperative of Apollonian creativity. In short, Marx was seeking a poetry of the future as he expressed it in 1852: "The social revolution of the nineteenth century cannot draw its poetry from the past, but only from the future."[5] That is, something in the present must transform man into the "creator-spirit" and inspire him to become the cosmic poet of the future.

The Promethean Quest

Marx formulated the problem in his Ph.D. dissertation entitled *On the Difference Between the Democritan and Epicurean Philosophy of Nature in General*.[6] In the Foreword to his dissertation Marx refers to Hegel as the first true author of a history of philosophy (E, I, 261–62). However, as all-inclusive as Hegel's history of philosophy is, there

4. Lewis Feuer has in effect attempted to interpret Marx's historical materialism as a function of his personal Promethean complex. See "The Character and Thought of Karl Marx: The Promethean Complex and Historical Materialism" in *Marx and the Intellectuals: A Set of Post-Ideological Essays* (Garden City, 1969), 9–52. Although I agree that much of Marx's theory is a reflection of his "personal" developmental problems, I will resist any reductionist temptations. I am interested in Marx's Promethean complex only insofar as it relates to the general anthropological need for a cosmological aesthetics.

5. Karl Marx, *The Eighteenth Brumaire of Louis Bonaparte* (New York, 1963), 18.

6. Although many commentators have discussed sections from the "Vorarbeiten" to Marx's dissertation, few have attempted to interpret the work as a whole. For some secondary sources on the dissertation see the chapter by Ernst Bloch, "Epikur und Karl Marx oder ein subjektiver Faktor im Falle der Atome" in *Über Karl Marx* (Frankfurt, 1968), 157–62; and Günther Hillmann, *Marx und Hegel: Von der Spekulation zur Dialektik* (Frankfurt, 1966), 103–308; Dick Howard, *The Development of the Marxian Dialectic* (Carbondale, Ill., 1972), 1–24; Heinrich Popitz, *Der entfremdete Mensch: Zeitkritik und Geschictsphilosophie des jungen Marx* (Frankfurt, 1967), 51–59; and van Leeuwen, *Critique of Heaven*.

nevertheless exists in it an inadequate comprehension of the meaning of the epicurean, stoic, and skeptic philosophies of the late Hellenic period following the total systems of Plato and Aristotle. Marx's thesis on Epicurus and Democritus was presented as a part of an intended comprehensive work on the matter. In Marx's opinion Hegel had failed to grasp the "speculative thought par excellence" of these Greek philosophies. Thus ostensibly it appears as if Marx simply wanted to fill in lacunae in Hegel's system of the history of philosophy.

There are various reasons for Marx's interest in Epicurus, and since the text of the dissertation proper is only remotely connected to the problem of the poetization of reality, I shall limit myself to the sections directly concerned with the problem. Suffice it to note that Marx was in part interested in the philosophy of Epicurus because it offered a path of philosophic salvation: "Epicurus is *satisfied* and *blessed in philosophy*. 'You must,' he says, 'serve philosophy so that true freedom will be your lot. He does not need to wait who surrenders and submits himself to it; immediately he will be emancipated. For this itself, the serving of philosophy, is freedom'" (E, I, 273). Epicurus' philosophy and physics constitute an interpretation of reality such that freedom is assured. Marx's interest in Epicurus is indicative of his interest in philosophy per se as a means of salvation. In the Foreword Marx mentions that he is also attaching a critique of Plutarch's polemic against Epicurus. Plutarch's criticism was false for Marx because it sought to conduct philosophy before the forum of religion, *i.e.* to ascribe cognitive and redemptive primacy to religion over philosophy. We shall presently determine why Marx has absolutized philosophy. At this point Marx gives us an insight into his conception of philosophy.

> Philosophy, so long as a drop of blood still pulsates in its world-conquering [*weltbezwingend*] and absolutely free heart will always call to its opponents with Epicurus: "He is not impious who gets rid of the gods of the crowd, but rather he who imputes to the gods the ideas of the crowd."
> Philosophy does not hide it. The confession of Prometheus: "In one word, I hate all gods" is its own confession, its own motto against all heavenly and earthly gods who do not acknowledge human self-consciousness

as the highest divinity. There shall be no others beside it.

To those sad March-hares who are happy about the apparently wors-ened civil position of philosophy, it answers again with that which Pro-metheus said to the servant of the gods, Hermes.

> I would never exchange my lot of suffering
> For your service of villeinage; hear it clearly, never!
> To be sure, it is better to be in bondage to the cliff
> Than to serve Father Zeus as a faithful messenger.

Prometheus is the most noble Saint and Martyr in the calendar of phi-losophy. (E, I, 262–63)

This quotation requires some clarification. The definition of phi-losophy as "world-conquering" and as possessing an "absolutely free heart" is indeed an unusual thesis, at least in the terms of twen-tieth-century philosophy. Philosophy is here obviously a "mental" activity that entails the pursuit of absolute value as its inspiration. In-deed, philosophy is of such a nature that it can have its own martyrs, namely Saint Prometheus. In the poem "Human Pride" we saw that Marx had equated human powers with those of the gods. Marx at that time had no poetic or mythic symbol for this defiant irony hurled at the gods. For such a symbol he turned to the Greek mythic figure of Prometheus. For after all, Prometheus had stolen fire from the gods and given it to man. He thus became a "cultural" hero. Prometheus continued to defy the gods even when he was cruelly punished. However, he was not in the last analysis a "true" hero for the ancient Greeks, in particular for Aeschylus, but rather a fool, a madman possessed by daemonic powers that could lead to cosmic destruction.[7] By the eighteenth century many Germans (Europeans in general) had come to misunderstand the significance of Prome-theus,[8] treating him as a hero to be emulated precisely because of his defiance of the gods (cf. Goethe's poem "Prometheus").

---

7. Cf. C. Kerenyi, *Prometheus: Archetypal Image of Human Existence*, trans. Ralph Man-heim (New York, 1963), and Paul Ricoeur's comments on Aeschylus in *Prometheus Bound* (Boston, 1967), 222–26. Because of Marx's misuse of the quotations from Aeschylus, Eric Voegelin considers him to be "an intellectual swindler." Cf. *Wissenschaft, Politik und Gnosis* (Munich, 1959), 38–39, 45–48. Such a thesis is not tenable because Marx's interpretation of Prometheus was widespread at the time.

8. For an excellent interpretation of German Idealism (*i.e.* Kant, Fichte, Hegel, Novalis,

In "Human Pride" Marx declared himself willing to step out upon the ruins of the universe with powers equal to those of the gods. This is, of course, man's pride, *i.e.* the absolutization of Apollonian individuation. In his *Scorpion and Felix* Marx at one point does identify the attitude of defiance with Prometheus although within an ironic context. "The ordinary person . . . fights with raging life, hurls himself into the billowing sea and seizes from the depths pearls of Promethean rights" (MEGA, I¹ , 696). However, in the Foreword to his dissertation Marx has Prometheus, the saint of philosophy, extend his defiance of the gods to the point of claiming human self-consciousness as the highest divinity. This is to say that man's own being, by itself, is the locus of death's conquering power. In the terms of the Oedipus complex as interpreted by Ernest Becker, Marx has totally committed himself to the narcissistic *causa sui* project. Consequently, man must be his own parent. It is better to suffer than to accept succor from Father Zeus. We can now see why Marx designated the heart of philosophy as "world-conquering and absolutely free." These two predicates are correlative. Man's freedom is precisely his ability to conquer the world (*viz.* objectivity). The term used by Marx for "conquering" is *bezwingend*, which implies "forcing." This is to say the Promethean spirit "forces" the world to be the locus of human freedom. Only by conquering the world can man create his cultural cosmos, the guarantee of his divinity and hence of his triumph over death.

This same Promethean mythos is evident in many of Marx's writings. For instance, in the great mythic drama of the *Economic Manuscripts of 1844* Marx returns to the theme of self-creation and independence (*viz.* freedom). "A being does not consider himself as independent until he stands on his own feet, until he owes his existence to himself. A man who lives by the grace of another considers himself as a dependent being. I live, however, entirely from the grace of another if I owe him not only the maintenance of my life, but if he has in addition created it, if he is the source of my life. My life

---

Schiller, Goethe, Hölderlin *et al.*) see Hans Urs von Balthasar, *Prometheus: Studien zur Geschichte des deutschen Idealismus* (Heidelberg, 1947). Unfortunately von Balthasar did not include Marx in his most penetrating analysis of German prometheanism.

necessarily has such a ground outside of it if it is not my own creation. Creation is therefore very difficult to expel from the consciousness of the people" (E, I, 544–45). Marx's rejection of the primacy
of an external "parent" is obvious. Traditional religion is grounded
in the belief that man is dependent for his existence and perfection
of his being upon the gods. It is an inevitable correlative to Marx's
prometheanism that he cannot tolerate the idea of being created, for
then he would not be the creator. Man must not, is not allowed to
have a "parent." There is no need to consider Marx's sophistic ar-
guments against the existence of God.[9] It suffices to note that Marx
simply never cared to raise seriously the question of God's existence
because, I believe, from the time of his dissertation (if not earlier)
the existence of a god beyond man (even if the objective existence of
such a being could be established) could have no value for him, simply because value meant for Marx man's self-consciousness of man's
being as the highest divinity. What importance can "proofs" have
for Saint Prometheus? Marx was convinced that socialism as the
ideal perfection of man needs no reference to a divine parent. Indeed,
socialism is not even atheistic, since to be atheistic implies that an
individual is interested in God, be it only to deny God. But Marx
believed that socialistic man would soon be beyond a negative need.
For this reason he writes:

Insofar as for socialist man the *entire so-called world history* is nothing but
the creation of man through human work and [is] the becoming of nature
for man, he has evident and incontrovertible proof of his *birth* through himself, proof of his own *process of origination.* . . . The question about an *alien*
being, about a being above man and nature . . . has become impossible in
practice. *Atheism* as a denial of this unessentiality has no longer any meaning because atheism is a *negation of God* and posits by means of this negation
the *existence of man.* But socialism as socialism no longer needs such mediation. It is the positive *self-consciousness* of man which is no longer mediated
by the dissolution of religion. (E, I, 546)

9. For an examination of Marx's proofs against God's existence see James Collins, *God
in Modern Philosophy* (Chicago, 1967), 249–57.

Man gives birth to himself! This, as Ernest Becker and Norman O. Brown have shown, is the driving force behind the Oedipus complex. Psychologically, it is a sign of a fixated "infantile narcissism." Such is the poetic inspiration of Marx's Marxism! Unfortunately, the narcissistic child also wishes to kill its parent, and the "triumph" of Marxism in the twentieth century has given birth to an enormous amount of death. At any rate, the development of Marx's Marxism is simply unintelligible apart from Marx's fanatical commitment to the Promethean mythos. How Marx sought to translate Promethean mythos into secular form will be dealt with presently. For the moment the mythopoetic nature of Marx's conception of philosophy must be stressed.

Philosophy for Marx was not an abstract and disinterested contemplation of general ontological principles. Philosophy is inspired by a world-conquering heart, by the desire to make man's self-consciousness into the highest divinity. Philosophy is the cognitive form of salvational consciousness and as such is highly Hegelian. In order to understand Marx better on this point we must briefly examine Hegel's concept of philosophy.

Marx and Hegelian Philosophy

Marx's letter of November 10, 1837, to his father not only announces his loss of faith in the gods of Romanticism but also proclaims his conversion to Hegelian philosophy. Marx writes: "I had read fragments of Hegel's philosophy whose grotesque, craggy melody had bothered me. Once more I wanted to dive into the sea, however with the definite intention of finding that mental nature just as necessary, concrete, and firmly grounded as corporeal nature and . . . of bringing the pure pearls into the sunlight" (E, I, 8–9). Marx further writes: "I had gotten to know Hegel from beginning to end, together with most of his disciples . . . and I became all the more firmly chained to the modern world-philosophy from which I had thought to escape, but all the plenitude of chords were silenced and a real rage of irony [*Ironiewut*] seized me as could easily happen after so much had been negated" (E, I, 10). What then had been "negated" by Hegel's "modern world-philosophy"? I agree with Hill-mann that Hegel's philosophy negated Marx's previous romantic *Weltanschauung*. The antithesis between Hegel and Romanticism was intense and any "conversion" to Hegelianism would certainly entail much ironic negation of what was. The nature of this negation will reveal for us the meaning of Hegelian philosophy for Marx. Relative to Romanticism, Hegel's philosophy constitutes a three-fold nega-tion while at the same time it preserves a central feature of Roman-ticism. Let us take up the first two forms of negation.

Directly after announcing the loss of his holy of holies and his need to find new gods, Marx writes: "Starting out from Idealism—which, it is said here in passing, I had compared to and nourished with Kantian and Fichtean Idealism—I came upon the notion of seeking the Idea itself in the real [*im Wirklichen*]. If the gods had be-fore dwelt above the earth, now they had become the center of it" (E, I, 8). Both the terms *Idea* and *real* are Hegelian. They refer to a specific relationship between the ideal and the empirical. The "Idea" is the essence of the divine, indeed, the telos of divine striving. Marx was not rejecting a spiritual concept of reality by discarding "Ide-alism," only one where spirit is not fully merged with the empirical. The attraction of Hegelianism—its so-called nonidealistic essence—resided in the fact that Hegel claimed philosophically to have grasped the Idea *in* the real. This claim needs further elucidation.

We have seen that Romanticism, called "Idealism" by Marx, en-tails a disparity between the "ought" and the "is." Furthermore, in the discussion of the crisis of Romanticism, it was shown that this disparity was a plausible outgrowth of the doctrine of irony. Sec-ondly, Romanticism, although philosophical, subordinated philoso-phy to poetry or, more specifically, to the immediate aesthetic intuition of the unconditioned in nature. Philosophy constituted for Romanticism an adumbration of an essentially supra-rational ex-perience. Feeling or immediate intuition, not thought or reason, is the ultimate instrument and form of revelation. Hegel's notion of philosophy contradicts Romanticism on both essential points.[10] Hegel

10. Concerning Hegel's criticism of Romanticism and romantics see Otto Pöggler, *He-gels Kritik der Romantik* (Bonn, 1956).

placed philosophy above art as the mode and content of revelation. Indeed, religion too was rated above art by Hegel. Art, religion, and finally philosophy, in that order of ascendancy, constituted for Hegel the hierarchy of "knowledge" of the absolute. Indeed, as Hegel himself claimed: "Philosophy may be said to be the unity of art and religion."[11] Hegel was acutely aware of the fact that the absolute or infinite could not be fully grasped in immediate intuition. As Hegel noted in his *Phenomenology of the Mind*, romantic intuitionism eventually leads to "frivolity and again ennui."[12] Therefore, Hegel rejected the romantic "faith" in the magical power of the aesthetic word to reveal in the fullest manner the divine, the Idea. Not the senses, not feeling, not intuition but man's power to think is the means of fully grasping the absolute. This lies at the basis of Hegel's famous thesis that the real is rational and the rational real. Thought as reason, according to Hegel, can comprehend (*begreifen*) the infinite in the finite by means of the concept (*Begriff*). Insofar as Marx was converted to the "craggy melody" of Hegel's modern world-philosophy, he accordingly had to reject the romantic belief (1) in the supremacy of the aesthetic word and (2) in the ironic as the ideal, *i.e.* in longing as the state of perfection.

In rejecting the primacy of feeling, Hegel did not reject feeling and its language, particularly in religious form, as a valid revelation of the divine. It is only an inadequate one. In Hegel's opinion "philosophy *thinks* what the [religious] subject *feels*. . . . Feeling is thus not rejected by philosophy; on the contrary, it simply gets through philosophy its true content."[13] Here is what Hegelian philosophy preserved from Romanticism. Hegelianism as well as Romanticism was seeking redemption in and through nature. Philosophy seeks to reveal ultimate value, to unite man with the highest good. Therefore Hegel contends: "The object of religion as well as of philosophy is eternal truth in its objectivity, God and nothing but God, and the explication of God. . . . Thus religion and philosophy come to one.

11. G. W. F. Hegel, *Encyclopedia of Philosophy*, trans. Gustav E. Mueller (New York, 1959), 284.
12. G. W. F. Hegel, *The Phenomenology of Mind*, trans. J. B. Baille (New York, 1967), 75.
13. G. W. F. Hegel, *Lectures on the Philosophy of Religion*, trans. E. B. Speiers and J. Burdon Sanderson (3 vols.; New York; 1974), III, 149.

Philosophy is itself, in fact, worship. . . . Philosophy is thus identical with religion, but the distinction is that it is so in a peculiar manner, distinct from the manner of looking at things which is commonly called religion as such."[14] Religion "looks at" God through feeling, intuition, and vivid metaphors, whereas philosophy views God through reason, by means of the *Begriff*. However much Hegel's notion of philosophy differed from that of Romanticism, he nevertheless, no less than romantics, was seeking the unconditioned in the empirical world. Philosophy is simply the form a fully "saved" consciousness assumes. "Philosophy is the liberation of the spirit from the insufficiency and one-sidedness of all forms of life; in passing beyond them they are nevertheless preserved and ultimately grounded. . . . This whole way of liberation is not only a preparation for, or a way toward, philosophy, but is also within philosophy."[15] In short, the consciousness produced by philosophical thinking is the "reconciliation"[16] between the absolute and the relative that Romanticism could never achieve but aimed for. Hegel is very adamant about the mission of philosophy: "The ultimate aim and business of philosophy is to reconcile thought or the notion with reality."[17] Hegel declares himself to be highly opposed to all forms of monism or pantheism that consider the empirical to be nonessential, to be illusion. "The notion of philosophy is the self-thinking Idea, the truth aware of itself—the logical system, but with the signification that it is universally approved and certified in concrete content as in its actuality."[18] Because all is reconciled in philosophical consciousness, philosophy is theodicy.

In [philosophical] apprehension the spiritual and the natural universe are interpenetrated as one harmonious universe, which withdraws into itself, and its various aspects develop the Absolute into a totality, in order, by the

---

14. *Ibid.*, I, 19–20.
15. Hegel, *Encyclopedia of Philosophy*, 284–85.
16. Hegel, *Philosophy of Religion*, III, 149.
17. G. W. F. Hegel, *Lectures on the History of Philosophy*, trans. E. S. Haldane (3 vols.; London, 1892), III, 545.
18. G. W. F. Hegel, *Philosophy of Mind, Being Part Three of the Encyclopedia of the Philosophical Sciences*, trans. William Wallace (Oxford, 1971), 313.

very process of so doing, to become conscious of itself in its unity, in Thought. Philosophy is thus the true theodicy, as contrasted with art and religion and the feelings which these call up—a reconciliation of spirit, namely of the spirit which has apprehended itself in its freedom and in the riches of its reality.[19]

From a twentieth-century point of view, Hegel's philosophy is Idealism par excellence. But for the young Marx, because it united the ideal and the real, Hegel's philosophy represented "science." However, it must not be forgotten that despite Hegel's disagreement with Romanticism concerning the form of salvific consciousness, he did not differ from Romanticism in believing in the primacy of the spirit. Man can and must transform finitude, oppressive objectivity, into a state of redemption by means of mental causality, in the way that he *thinks* things.

Before continuing on to ascertain the third point of negation, it is worth presenting further indications of Marx's essentially "religious" concept of philosophy. Philosophy for Hegel raises human consciousness to the infinite and thereby sets man into a state of exaltation. Indeed, exaltation is an essential ingredient of a philosophical "worship"; it is the product of rationally perceiving the reconciliation of the absolute with the relative. In one of the "Vorarbeiten" to his dissertation Marx, while talking about the philosophical exaltation [*Begeisterung*] of philosophers such as Aristotle, Spinoza, and especially Hegel "when he develops the eternal realization of the Idea, the magnificent organism of the universe of spirit," contends that this exaltation "is more profound, warmer, more beneficial for the mind than religious exaltation; for that reason [religious] exaltation burns on to culmination in ecstasy as its highest point and [philosophical exaltation] burns on to culmination in the pure ideal flame of science. That is why [religious exaltation] is only a hot water bottle of individual minds, while [philosophical exaltation] is the animating spiritus of world-historical developments" (E, I, 225). It goes without saying that Marx did not want to be left out

19. Hegel, *History of Philosophy*, III, 546.

of any "world-historical developments." It is also clear that Marx's concept of philosophy is "poetic" in the sense defined in Chapter I. Philosophy presents man with sacred power; for that reason it sets him in a state of exaltation. Philosophy does the same thing as religion, only better! Indeed, as Marx goes on to maintain, "every philosopher wants to liberate the soul from its empirical limitations" (E, I, 225). How clearly the mythic nature of Marx's "rational" ratiocinations sparkles forth. Suffering, death, and insignificance are, in my judgment, the contents of "empirical limitations." The philosopher liberates the human soul from such negation.[20] Philosophy for the young Marx was surely as much a matter of "worship" as it was for Hegel. Marx like any "true believer" was seeking the salvation of his "soul."

Philosophy is a salvific form of consciousness. But what does it cognize? What is the content of philosophic consciousness that can produce exaltation in the human mind? The content is, of course, sacred power, *i.e.* the world-conquering force. In the terms of my discussion of the poetic in Chapter I, philosophy reveals a cosmic meaning and is accordingly "poetic" in content, although not in form. Hegel's concept of philosophy does not deviate from that of Romanticism with regard to its salvific content and function. Romantics as well as Hegelians sought consciousness of a life-giving power in which man *qua* his finitude could submerge himself. However, Hegel deviated significantly in determining man's relationship to power. We have seen that romantics sought an essentially Dionysian relationship to power. As such, human individuation and apollonianism were a problem for romantics. Cut off from enrapturing power, many late romantics often languished in moods of despair. Schopenhauer's solution was for man to give up the Will to Life. Here we have the heart of the antithesis between Hegelianism

---

20. Ernst Topitsch has shown that the desire to escape the limitations of empirical existence is the formative principle of Marx's gnostic dialectics. See "Marxismus und Gnosis" in *Sozialphilosophie zwischen Ideologie und Wissenschaft* (Neuwied, 1961), 235–70. Topitsch also considers the desire to escape "empirical limitation" as the basic content of the mythos which generated the origins of philosophical speculation. See his *Vom Ursprung und Ende der Metaphysik* (Munich, 1972). Marx's philosophizing belongs to a tradition several thousand years old.

and Romanticism. Hegel conceived man's destiny as that of actively appropriating power. Power only becomes salvific for man when he experiences it as an extension of his individuation, of his subjection of the world to the dictates of his will. The reconciliation of subjectivity with objectivity results from the subject's "conquering" of objectivity. This active and *proud* attitude coincides with Marx's feelings as expressed in "Human Pride." Marx's conversion from Romanticism to Hegelianism parallels his shift from dionysianism to apollonianism. Let us examine in more detail the "Promethean" essence of the Hegelian Spirit.

Hegel defines Spirit in the following manner:

The nature of Spirit may be understood by a glance at its direct opposite—Matter. The essence of matter is gravity, the essence of Spirit—its substance—is Freedom. . . . Matter possesses gravity by virtue of its tendency toward a central point; it is essentially composite, consisting of parts that exclude each other. It seeks its unity and thereby its own abolition; it seeks its opposite. If it would attain this it would be matter no longer, but would have perished. . . . Spirit, on the contrary, is that which has its center in itself. It does not have unity outside of itself but has found it; it is in itself and with itself. Matter has its substance outside of itself; Spirit is Being-within-itself (self-contained existence). But this, precisely, is Freedom. For when I am dependent, I refer myself to something else which I am not; I cannot exist independently of something external. I am free when I am within myself. This self-contained existence of Spirit is self-consciousness, consciousness of self.[21]

What Hegel calls matter is essentially the Dionysian urge to find substance outside of the limits of the self. The extrapolation of Dionysian absorption is indeed "its own abolition," *i.e.* the self disappears the moment it is totally absorbed. This drive is derogatorily ascribed by Hegel to "dead" matter. Spirit, on the other hand, is the opposite, namely the exertion of power over "otherness," the total individuation of the self. Spirit is free insofar as it is independent, self-con-

21. G. W. F. Hegel, *Reason in History: A General Introduction to the Philosophy of History*, trans. Robert S. Hartman (Indianapolis / New York, 1953), 22–23.

tained, within itself. In short, Spirit locates power in its own center. Spirit is not attracted by gravity, it is gravity. The self-centeredness of Spirit is a plausible extention of the idealistic assumption that $I = I$. Hegel writes about the dynamics of self-consciousness: "In the formulation $I = I$ is enunciated the principle of absolute Reason and Freedom. Freedom and Reason consist in this, that I raise myself to the form of $I = I$, that I know everything as mine, as 'I,' that I grasp every object as a member in the system of what I myself am."[22] Spirit is able to fulfill the imperative of $I = I$ by appropriating all objectivity, by uniting it to its own center. Hegel accordingly defines the essence of appropriation:

To appropriate means at bottom only to manifest the pre-eminence of my will over the thing and to prove that it is not absolute, is not an end in itself. . . . When the living thing becomes my property, I give to it a soul other than the one it had before. I give it my soul. The free will, therefore, is the idealism which does not take things as they are to be absolute. . . . Even an animal has gone beyond this realist philosophy [which accepts the independence of objectivity] since it devours things and so proves that they are not absolutely self-subsistent.[23]

Spirit can bestow a soul (*i.e.* its own power) upon an object insofar as it proves that the object is not independent of Spirit's power, insofar as it "devours" objectivity. By exercising creative power over the object, Spirit comes to feel itself as power, *i.e.* as $I = I$. "The genuine truth is the prodigious transfer of the inner into the outer, the building of reason into the real world, and this has been the task of the world during the whole course of its history."[24]

It must be emphasized that the absorption of objectivity into the subject is a sacred act. This fact is fascinatingly symbolized in Hegel's "Lutheran" doctrine of the Eucharist. Hegel appreciated the Roman Catholic doctrine of the Eucharist insofar as it suggested a reconciliation of the finite and the infinite, but the doctrine was in-

22. Hegel, *Philosophy of Mind*, 165.
23. G. W. F. Hegel, *Philosophy of Right*, trans. T. M. Knox (London, 1967), 236.
24. *Ibid.*, 166.

adequate because it conceives the host as an objectivity transcending and existing independent of the believer. "And yet in Catholicism this spirit of all truth is in actuality set in rigid opposition to the self-conscious spirit. And, first of all, God is in the 'host' presented to religious adoration as an external thing."[25] Since Spirit is ruled by the principle of I = I, Spirit in man can obviously never accept any divinity outside of itself. This sublime truth is manifested in the "Lutheran" doctrine of the host. "In the Lutheran Church, on the contrary, the host as such is not at first consecrated, but in the moment of enjoyment, *i.e.* in the annihilation of its externality, and in the act of faith, *i.e.* in the free self-certain spirit: only then is it consecrated and exalted to be present in God."[26] Exaltation is, in short, the "enjoyment" of the self's own sacred power as is manifested by its "annihilation of . . . externality" and "the free self-certain spirit." In philosophy this is grasped rationally, in religion through feeling. Here we have the twin psychological features of absolutized apollonianism, of the narcissistic *causa sui* project. We have also seen such psychological urges in some of Marx's "romantic" poems, *i.e.* when he revolts against the "marble-rock of Being." Viewed in its active positivity, such "prometheanism" is also self-creation. No wonder Hegel conceives of the activity of Spirit as that of self-production. "In self consciousness . . . Spirit knows itself. It is the judgment of its own nature and, at the same time, the operation of coming to itself, to produce itself, to make itself (actually) into that which it is in itself (potentially)."[27] And what Spirit is potentially is God, sacred power. Freedom, annihilation of objectivity, and self-creation—these are the Promethean features we have found in Marx. No wonder Marx conceived the heart of philosophy as "world-conquering and absolutely free." As a "convert" to Hegelianism, Marx could conceive of philosophy in no other manner. Thus Hegelian philosophy must be viewed as the theoretical form assumed by Marx's romantic mood of defiance. In other words, insofar as the romantic Marx had opted for Apollonian defiance, he had to reject romantic passivity in

25. Hegel, *Philosophy of Mind*, 284.
26. *Ibid.*, 284–85.
27. Hegel, *Reason in History*, 23.

favor of a theory of power. For this reason, I believe, Marx's speculations of 1837 carried Marx, the fallen-away romantic, "like a false
siren into the arms of the enemy [*i.e.* Hegel]" (E, I, 9). Hegel, the
enemy of Romanticism, became the mentor of Marx, not because
Hegel had rejected the romantic imperative to subjectivize objectivity, but because he had offered an apparently effective way to seize
this power. Hegel's philosophy is, as Robert Tucker has so convinc-
ingly shown, a "dialectics of aggrandizement," that is, a theory that
transforms pride into a cosmogonic principle of man's universe.[28]

Sociality as Sacred Power

The above exposition of the content of philosophical consciousness
according to Hegel is incomplete. So far I have shown only that Promethean power and creativity belong to the essence of Spirit for Hegel. The question must be asked: How does Spirit relate itself to
man? Somehow, the dynamics of Spirit must become the dynamics
of man. Before considering the nature of such a "reconciliation," let
us first reconsider what is involved in the problem. Man, as Hegel
was well aware, is *qua* his finitude exposed to the transitoriness of
time. Man seeks permanent value, but objectivity seems to thwart
him. Man as an individual is mortal and cannot be the bearer of
death-conquering power. It would seem that he cannot appropriate
Promethean power because of individual mortality. Hegel was as-
tutely aware of the problem of individuality, knowing that the individual needs to participate in a supra-individual power and must
connect his "private" heroism with a universal justification. Hegel
consciously called such a locus of power *God*. Divinity is functionally the power to triumph over the insignificance caused by the absurdity of death. Divine power was, furthermore, Promethean power
for Hegel. The divine is, of course, its own parent, its own *causa sui*.
Hegel would seem to be faced with an insoluble problem. The individual human *qua* his particularity is clearly incapable of creating

28. Cf. Robert Tucker, *Philosophy and Myth in Karl Marx* (Cambridge, 1964), 57–72.

infinitude for himself. Yet Hegel seeks to locate human redemption in man's ability to appropriate divine power. The individual is weak and dependent, whereas the divine is its own parent. How is man to be elevated to the divine?

Hegel, like Schlegel and Novalis before him, accepted the idealistic thesis that One is All and All is One. In other words, the finite or the many is not an autonomous reality. Finitude is congealed infinitude. The universal One dirempts itself into the Many, into the plurality of finitude. This means that each concrete thing is ontologically composed of two components, finitude and infinitude. God is not for Hegel a reality ontologically distinct from the manifold of human realities but rather the universal force which forms the many into a structure, into an organic whole.

There is only one Spirit, the universal divine Spirit. . . . It must be understood as that which permeates through everything, as the unity of itself and of a semblance of its "other," as of the subjective and particular. As universal, it is object to itself, and thus determined as a particular, it is this individual: but as universal it reaches over this its "other," so that its "other" and itself are comprised in one.[29]

God has no existential locus "beyond" man.

There cannot be a Divine reason and a human, there cannot be a Divine Spirit and a human, which are absolutely different. Human reason—the consciousness of one's being—is indeed reason; it is the divine in man, and Spirit, insofar as it is the Spirit of God, is not a spirit beyond the world. On the contrary, God is present, omnipresent, and exists as Spirit in all spirits. God is a living God, who is acting and working.[30]

Just as God has no ontological reality distinct from finitude, God has no consciousness of the divine omnipresent in himself. "God is God only so far as he knows himself: His self-knowledge is, further, a self-consciousness in man and man's knowledge of God, which

29. Hegel, *History of Philosophy*, I, 72.
30. Hegel, *Philosophy of Religion*, I, 33.

proceeds to man's self-knowledge *in* God."[31] However, man does not possess immortal power *qua* his particularity, *i.e.* his finite being. "Man is an end in himself only by virtue of the divine in him—that which we designated at the outset as *Reason* or, insofar as it has activity and power of self-determination, as *Freedom*."[32] In short, the divine as the Idea is a supra-individual power that pulsates in and through individuals. The Idea is one "in its totality and in all its individual parts, like one life in a living being, one pulse throbs throughout all its members. All the parts represented in it, and their systematization, emanate from the one Idea; all these particulars are but mirrors and copies of this one life, and have their actuality only in this unity."[33] Mankind must be treated as a single living organism of which the individual is a member. Man is incarnate God.[34]

Ontologically, God is the one throbbing life in the plurality of individual human selves. God as the Being of beings "is the actual presence of the essential and self-subsisting spirit who is all in all."[35] Insofar as God subsists omnipresent in man, God possesses not only ontological reality but also anthropological being. God exists anthropologically in man as the spirit of a community, as social solidarity. "Absolute Spirit [is] realized in the plurality of distinct consciousness definitely existing. It [this spirit] is the community (*Gemeinwesen*) which . . . came before us as the absolute and ultimate reality. . . . It is spirit which is *for itself*, since it maintains itself by being reflected in the minds of the component individuals . . . *Qua* actual substance, that spirit is a Nation (*Volk*); *qua* concrete consciousness, it is the Citizens of the nation."[36] In other words, Spirit—creative power—resides in the social oneness bonding individuals into a collectivity. Yet this world is a spiritual reality, it is essentially the "fusion of individuality." It is this social "fusion," not the

31. Hegel, *Philosophy of Mind*, 298.
32. Hegel, *Reason in History*, 45.
33. Hegel, *Philosophy of Religion*, I, 28.
34. Hegel's conception of man as present incarnate God entices and enthralls Marxists. Cf. Ernst Bloch, *Subjekt-Objekt: Erläuterungen zu Hegel* (Frankfurt, 1971), 313–48. The subtitle to Bloch's chapter on Hegel's philosophy of religion is "Cur deus homo."
35. Hegel, *Philosophy of Mind*, 301.
36. Hegel, *Phenomenology of Mind*, 466–67.

individual in his uniqueness, that is divine. Hegel refers to such a social fusion as "the collective light [which] plays in fainter colors," or
simply as "the collective spirit."[37]

Inasmuch as the human locus of God is the collective social power
of the human species, this collective power triumphs over objectivity "through practical activity."[38] In other words, man creates himself
by appropriating collectively his environment. This transformed
environment is nothing else but culture, social objectivity. Social
objectivity manifests the imprint of man's inner life, *i.e.* the divine
power in him. By rationally contemplating social reality (and this is
the content of a philosophical consciousness), man becomes aware
of his absolute independence, of his divinity. The parallel between
Hegel's God becoming self-conscious in man's consciousness of
himself and "man's self-consciousness as the highest divinity" for
Marx is evident. The vehicle of immortality for both thinkers is not
a transcendent being but the social cooperation between men conceived as a self-creating force. Social collectivity is the "real" correlative to the mythic figure of Prometheus since it is the content of
man's consciousness of himself as divine.

What is then the role of the individual self vis-à-vis sociality as
God?

The specific particularity of a given nature . . . is something powerless and
unreal: it is a "kind of being" which exerts itself foolishly and in vain to
attain embodiment: it is the contradiction of giving reality to the bare particular, while reality is, *ipso facto*, something universal. . . . For the power of
the individual consists in conforming itself to [universal] substance, *i.e.* in
emptying itself of its own self, and thus establishing itself as the objectively
existing substance. . . . The self is conscious of being actual only as transcended, as cancelled."[39]

The individual *qua* his unique finitude is only a moment, a phase of
universal becoming. In itself, the individual is unreal, powerless, an

37. Hegel, *Philosophy of Mind*, 279, 281.
38. Hegel, *The Philosophy of Fine Art*, I, 42.
39. Hegel, *Phenomenology of Mind*, 515, 517.

illusion. The individual has no reality in itself upon which it can erect immortality. Its only destiny is to "empty itself" of any claims to permanence and to submerge itself in social universality. In this way it will fulfill its destiny to bring the divine to full self-consciousness. Expressed differently, the individual self is alone the subject of consciousness. The social collectivity has no awareness. The social collectivity is a living being only as it lives in and through individual beings. The destiny of the individual is to become the conscious mirror that reflects the divine creativity of the social collectivity. Conversely, the individual recognizes his "true and universal self" in the collective whole. He renounces all claims to particular autonomy and is thereby saved as an individual because he shares in the collective autarchy. Freedom is being a member of and determined by the social self.[40] The individual thereby transcends the limitations of empirical existence. We encounter the Dionysian attitude again. The individual cannot escape dependence upon a larger immortality vehicle. However, absorption means in this case an absorption into the collective's Apollonian creativity. This is a prerequisite for the individual's obtainment of Promethean self-consciousness, because it is the prerequisite of his being taken up into the social whole. The individual who becomes one with the *Volk* is thereby enabled to think rationally the reconciliation of Spirit with nature.

The State as a "Secular Deity"

We must proceed one step further in our analysis of the Hegelian reconciliation of subjectivity with objectivity if we are to understand the development of Marx's thinking. Marx (*ca.* 1840–1843) criticized Hegel within the framework of Hegel's own philosophy. But Marx did so by focusing upon the State, which within Hegelian philosophy fills a salvational function. Let us proceed to examine how Hegel's divinization of sociality culminates in the State as the "secular deity."

40. Cf. Richard L. Schacht, "Hegel on Freedom" in Alasdair MacIntyre (ed.), *Hegel: A Collection of Critical Essays* (Garden City, 1972), 289–328.

As shown above, the individual finds and participates in universal power insofar as he subsists in that which the social collectivity has created. The most general mode of life of the social collectivity is, as we have seen, culture. "That which, in reference to the single individual appears as his culture, is the essential moment of spiritual substance as such. . . . Culture is the soul of substance, in virtue of which the essentially inherent (*Ansich*) becomes something explicitly acknowledged, and assumes definite objective existence."[41] The culture of a community is the objective gestalt of man's *causa sui* powers and thereby mediates to the individual a universal identity. Culture is anthropological rationality. The individual participates in this objectified rationality by the self-conscious conformity of his will to universal life.

"Universal substance utters its universal language in the customs and laws of a nation."[42] Custom and law are the *Gestalten*, ethical or moral, that the "spirit of a community" assumes in its structuring of individual consciousness. Participation in such norms constitutes ethical life (*Sittlichkeit*) according to Hegel. "The ethical life is the divine spirit as indwelling in self-consciousness, as it is actually present in a nation and its individual members."[43] Indeed, one can say that the conformity of the particular individual to the "ethical" norms of the sociocultural order is divine life having become self-conscious because the individual is thereby aware of the "forming" or "creating" power of the social collectivity. Absolute forming power is now acknowledged by the particulars it informs. From this point of view, the ethical substance appears as "an absolute authority and power infinitely more firmly established than the being of nature."[44]

The norms of ethical life, of collective creating, are for Hegel the "appearance" of what I have designated as sacred power. Ethical life is what "fuses" individuals into a single, self-conscious collectivity. The social collectivity must, since it is incarnate Spirit, be governed by the principle of I = I, *i.e.* it must "cancel" the autonomy of all its parts by structuring them into a whole. Correlatively, the parts bring

41. Hegel, *Phenomenology of Mind*, 516.
42. *Ibid.*, 377.
43. Hegel, *Philosophy of Mind*, 283.
44. Hegel, *Philosophy of Right*, 106.

the collectivity to self-consciousness by recognizing the structuring power of sociality. But in any community particular individuals will always deviate from each other. Unity will be threatened. There must, accordingly, reasons Hegel, be an objective embodiment of absolute power, *i.e.* a social reality that is the highest and last resort of social unity. The ethical power of ethical powers for Hegel was first and foremost the State. "Government is concrete actual spirit reflected into itself, the self pure and simple of the entire ethical substance."[45] The State is the Spirit having become visible, having penetrated objectivity and hence existing as objectified. "The State is the actuality of the ethical idea. It is the ethical mind *qua* the substantial will manifest and revealed to itself, accomplishing what it knows and insofar as it knows it." Hegel even refers to the State as "this actual God" and pontificates: "Man must venerate the State as a secular deity." "The State must be treated as a great architectonic structure, as a hieroglyph of the reason which reveals itself in actuality."[46]

In the first chapter I described the poetic as the meaning which is manifested in and through a sensate medium. Hegel's State as a "hieroglyph," as a "secular deity," fulfills this definition. The State is absolute value become visible and hence that which man is to worship. We have seen that for Hegel both religion and philosophy worship God. Since God is incarnated in the State, philosophy ultimately comes to worship the State. Therefore salvational consciousness will entail the individual's sociopolitical recognition that the particularity of his finitude has been integrated into social universality *via* the State.

It is no wonder that Hegel writes: "The State does not exist for the citizens, on the contrary, one could say that the state is the end and they are the means. But the means-end relation is not fitting here. For the state is not the abstract confronting the citizens; they are parts of it, like members of an organic body, where no member is an end and none is means. . . . All the value man has, as a spiritual reality, he has only through the state."[47] Hegel should not be misun-

---

45. Hegel, *Phenomenology of Mind*, 473.
46. Hegel, *Philosophy of Right*, 155, 279, 258, 289.
47. Hegel, *Reason in History*, 52.

derstood. The individual exists *for* the state in the sense that his particularity can only have one function, namely to realize the dictates of collective creativity as structured by the state. But the state should not be experienced as a reality "beyond" and opposed to the individual, rather as that which lends transcending value to the temporality and finitude of individual activity. When the totality of the individual's particular existence is permeated by his being a "citizen" of a state, the individual is reconciled with the "secular deity." Consequently, salvation has not only philosophical but also social and political features. In short, "[the State] is the holy bond that ties the men, the spirits together. It is one life in all, a grand object, a great purpose and content on which depends all individual happiness and all private decisions."[48]

The Crisis of Hegelian Philosophy

The "poetic" motive informing Hegel's speculations is the desire to reveal the total fusion or "concretization" of the social universal in the particular. Since Spirit is all, there should be nothing that is not divine, that is not experienced as a manifestation of the universal. The "fusion" of sacred power with concrete life is precisely what Hegel understood by concrete universality. Concrete universality includes not only the metaphysical and logical aspects of Spirit but also its anthropological mode of existence. In other words, history, political structures, political economy, in short, social existence—all profane areas of human existence—should be on principle cognizable as full embodiments of universal spirit. The sciences that deal with the anthropological form of Spirit can be designated as sciences of the *real* life of man. Such sciences, including political theory, are regulated by "real" fact, that is they claim to explain what the empirical should be. Hegel's philosophical task was to subsume the empirical sciences of the *real* under the logical and metaphysical exigencies of the ideal. Relative to man, Hegel had to show rationally that the divine had become fully immanentized in human existence. The development of God is also man's socioempirical development. Politics was theology and theodicy for Hegel.

48. *Ibid.*

The identification of the sacred and profane was the cardinal theoretical danger facing Hegelianism. If a "gap" can be shown to exist between the human and the divine, between man and the State, Hegelianism as a *total* philosophy will collapse.[49] This was what happened to Hegelian philosophy in the course of the 1830s after Hegel's death. One group of Hegelians, called "young Hegelians," or "left-wing Hegelians," came to the conclusion that Hegel's ideal lacked any real locus and human matrix of mediation. Hegel's ideal was not surrendered. The "real" fact of the matter is that man has not yet reached such a state of self-consciousness. More importantly, Hegel's critics came to realize that Hegel's idealistic metaphysics of Spirit could not be translated adequately into the language and concepts of empirically oriented science. No left-wing Hegelian (and Marx belongs to this group) doubted that the "elevation of the finite to God" was the *eschaton* of history; they just doubted the proofs Hegel had constructed in order to demonstrate that this *eschaton* had been reached. A new theoretical position had to be developed if redemption were to be realized.[50] Such is the background to Marx's Ph.D. dissertation. Marx too was seeking to critique Hegel's concept of philosophy without giving up its ideal. Before examining Marx's dissection of "philosophy" as a problem, we must first grasp more fully the nature of the crisis in Hegelian philosophy.

The "Discordant Note"

In the concluding pages of his *Philosophy of Religion* Hegel admits something of enormous significance. According to Hegel, on a level of religious consciousness the "Holy Spirit" should penetrate human

---

49. For an excellent analysis and critique of the fragile "Hegelian middle," see Emil L. Fackenheim, *The Religious Dimension of Hegel's Thought* (Boston, 1967), 223–42. Concerning the theodicean crisis inherent in Hegel's inability to show the world as reconciled with itself, see Iwan Iljin, *Die Philosophie Hegels als kontemplative Gotteslehre* (Bern, 1946), 305–82.

50. I shall not enter into the history of "young Hegelianism" and Marx's relationship to it. Suffice it to note that Hegel's "left-wing" followers were concerned with the antinomy between the real and ideal. Their speculations were political and eschatological (*i.e.* political being formed the locus of the *eschaton*). The question was: How is human consciousness to be raised to awareness of its autarchic freedom? Cf. William J. Brazill, *The Young Hegelians* (New Haven, 1970), and Jürgen Gebhardt, *Politik und Eschatologie: Studien zur Geschichte der Hegelschen Schule in den Jahren 1830–1840* (Munich, 1965).

consciousness. The oneness of man with the Absolute in the State should religiously be manifested by a note of spirituality in the religious life of contemporary man. But philosophy is faced with a "discordant note," namely the decline of religious life in modern times. "This discordant note is actually present in reality."[51] Just as "universal unity in religion" disappeared in the time of the Roman Empire and just as "the Divine was profaned," so too is it in Hegel's time. Political life needs a religious basis. Indeed, the reconciliation of man with God in political life is the secular form of the doctrine of incarnation. But "the unity of the outer and inner no longer exists in immediate consciousness, in the world of reality." Even the modern State cannot reawaken the universal oneness of the religious consciousness: "the process of decay has gone too deep for that."[52] Instead of there being universal consciousness in each individual, man's consciousness has fragmented and dirempted into spheres of "private" concern. The fragmentation of modern culture (of which Schiller complained) appears not to be healed in actuality. What then is the real relationship of philosophy to such real fragmentation?

For us philosophical knowledge has harmonized this discord. . . . But this reconciliation is itself merely a partial one without outward universality [*i.e.* without empirical embodiment]. Philosophy forms in this connection a sanctuary apart, and those who serve in it constitute an isolated order of priests, who must not mix with the world, and whose work is to protect the possessions of Truth. How the actual present-day world is to find its way out of this state of disruption, and what form it is to take, are questions which must be left to itself to settle, and to deal with them is not the immediate practical business and concern of philosophy.[53]

Emil L. Fackenheim has aptly described this admission by Hegel: "What an incredible, what a shattering turn of thought! "[54] It is indeed incredible because it is the announcement of the failure of Hegel's

51. Hegel, *Philosophy of Religion*, III, 150.
52. *Ibid.*
53. *Ibid.*, 151.
54. Fackenheim, *The Religious Dimension*, 235.

philosophical project, of the *causa sui* project. All of Hegel's recriminations against Romanticism and its inability to transcend subjectivity can be (and were in effect by Marx and others) directed at Hegelian philosophy. Philosophy is in the above citation no longer the manifestation of the life of a community but a "sanctuary" inhabited by philosophical priests who do not possess the slightest idea how the "actual present-day world" is to be saved from its current "state of disruption." Indeed, the Hegelian philosopher does not even know what type of questions to ask; instead the world "must be left to itself to settle" the problem of discord in modern life. Hegelian philosophy may be a "totality," but only one in thought, not in empirical actuality. Hegel's confession of philosophical failure would indeed be "shattering" for any true believer who seriously was seeking consciousness of man's creative energies as sacred power. To state that the reconciliation of thought with the real "is not the immediate practical business and concern of philosophy" is to confess the bankruptcy of Hegelian theory.

Marx's Opposition to the "Discordant Note"

Marx claimed to have become acquainted with Hegel from one end to the other. Whether Marx was aware of Hegel's confession of failure, he was, to be sure, aware of the failure of Hegelian philosophy. In one of the "Vorarbeiten" to his dissertation Marx writes:

By the fact that philosophy has closed itself into a completed, total world . . . the totality of the world per se is dirempted in itself, and to be sure this diremption is driven to extremes, for spiritual existence has become free, has been enriched to universality; the heartbeat has become in a concrete way the division which is the entire organism. The diremption of the world is only total when its sides are totalities. The world is therefore one ripped to pieces [*zerrissen*], which encounters a philosophy total in itself. The appearance of this philosophy's activity is divided [*zerrissen*] and contradictory; its objective universality returns into subjective forms of individual consciousness in which it is alive. (E, I, 215–16)

Hegelian philosophy had claimed to be a "total world" in the sense that it reconciled subjectivity and objectivity, thought and actuality. But if Hegelian philosophy in effect has its totality only in thought and not in actuality, then its claim to totality must also signal the diremption of the totality of the world. In the case of Hegelianism, the split between the actual and thought must be driven to the extreme because philosophy claims to make man absolutely free—*i.e.* to be world-conquering. The contradiction between subjectivity and the realities of objectivity are the "heartbeat" of Marx's times. In other words, the "discordant note" between thought and reality constitutes the consciousness and volitional dynamics of Marx's contemporaries. Marx can speak of the sides of the world (thought and actuality) as being "totalities" because they seem to have no point of intersection, no mediation. This ensures the total diremption of the world. Insofar as philosophy informs an individual's consciousness, such a consciousness is no more than a "subjective form" that must oppose objectivity in a contradictory and divided manner.

Such an opposition between philosophy and reality after the claims of a total philosophy is seen by Marx as a necessary law of philosophical development. Marx never really proves this assertion, but it is a necessary belief if philosophy is to have any task after a total philosophy. "Who does not understand this historical necessity must consequently deny totally that after a total philosophy men can still live. . . . Without this necessity one cannot comprehend how after Aristotle a Zeno, after Epicurus, even a Sextus Empiricus, after Hegel the baseless and wanting attempts (for the most part) of recent philosophers could appear" (E, I, 216). Marx's treatment of Epicurus is partially his attempt to understand how after the total philosophies of Aristotle or Plato a late Greek philosophy could appear that often returned to ideas prevalent before the total philosophies (E, I, 267). Presently we will consider the importance of the Socratic method in the construction of new systems of philosophy.

As was evident from the Promethean quotation given above, Marx did not give up the philosophical project inasmuch as it was the form in which he sought to realize the *causa sui* project. Prometheus, the symbol of philosophy, will conquer the world. But how? If Hegelian philosophy is only correct as an ideal, if it has failed to render the actual world philosophical, how is a remedy to be found? We have seen that Hegel himself rejected the task of overcoming discord by means of philosophy.

There could be no solution to the antinomy between the real and ideal within the terms of Hegelian philosophy, because philosophical knowledge for Hegel is essentially not dialectical, *i.e. not* creative. Alexandre Kojève, in his brilliant exposition of Hegel's concept of philosophical wisdom, has written: "The attitude of the [Hegelian] philosopher or the 'scientist' (= Wise Man) with respect to Being and to the Real is one of purely passive contemplation and that philosophic or scientific activity reduces to a pure and simple *description* of the Real and of Being. The Hegelian method, therefore, is not at all 'dialectical.' " [55] Being itself is, to be sure, dialectical; it is the process whereby Spirit comes to create itself. This process is the result of the will. Will and thought are one for Hegel, although the function is different. Will as a creative force precedes thought. The function of philosophical thinking is simply to comprehend what will has achieved. "To comprehend what is, this is the task of philosophy, because what is, is reason." [56] The development of Spirit as human history is, of course, a function of will, but will creating unconsciously or not fully conscious. World history progresses toward its end only "as an innermost unconscious instinct. And the whole business of history . . . is to bring [the idea of Spirit] into consciousness!" [57] Only after man at a particular historical stage has collectively conquered nature and brought forth a thriving culture can a reflective and essentially contemplative consciousness come into being. The discovery of the focal points is the coming into being of philosophical consciousness. Philosophy is, therefore, the self-reflection of a historical stage upon itself. "Whatever happens, every individual is a child of his time; so philosophy too is its own time, apprehended in thoughts." [58] Philosophy is thus the dialectical process of will reflecting upon its com-

55. Alexandre Kojève, *Introduction to the Reading of Hegel*, trans. Allan Bloom (New York, 1969), 171.
56. Hegel, *Philosophy of Right*, 11.
57. Hegel, *Reason in History*, 30.
58. Hegel, *Philosophy of Right*, 11.

pleted movement. Philosophical consciousness itself is *not* dialectical; rather it is passive contemplation of that which has already come to be. "It is only when actuality is mature that the ideal first appears over against the real and that the ideal apprehends this same real world in its substance and builds it up for itself into the shape of an intellectual realm. When philosophy paints its grey in grey, then has a shape of life grown old. By philosophy's grey in grey it cannot be rejuvenated but only understood. The owl of Minerva spreads its wings only with the falling of dusk."[59]

Hegel quite consistently rejects the notion that philosophy can act as a causal power in erecting an ideal to be realized. "It would be as absurd to fancy that a philosophy can transcend its contemporary world as it is to fancy that an individual can overleap his own age, jump over Rhodes. If his theory really goes beyond the world as it is and builds an ideal one as it ought to be, that world exists indeed, but only in his opinions, an unsubstantial element where anything you please may, in fancy, be built."[60] (Romantics of course held that "fancy" indeed builds worlds.) Since philosophy cannot effect a reconciliation between the "is" and "ought" that is not already present, any attempt to construct an ideal must be a matter of errant subjectivity, of "fancy." This quotation quite clearly reveals the noncreative and passive concept of philosophy in the mature Hegel's thought. Philosophy is simply the reflective awareness of the creative process at a given nodal point of history, and not a causal factor in this process. Philosophy's task is simply "to recognize" what has become (what is), not to create it. "To recognize reason as the rose in the cross of the present and thereby to enjoy the present, this is the rational insight which reconciles us to the actual."[61]

But what if the "is" is in actuality not informed by the "ought"? Then there would be, on Hegelian premises, no rationality, no real reconciliation, for philosophy to recognize. Philosophy would then either degenerate into despair or escape into the haven of "one-sided" thought (*viz*. illusion). Indeed, so long as philosophy remains passive

59. *Ibid.*, 13.
60. *Ibid.*, 11.
61. *Ibid.*, 12.

contemplation, there will always remain a "cross of the present" in the "rose" of enjoyment, which is to say there will be no true enjoyment of sacred power.[62] As long as Marx persisted within Hegel's nondialectical conception of philosophy, he was faced with an impasse. However, Marx transcended Hegel. Marx, in my judgment, retained the Hegelian ideal of reconciliation between thought and actuality. He returned, however, to a romantic conception of philosophy, that is to philosophy as the dialectics of irony. Whether this return was done in full consciousness or not, there is some indication that Marx was aware of the historical background to what he was doing.

In one of the "Vorarbeiten" Marx discusses critically Bruno Bauer's association of Socratic philosophy with Christianity. In the process of refuting Bauer, Marx defines Socratic irony:

Socratic irony . . . is nothing but the form of philosophy as it relates itself subjectively to common consciousness. That it has in Socrates the form of an ironic human or wise man follows from the fundamental character and relationship of Greek philosophy to actuality [*zur Wirklichkeit*]; amongst us, irony in Fr. v. Schlegel has been taught as a general immanent formula, so to speak, as philosophy. However, objectively, or according to content . . . Fichte with his world-creating ego (although Nicolai recognized that he should not create a world), every philosopher who asserts immanence against the empirical person is an ironist. (E, I, 220)[63]

It is not known how much Schlegel was read by Marx. Marx may have derived his ideas on Schlegel and irony from someone else such

62. For a penetrating examination of Hegel's concept of the rose and the cross, see Karl Löwith, *From Hegel to Nietzsche: The Revolution in Nineteenth-Century Thought*, trans. David E. Green (Garden City, 1967), 13–28. Herbert Marcuse accuses Hegel of betraying his highest philosophical ideals because he ultimately tries to justify a world dirempted instead of negating it. Cf. *Reason and Revolution: Hegel and the Rise of Social Theory* (Boston, 1968), 218–23.

63. None of Marx's commentators have commented upon Marx's reference to "irony in Fr. Schlegel." Van Leeuwen in his lengthy paraphrase of the quotation from Marx simply omits any reference to Schlegel. (Cf. *Critique of Heaven*, 121.) The one exception, so far as I can determine, of an interpreter seeking to illuminate Marx in the light of Schlegelian irony, is Ernst Behler, *Klassische Ironie, Romantische Ironie, Tragische Ironie*, 125–27. Behler is interested in Marx's positive evaluation of Schlegelian irony, and his attempt is not to ascertain the meaning of this evaluation for Marx's evolving thought.

as Hegel, Solger, or even indirectly through Heinrich Heine. Also, as a student at Bonn (1836–1837), which was known as a center of Romanticism, Marx did attend two courses taught by August von Schlegel, Friedrich's older brother and a leading theorist of German Romanticism. As already noted, Marx had intended to write an essay *de romanticis* (much of which he probably did write) to be printed in Arnold Ruge's *Anekdota philosophica*. Marx did, of course, write over 140 poems (1833–1837) in the vein of late Romanticism, and there is his November 10, 1837, letter to his father. In short, biographical evidence suggests that Marx was well acquainted with the romantic movement, though the details of such an acquaintance cannot be ascertained. Also, Marx was aware (as the immediately previous citation shows) that irony was the form of philosophy for Schlegel. We can, I would contend, gain a deeper insight into Marx's revision of Hegelian philosophy if we investigate Schlegel's concept of irony as the form of philosophy. Whatever the specifics of Marx's knowledge of Schlegel were, there are some striking parallels between the two thinkers. Schlegel's concept of philosophy unites theory and praxis, thought and will into one evolving and often revolutionary movement.[64]

Schlegel and Philosophy as Irony

According to Marx, Socratic irony is "the form of philosophy," and irony in Friedrich Schlegel has been taught "as philosophy." Schlegel himself in a historical discussion of Socrates wrote: "Since reflecting [*Nachdenken*] was, according to Socratic doctrine, an inner self-thinking [*Selbstdenken*], its dialectic or art of reflecting could not be a particular science, or a special part of philosophy; rather it was the

64. Some of the important writings of Schlegel that Marx could have read before writing his dissertation are: *Lyceums-Fragmente* (1796), *Athenäum-Fragmente* (1798); *Ideen* (1800); *Gespräch über die Poesie* (1800); *Die Entwicklung der Philosophie in Zwölf Büchern* (1804–1806—first printed 1836); *Geschichte der alten und neuen Literatur* (first printed 1822); *Philosophie des Lebens* (1828); *Philosophie der Geschichte* (1829), and *Philosophie der Sprache* (1830). During the years 1822–1825 Schlegel published his *Sämtliche Werke* in ten volumes. I shall also cite from a group of aphorisms and notes known today as *Philosophische Lehrjahre*. Marx could not have read these aphorisms. However, they cast light upon Schlegel's evolving conceptualization of ironic philosophy.

form of all philosophy per se. The philosophy of Socrates was . . . a continuously progressing philosophizing . . . a methodical forming and perfection of thinking and reflecting" (KA, XIII, 204–205). Also, in a fragment Schlegel wrote: "This is the FORM *of philosophy* . . . irony here entirely dominant" (KA, XVIII, 464). Irony was, therefore, for Schlegel more than a poetical category; it was also an essential ingredient in philosophical consciousness. "Irony has in systematic philosophy its real place" (KA, XVIII, 109). "Irony is the duty of philosophy which is not yet history or a system" (KA, XVIII, 86). The "real place" irony assumes in philosophy is that of the *form* of philosophizing. In order to explain what Schlegel meant, I will seek to explicate the three basic features of philosophy for Schlegel: "What truly makes a philosopher is the transcendental and the practical and the critical" (KA, XVIII, 111).

The Transcendental The term *transcendental* is ultimately derived from Kant, though Schlegel gives it a Fichtean twist. The transcendental method of philosophizing is identified by Schlegel with the "process of irony," and indeed "Socratic irony" has "transcendental form" (KA, XVIII, 468, 79). The transcendental philosopher seeks to justify theoretical knowledge by grounding it in consciousness, by focusing upon the pure conditions in the subject for knowing an object. Schlegel enunciated the transcendental principle of philosophy when he wrote that "philosophy must proceed from the I, and its content should be nothing but the *history of consciousness*" (KA, XII, 398).

The grounding principle of romantic idealism is I = I. Therefore, the act of knowing is teleologically directed to the production of self-consciousness. Knowing is the process of grasping the self exteriorized in objectivity. Irony is a constitutive principle of philosophy as well as of poetry because it is a transcendental condition of consciousness per se. In other words, philosophy and poetry are two modes of thinking and irony is the form of thinking per se. But as we have seen in Chapter II, mental activity, human as well as divine, is constitutionally oriented to infinity. "The necessary in man is precisely just the longing for the infinite." "The foundation of consciousness = the view of infinity." Consequently, Schlegel concludes:

"The essence of philosophy consists in the longing for the infinite and the education [*Bildung*] of reason" (KA, XVIII, 420, 415, 418). Philosophy is the theoretical and conceptual manner in which the human mind longs for and pursues infinity. Indeed, philosophical theorizing as transcendental thinking is the "process of irony." This process is nothing other than the "history of consciousness." And the logical form of this process constitutes the dialectics of Socratic irony. "All logic should be dialectics and all dialectics should be Socratic" (KA, XVIII, 366). What then is the transcendental condition for the dialects of irony? This condition is a function of the structure of the self.

In Chapter II it was shown that the human self is in romantic theory an ontological composite. The human self is a momentary congelation of the divine in empirical form. As such an *Ich* and *Ur-Ich*, the finite and infinite, constitute the structural poles of the human self. This structural duality is reflected in the dynamics of human willing and thinking. Indeed, the "gap" between the exigencies of infinitude and the actuality of finitude generate in the human self activity, be it theoretical, poetic, or practical. The transcendental duality of the human condition translates itself into a mental movement toward unity. This mental movement is the anthropological *modus essendi* assumed by ontological becoming. The conceptual form of this movement is the act of philosophizing.

The polar structure of the human self manifests itself in a series of antithetical tendencies which mediate each other in seeking reconciliation. "Irony is a lawful change; it is more than mere oscillation." Transcendental thinking as philosophy is an "eternally mobile" principle. "That idealism must be eternally mutable . . . is clear from its own view of the identity of philosophy and spiritual-mental activity [*geistige Tätigkeit*]" (KA, XVIII, 77, 468, 344). Schlegel derived the basic antithetical duality of spiritual-mental activity from Fichte. "The good in Fichte's form is positing, and then the going out of and returning into the self—the form of reflection" (KA, XVIII, 476). "*Reflection* in the right sense [is] already an artificial consciousness—the going out of the self and the returning again into the self" (KA, XVIII, 437).

The centrifugal and centripetal movement of consciousness permeates all of human activity including philosophy. For instance, relative to the exigencies of finitude and infinitude, the human self goes out of itself and sinks itself in the finite objects. In other words, the human self focuses its psychic energies upon definite, determinate, and limited contents of consciousness which it seeks to appropriate philosophically through theory. In order to exist, the human self must have an "objective" content to satiate its selfhood. But this self is simultaneously impelled by its longing for the infinite to seek an endless and illimitable content of consciousness. Therefore, the self must return itself from its fixation in "outer" form and thereby free its "inner" substance from limiting and oppressive objectivity in order to immerse itself once again into objectivity on a higher level. Consequently, the self possesses the tendency and ability to transcend every limitation, to progress ever higher. The impulse to transcend is derived from the dialectical awareness of the contradiction between the centripetal and centrifugal tendencies. The tension is resolved insofar as the dialectical impulse is transformed into an act of annihilation. But the self is one and as such must seek to regain psychic integrity, which it does by higher creativity following the act of annihilation. This the self accomplishes insofar as the active, infinite, creative self can encounter itself incorporated in the manifold of determinate and finite objects. The repeated encounter of affirmation, negation, and transcendence assumes philosophical form as knowledge. The transcendental or dialectical movement of the self is like a spiral. Its movement is a product of the self's ability and necessity to transcend the limitations of any "is." "And so the freedom of the self in relation to the [objective] world transforms itself into the ability *to expand and to contract* itself *at will*" (KA, XII, 360). This freedom is the "process of irony," as the formal causal power of thinking. This is why irony "is a lawful changing."

Furthermore, the centripetal and centrifugal movement of the self shows itself in the very goal of consciousness, namely in infinity. Infinity as a concept is characterized by transcendental polarity. Schlegel called these poles "the idea of *infinite unity* and of *infinite fullness*" (KA, XIII, 245). In seeking the infinite the self longs to cognize an endless richness. Richness implies multiplicity, division, and distinction. It is for this reason that the self had to turn to the world of objects. But multiplicity without commonality, without unity, cannot quench the need for infinity because every element of the manifold implies separation. Fullness without unity must metamorphize into an empty chaos, since infinite fullness is also infinite isolation. Therefore, the self must seek infinite unity dialectically, that is by incorporating total unity into manifoldness. This, on the level of philosophy, is the principle of system. But, any given "system" is incomplete because it can never exhaust infinite fullness. Every system is accordingly finite. The self must then relate itself "skeptically" to any given system, *i.e.* render it chaotic. "The ideal of an infinite analysis is nothing other than the ideal to make all sciences chaotic" (KA, XVIII, 281). Therefore, the course of philosophical development "should be in several cycles, always wider and greater. When the goal [of creating a system] is reached, it would *begin again and again from the beginning*—alternating between chaos and system, chaos preparing for a system and then new chaos" (KA, XVIII, 283). Thus Schlegel describes the form of philosophy: "The absolute unity would perhaps be a chaos of systems" (KA, XII, 5). This chaos of systems is the form of philosophy as ironic activity. Or as Ernst Behler has noted: "The dialectics of romantic irony grew first of all out of the tension between infinite fullness and infinite unity."[65] The awareness of this tension assumes the form of a volition which impels man to transcend and to sublate it. This tension is what Schlegel called Socratic irony. "Socratic irony . . . contains and incites a feeling of the insoluble conflict between the unconditioned and the conditioned, of the impossibility and necessity of total communication" (KA, II, 160). Schlegel seeks to resolve this antinomy through the notion of progressive circularity. The self, inspired by Socratic irony, relates itself as a subject first annihilatingly toward objectivity and then it re-creates a higher unity, only to repeat the circle endlessly. "The consciousness of infinity must be constituted by annihilating [its] opposite. One must constitute oneself by means of an act and this

---

65. Cf. "Einleitung," KA, XVIII, xvii.

act is no other than the annihilation of every phantasy of finitude"
(KA, XVIII, 412). And any given philosophical system is indeed a
"phantasy of finitude." The power of annihilation that brings the self
closer to infinitude is, of course, irony, Socratic irony.

Marx had stated that "Socratic irony . . . is nothing but the form
of philosophy as it relates itself subjectively to common consciousness" and that the ironist is "every philosopher who asserts immanence against the empirical person." This form of philosophizing is
the annihilating power of irony. It relates itself subjectively to "common consciousness" (consciousness absorbed in finitude) by negating this consciousness. In this sense, it can be said to assert
immanence (the awareness of man's inner infinitude) against the
empirical person (the person mired in objectivity). The "general immanent formula" of irony is to negate in order to posit anew. Schlegel's concept of Socratic irony coincides with and gives depth to
Marx's brief definition. The question that must now be answered
is how philosophy can ironize an inadequate philosophical consciousness.

The Critical   It should be obvious from the above that the philosophical act for Schlegel differs from Hegel's conception. For Hegel,
philosophy is the self-reflection of a completed phase of development. As such the philosopher cannot transcend his age. Schlegel, on
the contrary, contends: "The individual can never completely deny
his age; nevertheless he can elevate himself above it. He is not bound
in inalterable necessity to his time, and so it must really be, since it
would be a poor freedom if one did not even have the energy to pro-
cure it [freedom]" (KA, XIII, 28). Philosophical thinking is consequently an integral force in the "procuring" of a transcendence of a
given age. This is because philosophy is a dialectical (active), rather
than a contemplative (passive) power. But how is philosophy active?
The answer: "If the contention stands firm that the object of philosophy is inexhaustible, that philosophy approaches only gradually
the infinite goal of its vocation, it would be a necessary law for the
manner of considering and method of philosophy that it is critical"
(KA, XIII, 317). Insofar as philosophy tries to comprehend reality,
it must erect a system. However, every system is incapable of unify-

ing infinite fullness. Therefore, any given system must be "annihilated," rendered chaotic, before a new and more adequate one can be formulated. The act of annihilation is irony. But this irony is carried out within and by means of philosophy itself. Consequently, the philosophical act or ironizing is criticism. The "is" of a given philosophy is criticized as inadequate in order to create a new and closer approximation to the "ought." Critique as irony is the means by which philosophy approaches actuality.

Philosophical criticism entails three basic features. First, critical irony must "attack and refute" the mode of philosophy (that in effect accepts the empirical world the way it is) "as totally false and perverted; [philosophical method] must strive to show most thoroughly the superficiality, emptiness, nothingness . . . of this opinion in order to pave and break the way for the knowledge of the highest truth. . . . [Philosophical method] must accordingly also be the critique of all philosophical movements" (KA, XIII, 318–19). In short, the error eradicated by critique "consists according to content in the fact that the permanent, the thing, non-being [*i.e.* that which is] is considered to be real" (KA, XIII, 22). Secondly, philosophical critique is able to reach its goal by constructing a genetic explanation of what is. The philosopher understands his object when he "has ascended to its origins and initial origination, and can explain from this the gradual development of all its properties and features as well as derive its entire present form" (KA, XIII, 322). Philosophy, because it seeks genetic explanations, is accordingly concerned with history. "Philosophy is only really and truly constructed when it is at the same time historical" (KA, XIII, 323). Philosophy, in short, ironizes itself when it comprehends itself in and as its history. Thirdly, philosophical critique seeks to grasp its object not only in itself but in its relationship to other things, particularly "in its relationship *to us* and *to the world in general*" (KA, XIII, 324). Philosophical criticism has, therefore, a "practical" meaning for man. In what sense is philosophy practical?

The Practical "The destiny of man can only be reached through praxis [*praktisch*]" (KA, XIII, 20). Praxis is defined by Schlegel as "the activity of a striving in opposition to contrary fighting. . . .

Praxis is the effort of a drive . . . which, if it is to succeed, must be grounded in knowledge and method" (KA, XIII, 20). As Schlegel notes, praxis is ultimately concerned with the realization of "the visible Kingdom of God" on earth (KA, XIII, 34). Praxis is simply irony become practical. Praxis is the ironic form of philosophy. "Praxis has indeed the task to dissolve the permanent, to annihilate the limited, the earthly, the thing [the 'is']" (KA, XIII, 20). The law of praxis is progressivity since it seeks the visible Kingdom of God.

Schlegel stresses at this point that history *qua* history is not progressive. For Hegel history was progressive and philosophy was accordingly the reflection of this progressivity. For Schlegel, in contrast, "a steady development and perfectibility does not fit history at all; it is the general method of praxis" (KA, XIII, 22). The creative power of perfection resides in the application of theory to history by philosophy. "The tendency of Idealism is to make all theory praxis, and all praxis theory. Praxis and theory are factors of philosophy" (KA, XVIII, 397). Therefore, philosophical critique itself is a perfecting force in history insofar as praxis (*i.e.* the effort to overcome the "is") is given theoretical direction. "Praxis has, as stated, no other goal than to clean up all hindrances which stand in the way of man's striving after the infinite; it must, however, if it is to have the desired success, be grounded on knowledge and methodologically directed" (KA, XIII, 23). Philosophically guided praxis would appear to be nothing but applied irony.

Schlegel grows vague at this point. He does not treat praxis as the concrete use of physical force to alter social, political, or economic conditions through, for example, revolution. The concept remains for the most part within the realm of thought. That is, praxis *seems* to entail a theoretical critique of the forms of human existence that hinder human progress. Praxis seems to imply a reform of consciousness rather than a material reform of "objects." Yet a very suggestive statement sticks out: "The application of [the] laws [of human consciousness] to the history of man would itself lead to history, and this demands a lot of critical spirit" (KA, XIII, 27). The laws of human consciousness are the dialectics of irony. This is also the program of Marx's maturing Marxism. Of course, the nature of the laws of human consciousness differed for Marx, but the notion that critique itself can become history hints at the "Marxist" notion of irony via real revolution. Let us now return to Marx's conception of philosophy in his Ph.D. dissertation.

Socrates as an Ironist

Parallels can be drawn between Schlegel's conception of philosophy as dialectics and Marx's interpretation of the meaning of Socrates for philosophy. "Socrates is personified philosophy," avers Marx, and as such he is a representative par excellence of Greek philosophy. Philosophy assumes in Socrates "the form of an ironic human or wise man" (E, I, 220). In the second "Vorarbeit" to his dissertation Marx discusses the nature of the Greek wise man, particularly as exemplified in Socrates.

According to Marx Greek wise men not only cognitively sought to grasp "ideal substance" (*viz.* sacred power), but also to become it, transforming subjectivity into substantial power. Marx claims that the first Greek wise men "are the real spiritus, the embodied knowledge of substance. . . . This embodiment of the ideal substance takes place in the philosophers themselves who proclaim it; not only is its expression plastically poetic, but [ideal substance] is reality in this person. . . . They themselves are living images, living works of art" (E, I, 80). The Greek philosopher is a "living work of art" because the unity of his existence, his subjectivity, is informed and structured by the awareness of absolute value. Spirituality permeates the philosopher's empirical activity. Such spiritualized activity can well be designated as poetic, at least in the sense given to the term in Chapter I. The first Greek philosophers could, of course, express their understanding of reality in strange ways, as in Thales's claim that everything is water, even though it is empirically clear that this is not so. Such formulations reveal, however, the theoretical certainty of the philosopher *qua* his subjectivity that the immediate empirical given of objectivity is not absolute. The philosopher negates objectivity by philosophically reducing it to the appearance of the One. This certainty is the ideality of substance having become the principle of subjective existence. In other words, the underlying premise of the Greek wise man is in effect that spirit is primary and the world must acknowledge this primacy. In this sense philosophy is subjectivity that turns against the objective (empirical or social) world. In short, the wise man is "subjectivity which posits itself as the principle of philosophy. This subjectivity, turned against the substantial powers of the people . . . turns itself outward against reality [*Wirklichkeit*], is entangled in practice in it, and its existence is movement" (E, I, 82). And how is a philosopher in movement? He philosophizes and thereby negates in and by thought the claims of the empirical world, even of the social collectivity, to absoluteness.

The wise man is seeking to experience sacred power via philosophy as the power of spirit. This is the philosopher's inner necessity. It is the volitional principle directing his reflective consciousness and hence turns him into a living work of art. The philosopher is impelled to realize the exigencies of subjectivity. As such philosophy is subjective spirit. "Subjective spirit itself is as such the container of substance, but because this ideality confronts reality, it is present objectively in minds as a Must [*Sollen*], subjectively as striving" (E, I, 82). The Greek wise man knows that he contains ideality in himself and that his inner "must" is also the "must" of outer reality. "This must of reality is equally a must of the subject that has become conscious of this ideality, for it itself stands in this reality and the reality outside of it is its own" (E, I, 83–84). The philosopher is fully imbued with substance (sacred power), but only as ideality. Reality does not acknowledge this power. Accordingly, the philosophical subject must free itself from the absoluteness of reality by negating outer autonomy. This philosophical striving, this axiological *must*, turns against and opposes reality by means of philosophy. Because the philosopher is aware of substantiality as a "must," not as an "is" embodied in reality, he must liberate subjectivity from empirical reality.

On account of the opposition between ideality and reality, "the ideality of substance in subjective spirit" must be conceived as a "falling away from substantial life" (E, I, 84), *i.e.* from substantiality as objectivity. The inner urge of subjectivity is to maintain the primacy of subjectivity over objectivity. This imperative of subjectivity can appear to the philosophizing subject *qua* his finitude as "an alien power, the bearer of which it finds itself, as the daemon of Socrates. The daemon is the immediate appearance of the fact that philosophy is for Greek life just as much an inner as an outer matter" (E, I, 84). Schlegel himself had written: "No one, indeed, can have irony who does not have a daemon" (KA, XVIII, 217). Philosophy as an activity of subjectivity directed against the empirical world, is to be sure, an act of irony. As we have seen, irony, as a volitional force in an individual, originates out of the contradiction between the inner need for absoluteness and the outer (empirical) relativity of things. The self is, accordingly, driven to negate the confines of "profane" reality. Although the need for ideal substance is located in the individual self, it is a supra-individual power, a transcendental feature of human selfhood. Indeed, it is the divine congealed in man striving to come to self-awareness. As a universal property and hence as psychological volition toward universality, it can appear to the individual thinker as an alien power, as a daemon that directs and, indeed, compels his activity. The daemon in Socrates is in effect irony felt as an urge to activity. Marx describes Socrates: "Socrates is the substantial manner in which substance has lost itself in the subject. He is, therefore, just as much a substantial individual as the earlier philosophers, however in the wisdom of subjectivity, not closed off, not an image of the gods but a human one" (E, I, 84). Socrates is, in short, the subjective spirit in which substance has become concrete. He is certain of the primacy of spirit, aware of the false appearance of reality, and therefore he is inwardly compelled to act by means of philosophy upon his environment in such a way that he can defend the ideality of the subject, *i.e.* can assert spiritual immanence against the oppressive determinateness of objectivity. Now, the form of oppressive reality that concerned Socrates is the claims of collective life to substantiality. Accordingly, Socrates manifests subjective spirit by teaching: "[Socrates'] philosophy is his leading [others] out and beyond substantial existing notions, distinctions, etc., into determination-in-itself which has no other content than to be the vessel of this dissolving reflection" (E, I, 86). In short, Socrates raises the ideality of subjectivity to consciousness by dissolving (*i.e.* ironizing) the false social consciousness of his contemporaries. In this way Socrates, as an ironist, "asserts immanence against the empirical person."

In the sixth "Vorarbeit" Marx elaborates upon Plato's modification of Socratic dialectics. Marx notes that Plato felt the desire "to provide a positive, above all mythical foundation for that which is known by philosophy." This positive element is myth or the allegorical attire of philosophical truths. But why did Plato feel this need? "Externally one can find the answer to this in the subjective form of the Platonic system, namely in the dialogic [form], and in irony" (E, I, 226). A positive interpretation of philosophy, that is the embodiment of ironic activity in concrete images, enables the individual more easily to ironize objectivity. Mere negation is too abstract. The positive, on the other hand, "becomes a medium through which absolute light shines. . . . The positive points to something other than itself, has in itself a soul for which this transformation is marvelous; the entire world has become a world of myths" (E, I, 228). The mythologization of the world is, in effect, Plato's attempt to reconcile subjectivity and objectivity, to realize the Socratic "must." In this context, Socrates himself, claims Marx, became for Plato a mythical expression of wisdom. Socrates became "the philosopher of death and love" (E, I, 228). In other words, irony as creation through annihilation was mythically expressed as the dialectics of death and love, about which Marx writes:

Death and love are myths of negative dialectics, for dialectics is the inner simple light, the penetrating eye of love, the inner soul, which is not crushed by the body of material diremption, the inner location of spirit. Thus love is the myth of [dialectics]; however, dialectics is a torrent which breaks to pieces the many and their limits, which topples independent forms, sinking everything down into the sea of eternity. Therefore, the myth of it is death.

It [dialectics] is thus death, but at the same time the vehicle of vitality, the blooming in the gardens of the spirit, the foaming in the bubbling tumbler of tiny seeds out of which the flower of a spiritual flame bursts forth." (E, I, 228)

Marx was wrong in my judgment. Death and love are not so

much mythic expressions of dialectical philosophy as such philosophical forms are "scientific" mythologizations of psychological terms. Ludwig Feuerbach once, quite correctly, designated Hegel's philosophy as "esoteric psychology," that is, Hegel's philosophical categories (substance, appearance, essence, etc.) are in actuality psychological principles dressed in logical language. And the model for Hegelian psychology is the Promethean ego. Therefore, the process of dialectics is simply the psychological unfolding of Promethean spirit expressed in logical categories. Love and death express more honestly and accurately, in my opinion, the poetic and psychological activity of selfhood than do Hegel's logical terms. I might also mention that Marx's concept of philosophy is also "esoteric psychology," though he does not, at least at this point, recognize it.

At any rate, the dialectics of death and love describe the ironic act. The ironic self as a Socratic philosopher, secure in the self-conscious sufficiency of its subjectivity, smashes to pieces an oppressive reality. The self can accomplish this because love gives it power to see through the superficiality of reality. We have already encountered this attitude of death and love, annihilation and creation, in "Human Pride" and other poems by Marx. On his own terms, Marx in "Human Pride" was simply poetizing in a Socratic manner. But the "death" of objectivity is not a movement into pure nothingness, into pessimism, but into "the sea of eternity." Once again we come upon fluidity imagery. Schlegel had said that all systems must be rendered chaotic. Chaos and fluidity are but two different expressions for the same creative but unformed energy of love. Therefore, death is also the vehicle of vitality. That which had been killed becomes the fertile ground upon which the gardens of spirit flourish. In utilizing two agricultural symbols, Marx was making use of a very ancient myth of rebirth.[66] The dialectics of love and death is simply the creative act of irony. Socrates, the philosopher of life and death, is indeed an ironist par excellence.

Whether Marx was directly conversant with Schlegel's ideas or had only secondhand knowledge, his identification of Socratic irony

---

66. Cf. Eliade, *Patterns in Comparative Religion*, 331–66.

and irony in Schlegel with the form of philosophy was a stroke of genius. Marx's own interpretation of Socrates the ironist has many similarities with Schlegel's ironic philosophy. The most important thing is that ironic philosophy presented Marx with a concept of philosophy as an active, creative, and dialectical force. Ironic philosophy is not conceptual contemplation of a completed movement; rather it is the motor of the very movement itself. Ironic philosophy is creative insofar as it alters the consciousness of others through rational critique by showing that the pretenses of reality to absoluteness are false. This is the manner in which the ironic philosopher relates his subjectivity "to common consciousness."

However much Marx appreciated the Socratic method, he still could not accept it as the final word. Socrates was for Marx an expression of the "inner limits" of Greek philosophy. In this connection Marx avers: "It is clear how foolish it was, when in the most recent period, the relationship of Hegelian philosophy to life was compared to [Socrates], and consequently a justification for its condemnation was deduced. It is precisely the specific failing of Greek philosophy that it stands in a relationship only to substantial spirit; in our times both sides are spirit and both want to be acknowledged as such" (E, I, 86). What Marx means can be explained by comparing his position with his rejection of romantic idealism. It will be recalled that Marx rejected the "idealistic" opposition of the "ought" to the "is." I have sought to show in Chapter II that this opposition is constitutive of Romanticism. Irony can be taken formally or materially. Irony as the form of spiritual activity is the ability and inner necessity of the self to transcend the limitations of the given by negating them. By means of irony the self moves ever closer to sacred power. The ironic self is, consequently, to a degree self-contained as "the subjective form of substance"; it is sacred power as it creates. This superiority enables the self to transcend the world by annihilating it. It is clear from Marx's interpretation of Socrates that Socrates too was an ironist. However, the paradox of Romanticism is that the material content of ironic philosophy—the direct consciousness of which manifests sacred power—is irony itself. Irony in Romanticism is both the form and material content of philosophy. But irony is the product of the contradiction between the "ought" and the "is": it is longing. Insofar as irony is raised to the absolute, the absolute can never be fully possessed. Correlatively, reality must always possess being that is not truly "substantial." Thus philosophy can never mediate an awareness of the reconciliation of the "is" and "ought." Philosophical consciousness cannot be the highest form of consciousness. As Schlegel says: "Every system is only an approximation of its ideal. Skepticism is eternal" (KA, XVIII, 417). Skepticism is the philosophical mode of the opposition between "is" and "ought." Skepticism is the means by which the philosopher negates philosophical consciousness, which he must do if an inkling, a feeling, of the infinite is to be maintained. This is also the reason why romantics valued aesthetics higher than philosophy. Aesthetics is the form in which such an inkling presents itself to consciousness. Marx rejected the romantic or idealistic antinomy for Hegel's notion of philosophy as the rational awareness of *realized* totality.

In the light of the above, it is easy to understand Marx's reference to "the specific failing of Greek philosophy." Greek philosophers could not, in Marx's opinion, do more than make the subject substantial. The world of objects remained unredeemed, contingent, insubstantial. As such there could be no reconciliation between subject and object. Plato, for instance, could not make reality substantial by inventing the supraempirical realm of pure ideas, leaving empirical reality untouched. Platonism effects no real solution of the subject-object problem; it simply transcends it. This, according to Marx, is the connection between Platonism and Christianity. In my own terms, Greek philosophy remained for Marx within the confines of irony. It succeeded in elevating the subject above reality, in securing spiritual immanence against empirical consciousness. But it failed to make objective reality substantial. Therefore, as Marx noted, the content of Socratic philosophy is to be the "vessel of this dissolving reflection." In short, Greek philosophy failed to make the real ideal. As such it only presents a "negative dialectics."

The specific success of Hegelian philosophy is to recognize that collective life (reality), not only individual subjectivity, must be idealized. Not only must the subject be embodied spirit, but objectivity, particularly social reality, must be spiritualized. The failure of Hegelian philosophy is that reality is not in fact reconciled with ideality. For Marx, who viewed the world as divided into opposing parts, philosophy as a totality stands in opposition to reality as a totality. Furthermore, in Hegel's nondialectical concept of philosophy there is no way in which the antinomy in philosophy can be philosophically overcome.

In my judgment, Marx was interested in Greek philosophy that developed after the total systems of Plato or Aristotle because it represents a revival of the ironic outlook toward reality. Epicurus' whole philosophy is, in Marx's opinion, directed toward the philosophical emancipation of subjectivity from the repressive chains of objectivity. "The principle of Epicurean philosophy is . . . the absoluteness and freedom of self-consciousness, although self-consciousness is only conceived in the form of individuality" (E, I, 304). This for Marx, the young Hegelian, is a one-sided and abstract freedom, in that it is freedom from, not within empirical reality. Empirical reality remains a pure negative; it is not the positive manifestation of substantial life. But it must be stressed that Epicurus was able to obtain freedom by means of philosophy, that his philosophizing itself was a creative force in his emancipation from empirical limitation.

My thesis is that Marx saw as his post-Hegelian task the development of a dialectical, Socratic, or ironic concept of philosophy. Only then could he escape the blind alley of Hegel's nondialectical concept of philosophy. However, as a modern, rather than as a resurrected Greek, Marx did not want to surrender the Hegelian imperative of reconciliation. In his *Economic and Philosophical Manuscripts of 1844*, Marx described communism in the following manner: "It is the true resolution of the antagonism between man and nature, and man and man, the true resolution of the fight between existence and essence, objectification and self-affirmation, freedom and necessity, individual and species. It is the solved riddle of history and knows itself as this solution" (E, I, 536). This is pure Hegel, the reconciliation of "ought" and "is." It is also poetry and religion, albeit secularized and hidden in "scientific" terminology. Indeed, few works testify more to the magic of Marx's poetic genius. The *Economic and*

Philosophical Manuscripts have "bewitched" not only Marxists but Marx himself into believing he was talking scientific materialism, when in fact he was poetizing matter.

At any rate, the problem facing Marx in 1840–1841 was how to accept Hegel's philosophical imperative and yet find a way to realize it by means of philosophy. Marx, in my judgment, sought to "reconcile" or synthesize the romantic and Hegelian conceptions of philosophy. Philosophy in its formal aspect is ironic and hence creative. However, the ideal that philosophy seeks to realize is the transcendence of irony. That is, the reconciliation of the ideal and real is the *material* principle of philosophy. Philosophy must become worldly (actual) and the world must become philosophical (ideal). The instrument of redemption as well as the content of redemption is philosophy. For this reason philosophy possesses "a world-conquering and absolutely free heart" for Marx. The dynamics of this heart is the life of the dialectics of love and death.

The Task of Philosophy: Irony

The philosophical rhythm according to Schlegel is a pattern of chaos, system, and renewed chaos. The transition from system to chaos is necessitated by the inadequacy of philosophy *qua* system to encompass fully the real and the ideal. The instrument of transition is irony—the criticism of the real in the light of the ideal. Marx describes the philosophical situation of his own times in a similar manner. "Just as there are nodal points in the history of philosophy which raise themselves to concretion, which work abstract principles into a totality, and consequently sever a straight linear progression, so too there are moments in which philosophy turns its eyes to the external world. No longer reflectively but like a practical person, it spins intrigues with the world, it emerges out of Amenthe's transparent realm and hurls itself on the heart of the wordly siren" (E, I, 214). Such a nodal point is, of course, Hegelian philosophy. As a system Hegelianism is a totality of abstract principles. But, alas, it is only abstract. Marx treats Hegelian philosophy not as the self-reflective consummation of history but as a moment within the historical continuum, as a phase in the rhythm of history itself. This rhythm is the self's centripetal and centrifugal movement, system and skepticism. Hegelianism as a totality (albeit an abstract one) is philosophy self-contained in itself, is the subject having become substantial. The next phase of the philosophical rhythm is for the philosopher to confront the world. Philosophy is no longer content to interpret the world as it is, to contemplate completed being, but strives in some sense to transform things into what they ought to be. Philosophy must become will. This is the meaning of the assertion that philosophy spins intrigues with the world.

Marx describes such intrigues in a semi-allegorical manner: "It is essential for [philosophy] to put on character masks. . . . As Deukalion at the creation of human beings threw stones behind himself, so philosophy casts its eyes behind itself (the bones of its mother are sparkling eyes), when its heart has been strengthened to create a world. However, as Prometheus stole the fire from heaven and began to build houses and to settle on earth, so philosophy, which has expanded itself to the world, turns against the apparent world. So now Hegelian philosophy" (E, I, 214). In the next chapter we will see that one central problem that the proletariat alone can solve is how philosophy can strengthen its heart so that it can create a world. Let us recall that the heart of philosophy is "world-conquering and absolutely free." For the moment, I wish only to note that Marx's conception of the philosophical task is quite poetic, mythic, and dramatic. First of all, it is necessary for philosophy to put on character masks if it is to carry out its intrigues with the world. Philosophy is, in other words, not simply a matter of "cold" and "value-free" ratiocinations. Philosophy entails the categorical imperative that man must come to "acknowledge human self-consciousness as the highest divinity," that man become his own *causa sui*. In turning against the world, philosophy is thereby entering into a dramatic tension with externality. Philosophy must conquer externality and make its heart absolutely free. Here we have the reason why philosophy has put on character masks. Marx was referring to the custom of Greek actors of wearing masks representing the characters of a given drama. In his *Poetics* Aristotle referred to the poetic principle which integrates characters, actions, dialogue, etc., into a dramatic whole as mythos.[67] The term *mythos* has been translated into English as "plot" or "fable." Such a translation is wholly misleading. In the context of Aristotle's usage, *mythos* refers more to the "dramatic" per se; *i.e.* it is the *form* of dramatic action. And all such action evolves out of the tension between contending parties. Drama is the representation of compromised value and its effects within the flow of time.[68] At this point in Marx's thinking, "philosophy" and the "world" are the antagonistic actors of the great drama of salvation. In the next chapter I shall show that the proletariat and the capitalist become the socioeconomic embodiments, the positive actors, of the dialectical mythos. Marx's reference to Greek drama clearly shows that the problem he was seeking to solve was essentially poetic. Insofar as he wanted to actualize philosophy in the empirical world, he wanted to experience aesthetically sacred power; he wanted to poetize the world.

Even though Marx was attempting rationally or philosophically to understand things, he was, nevertheless, directing himself to a problem that had plagued romantics. Schlegel, as noted in Chapter II, had stated: "Whatever has no relationship at all to the Kingdom of God is . . . only a secondary matter" (KA, II, 201). Romantics desired to perceive modern culture as a vehicle of the Kingdom of God on earth. In this way the empirical, the finite, would manifest the eschatological story—mythos—of man's redemption. An object or event is mythic when it points to a higher meaning, when it is the vehicle of sacred power. But, Schlegel complained, modern poetry lacks any mythology as a symbolic system that "truly" represents the ideal. Schlegel called upon his contemporaries to bring forth a new mythology. But from where? "The new mythology must be fashioned out of the deepest depths of spirit; it must be the most artistic of all works of art, for it must encompass all other things, a new bed and container for the eternal fount of poetry, and even for the infinite poem which is the seed of all other poems" (KA, II, 312).

67. S. H. Butcher, *Aristotle's Theory of Poetry and Fine Art with a Critical Text and Translation of the "Poetics"* (4th ed.; Dover, 1951), 26, 28, and 27, 29.
68. Cf. Susanne Langer, "The Dramatic Illusion" in *Feeling and Form* (New York, 1953), 306–25.

And that which belongs to the depths of spirit is creativity. This is the legacy of idealism. The Hegelian version of this mythos is, as we have seen, decidedly Promethean. Creative power is its own object of worship. Concerning this "poetic" inspiration of Marxism, the Marxist Roger Garaudy remarks: "This Promethean ambition characterized Hegelian humanism, the philosophy of confidence and pride in the self. Morality is man made divine. And science is the act by which man discovers himself in every object, in a world perfectly transparent to reason."[69] Rationality is for Hegel nothing but pride become visible to itself through its creations. This is also simply the narcissistic *causa sui* project functioning as the fount of poetry. Marx did not reject the ideal of Hegelian rationality; he only was seeking to reveal conceptually how it was to be actualized. Marx's assertion that philosophy must put on character masks is a phase in his gradual mythologization of science. This dramatic imperative is the "seed" of all his "scientific" poems, including *Das Kapital*. Let us focus more clearly upon the structure of this dramatic tension.

Marx compares Hegelian philosophy with the myth of Prometheus. At this state in his theoretical peregrinations Marx cannot provide philosophy with any worldly positivity. Consequently he must make use of the mythic figure of Prometheus in order to put some dramatic substance into the abstractly formulated antinomy. The Promethean striving to absolutize the self as God is, as Garaudy notes, Hegel's legacy to Marx. Prometheus' theft of fire and his settlement upon the earth symbolize the *causa sui* project. This project now should be the task of Hegelian philosophy. But why would the Hegelian philosopher feel himself compelled to turn against the apparent world? The reason is, the philosopher feels a tension within himself, one mediated to him by his very philosophical consciousness. Subjectively he is free; objectively he is demeaned. He is accordingly unhappy and happy. Marx explains this tension. "The kernel of this unhappiness is, however, that the soul of the time, the spiritual monas, is satiated in itself, is ideally formed in all directions, can acknowledge no reality that has come about without it. The

69. Garaudy, *Karl Marx*, 20.

happiness in such unhappiness is, therefore, the subjective form, the modality in which philosophy as subjective consciousness relates itself to reality" (E, I, 216, 218). Philosophy proclaims the Apollonian imperative to become a creator. It is for this reason that the "soul of the time" cannot acknowledge what it has not created. The soul's refusal to acknowledge what has become without it is the negative form of the positive imperative only to acknowledge human self-consciousness as the highest divinity. Human pride mediates between the positive and negative, that is to say grounds them both as aspects of the selfsame unity, namely the *causa sui* project. The soul faces a reality that it has not created and hence it is not realized creativity. This is its unhappiness. Yet, paradoxically, it is happy because it is aware (thanks to philosophy) of its autonomy and hence it is inspired to relate itself *annihilatingly* to the world. The tension, cognitively possessed, between the philosophers' subjective form and oppressive reality transforms itself into practical energy, into Will. Philosophy having become negating Will is precisely irony.

The struggle of the subjective consciousness with a recalcitrant world can only be described as a titanic battle. No wonder Marx could typify the period after total philosophies as an iron age marked by battles of titans. "Titanlike are the times which follow a philosophy total in itself and its subjective forms of development, for the diremption which is its unity is gigantic. . . . They are unhappy and iron times, for the gods have died, and the new goddess has still the dark form of fate, of pure light or of pure darkness. She is still lacking the colors of the day" (E, I, 216). What was but a hint in "Human Pride," a bold proclamation in the Foreword, has now become involuted into the realm of titans. Out of this struggle between titan and chaos, a new cosmos will emerge, a new creation shall arise. Garaudy was absolutely correct that the key to Marx's philosophy, economics, and politics, is the Apollonian imperative to turn man into a creator, an "untroubled god," which implies that Marx imagines man to be a titan. Phantasy is, indeed, the creator of worlds. The young Marx's philosophical imagination has projected the outlines of a cosmic poem of redemption, one in which man struggles against the powers of chaos. Marx's theoretical reflections were simply his attempt to write this Promethean poem in secular or prosaic language. The true poetic genius of Marx lies in his ability to create a scientific mythology, to dramatize the human condition in the exoteric dress of science.

Marx translates the dramatic tension into a psychological law. "It is a psychological law that the theoretical spirit [*Geist*], having become free in itself, turns into practical energy, and, emerging as *Will* out of Amenthe's realm of shadows, will turn against existing reality" (E, I, 326). Klaus Hartmann, in his massive study of Marx's theory, correctly designates such a psychological law as "unhegelian."[70] Like most expositers, however, Hartmann leaves the matter at that. Marx's psychological law is, to be sure, "unhegelian"; it is not unromantic. Indeed, philosophy for romantics is but a conceptual longing for infinity. As such the Will is an integral factor in the philosophical project. Once spirit has gone outside itself and subsumed reality under a system, it must come to experience this aspirant totality as inadequate. Such inadequacy awakens in spirit the urge to transcend the given. This urge to transcend must exist first as Will before it can be translated into the conceptual negation of the "is." Insofar as philosophy is metamorphized into Will, it comes to oppose all reality whose being has not been created by itself. This is its praxis. Hegelian philosophy has made spirit free as a subjectivity. Spirit is to be all in all. This is the infinite totality for which spirit longs. But reality possesses autonomy, albeit only apparent, outside of spirit. Spirit's pride must clash with the demeaning reality. This tension can be resolved insofar as spirit *wills* to oppose reality. And this psychological event is necessary because of the contradiction which generates it. Marx can, indeed, validly talk of a psychological law following philosophy, but only as an ironist.

In what sense, though, is philosophy, as energized Will, able to oppose reality? "But the *praxis* of philosophy is itself *theoretical*. It is *criticism* which measures the individual existence, the particular reality against the Idea. But this *immediate realization* of philosophy is in its innermost essence loaded with contradictions, and this, its es-

70. Cf. Klaus Hartmann, *Die Marxische Theorie: Eine philosophische Untersuchung zu den Hauptschriften* (Berlin, 1970), 15.

sence, structures itself in appearance and presses its stamp upon it"
(E, I, 327–28). At this point Marx was obviously not thinking of a
physical revolution. He was still thinking in idealistic paradigms.
Nevertheless, his concept of philosophical praxis as criticism is clearly
romantic. Philosophy is creative irony. The similarities between
Schlegel and Marx are quite startling. Both philosophers conceived
philosophical criticism as a means of actualizing the Kingdom of
God on earth. Marx, of course, since he identified the Idea with the
state, gave his philosophical criticism a decidedly political accent.

The existing world is actualized philosophy, only loaded with
contradictions. By showing what is essential in what is mere appearance, Marx hoped to emancipate his contemporary world. Consciousness is liberated by being freed from false notions about reality.
In an exchange of letters with Mikhail Bakunin, Ludwig Feuerbach,
and Arnold Ruge (published in 1843 in the *Deutsch-Französische Ja-
rhbücher*), Marx revealed clearly his "idealistic" concept of praxis and
the function of political criticism:

> Nothing hinders us from connecting our criticism with the criticism of
> politics, with the assumption of sides in politics, with real battles, and to
> identify ourselves with them. . . . We will show why the world is really
> fighting; and this consciousness is a something that it *must* appropriate,
> whether it wants to or not. . . .
>
> Our motto must be: reform of consciousness, not through dogmas but
> through analysis of the mystical consciousness which is unclear about itself,
> whether it comes to the fore in religion or in politics. It will then be evident
> that the world has long possessed the dream of a matter of which it has only
> to possess consciousness in order to possess it. It will be evident that it is
> a matter . . . of *realizing* the thoughts of the past. It will be evident that hu-
> manity does not begin a *new* work but rather achieves with consciousness
> its old work. (MEW, I, 345–46)

Marx obviously still is segregating physical praxis from theoretical praxis. Philosophy is a revolutionary force only insofar as it re-
forms the mind. That which stands between philosophy (as an ideal)
and the world (as the real) is simply the theoretically mystified and

muddled consciousness. Reform a confused consciousness and it will enact that of which spirit has always dreamed, namely its freedom.

Marx can be criticized for his "idealistic" thinking. The concept of philosophy as theoretical praxis is full of difficulties. But what is important is that philosophical praxis is *ironic* criticism—the total annihilation of what is, albeit only in theory. Hence Marx in the letter just quoted projected the mission of philosophy as: "*The relentless criticism of everything that exists* [*des Bestehenden*], relentless in the sense that criticism is not afraid of its results and just as little afraid of conflict with the powers-to-be" (MEW, I, 344). Is this ironic imperative very distant from Schlegel's notion of philosophical criticism becoming history? Let us return to the development of Marx's position in his dissertation.

What is the relationship of philosophy to the world once philosophy has become praxis?

Insofar as philosophy as will has turned outward against the apparent world, the system has been reduced to an abstract totality, *i.e.* it has become one side of the world which stands opposed to the other side. Its relationship to the world is a relationship of reflection. Inspired [*begeiste[r]t*] with the impulse to realize itself, it [the system] enters into a tension against everything else. The inner self-contentedness and roundedness is broken. What was an inner light turns into a consuming flame which is directed outward. The consequence results in the fact that the becoming-philosophical of the world is at the same time the becoming-worldly of philosophy, that its realization is at the same time its loss, that what it battles outside is its own inner deficiency. . . . Whatever [philosophy] opposes and fights is always the same thing that it is, only with reversed factors. (E, I, 328)

Marx's discussion of the relationship of philosophy to the world is also a description of irony. Philosophy should be the recognition of the reconciliation of subject and object, of ideality and reality. This is its roundedness present in its systematic totality. But there is no such de facto reconciliation, only the awareness of man's ought-to-be-divinity. This is the one-sidedness of philosophy and is simultaneously the source for the willing to oppose the world. This willing is inspired (*begeiste*[r]*t*). The German literally means "filled with spirit" or "spiritized." In other words, the philosophical subject has developed a full awareness of its subjective substantiality, its Promethean imperative. This is the "inner light" which now must turn outward as a "consuming flame" against the existing world. This "consuming flame" is but a poetic term for all-annihilating irony. Insofar as the philosophical self turns against the world, the world is thereby made philosophical. In other words, a world that has lost its independence is a world that has become subjectivized. The very act of subsuming the world under the unity of the subject is the world's becoming philosophical. Conversely, this is also the becoming-worldly of philosophy. The dramatic tension is resolved and a denouement of redemption is produced. Such is the task of post-Hegelian philosophy. What philosophy fights in the external world is "its own deficiency," the outer world's failure to embody what ought to be. Philosophy itself is also permeated by this selfsame deficiency: it lacks objective substance. The world's deficiency is philosophy's deficiency, only in a reversed manner. The two can be reconciled by negating and synthesizing each other. This process indicates the task of contemporary post-Hegelian philosophers for Marx.

Marx describes the effects of the duality of philosophy upon its bearer, the philosopher. "There results from this relationship—which lies in the realization of philosophy itself in opposition to the world— that these individual consciousnesses [*i.e.* philosophers] always have *a double-edged demand*, of which one edge turns against the world and the other against philosophy. . . . Their liberating the world from non-philosophy is at the same time their own liberation from the philosophy which enchains them in a definite system" (E, I, 328). Otherwise expressed, human consciousness demands nothing less than the apperception of realized totality, the fusion of individuality with sacred power. This cannot be mediated until the subject and object, theory and reality, are reconciled as one. Hegelian philosophy as a systematic and logical totality had claimed to have achieved this ideal. But it has not. As a result, philosophy itself is now one-sided and abstract. The task is to make the world philosophical. But how? This cannot be accomplished in the terms of philosophy as it now stands in its one-sided completeness. Therefore, if the knowing subject is to form his world rationally, he must not only criticize the world but he must also criticize philosophy for its deficiency. Philosophy, as heretofore carried out, is an inadequate mechanism for enacting its own realization. Therefore, the generative paradigms of philosophical thinking must also be ironized and thereby transformed into a "world-conquering" force. The Hegelian philosopher had not been able to alter the world, only to interpret it. How is such a philosopher to actualize the ideal, how is he to transform his subjectivity into objectivity? Insofar as the philosopher leaves his Hegelian sanctuary, renounces his merely priestly role, and actively turns against the apparent world, must not this creative demiurge cease being a philosopher in the traditional sense? In other words, can the philosopher in the strict sense as a theoretician be the efficacious instrument of redemptive irony of history's *eschaton*? The answer soon became apparent to Marx: No! In effect, this was the meaning of Marx's reflections upon the becoming-worldly of philosophy and becoming-philosophical of the world.

Marx did not surrender the religio-poetic ideal, namely the experiencing of sacred power in human culture. Marx never seriously asked himself "existential" questions—whether, for example, the cultural world could truly be a vehicle of immortality. His only task—and it was a veritable *idée fixe*—was to reveal the nature of the final battle between order and chaos, good and evil. After his romantic phase Marx sought this path in rationality. As a follower of Hegel, Marx identified rationality with philosophy. But philosophy had failed. Therefore, rationality had to be given another theoretical foundation. This theoretical basis, if it were true, had to prove itself by transforming itself into a practical power of annihilation and recreation. The problem facing Marx from about 1841 on was to discover the *real* basis that would enable thought to actualize itself. After much theoretical agony, Prometheus, the titans, and even philosophy, lost their mythic masks in the salvational drama. In the next chapter we will examine how Marx, the dramatist of world history, came to dismiss the old actors and introduce new characters into his great melodrama.

V
Irony as the
Proletariat

Marx's conversion to Hegel and his subsequent denial of the Hegelian claims that the ideal is de facto reconciled with the real presented him with a momentous problem. How is the world to be made philosophical and philosophy made worldly? This problem is in a broad sense poetic, dealing as it does with the aesthetics of human salvation. How can absolute value be infused into man's empirical existence? The very formulation of the question implies some sort of activity as an answer. Philosophy with its world-conquering heart must ironize the opposition between the "is" and "ought." But what character masks should irony put on if it is to spin intrigues with the world? The first mask put on by irony was criticism. The ironic imperative is, however, double-edged. Theory must criticize reality, but it also must criticize itself. Insofar as Hegelian philosophy has falsely understood reality, this philosophic method of rationality must be inadequate; it cannot truly grasp the nature of the opposition between the ideal and the real. What is wrong with philosophy? What is wrong with the world? Just where and with what principles can the ironist begin criticism of the established order? The development of Marx's thought is an outgrowth of his answers to such questions.[1]

1. A great deal has been written on the development of the young Marx's thinking between 1840–1845. Since I do not intend to discuss critically the various directions in the secondary literature, I will suggest a few sources on the matter. Cf. Bernard Delgaauw, *The Young Marx*, trans. F. Schütz and M. Redfern (London, 1967); Louis Dupré, *The Philosophical Foundations of Marxism* (New York, 1966), 87–149; Howard, *The Development of the Marxian Dialectic*, 48–170; Paul Kägi, *Genesis des historischen Materialismus* (Vienna, 1965), 117–278; Nicolas

The evolution of Marx's thinking during 1842 and 1843 exhibits a twofold direction. Marx continually seeks out a point of departure for criticism of the real and then he criticizes such a standpoint. The actual philosophizing was similar to Schlegel's concept of philosophy as system, chaos, and system. In the ensuing presentation, I will schematically and briefly trace the cyclical progression of Marx's theorizing relative to the problem of the real and the ideal. I am not seeking to exposit comprehensively Marx's theoretical peregrinations or to trace influences upon him. Here I am only interested in Marx's reflections upon how philosophy is to be realized.

1842—Early Years of Journalism

Having completed his dissertation and having failed to obtain a teaching position at a university, Marx turned in 1842 to journalistic writing, reviewing critically a series of topical questions in a polemical manner, *e.g.* censorship, divorce laws, wood laws, religion. Although such analyses ostensibly were concerned with concrete and "burning" questions of the day, Marx's underlying concern was of a decidedly philosophical interest. Philosophy, Marx had said, "measures individual existence against essence, particular actuality against the Idea" (E, I, 326, 328). Marx's basic line of argumentation was twofold: (a) He attempted to defend the objectivity of rationality against any value-free interpretation of history or human society and (b) he criticized the actual Prussian state in the light of the rational Idea of the State.[2] This conception of the state as the incarnation of human perfection and freedom was essentially Hegelian in spirit.

In the *Philosophical Manifesto of the Historical School of Law* Marx attacks all forms of historical positivism, *i.e.* any theoretical position

---

Lobkowicz, *Theory and Practice: History of a Concept from Aristotle to Marx* (Notre Dame, 1967), 259–400; Georg Lukács, *Der junge Marx: Seine philosophische Entwicklung von 1840–1844* (Pfullingen, 1965); McLellan, *Marx Before Marxism*, 72–161; Heinrich Popitz, *Der entfremdete Mensch* (Frankfurt, 1967), 67–141; Erich Thier, *Das Menschenbild des jungen Marx* (2nd ed; Göttingen, 1961); and Tucker, *Philosophy and Myth in Karl Marx*, 123–64.

2. In his writings of 1842 Marx developed a "primitive ethic." Eugene Kamenka has worked out the outline of this in *The Ethical Foundations of Marxism* (London, 1962), 17–50.

which ascribes primacy to mere historical factuality. In specific, he attacks a certain Gustav Hugo, whom Marx treats as the father of the historical school of law, charging that Hugo uses the mere positivity of facts as a justification of their existence. In other words, Hugo does not measure the actual by the ideal but allows the actual to be its own authority. Indeed, to defend this position Hugo must deny the rationality of historical existence. "[Hugo] seeks in no way to prove that the *positive* is *rational*; he does try to prove that the *positive is not rational*. With self-satisfied industry he brings together facts from all the areas of the world to use as evidence that positive institutions, *e.g.* property, the constitution of the state, marriage, *etc.*, are not animated by any rational necessity, that they even *contradict* reason" (MEW, I, 79). No reference is made by Hugo to any alleged rationality which teleologically structures history and which serves as a criterion for judging historical development and for pointing out the direction which history *should* take. "If the *positive* is to be *valid because* it is *positive*, then I must *prove* that the *positive* is *not* valid because it is *rational*, and how could I prove this with more evidence than by proving that the nonrational is positive and the positive is nonrational, by proving that the positive does not exist *through* reason but *in spite of it*? If *reason* were the *measure of the positive*, then the positive would not be the measure of *reason*. . . . Hugo *destroys* everything that is holy to lawful, moral, political man . . . in order to do it honor as a *historical relic*" (MEW, I, 79). In short, Hugo as a historical skeptic doubts Marx's philosophical *faith* that the ideal should and does inform the real. "*Hugo* is consequently a *perfect skeptic*. The skepticism of the *eighteenth century* concerning the *rationality of that which exists* appears in him as *skepticism* concerning the *existence of reason*" (MEW, I, 80). Marx's attitude toward Hugo's historical positivism gives evidence of his concept of what a science of history should be. History as a part of reality is rational, and the essence of rationality is human perfection. Therefore, any scientific analysis of history must seek out the rational in the apparent irrationality in/ of history. But where is the rational to be found in history? Marx follows Hegel in locating it in the state, for after all had not Hegel maintained that the state is the appearance of the divine on earth, the goal of history, and as such it should be worshipped? Therefore, that which comes under the rubrics of politics is the area that should be investigated if the conflict between the ideal and the real is to be resolved. In other words, the *real* basis for such a contradiction lies in the realm of the political, more specifically in the failure of the state to inform fully the civil society. The state remains, however, as the bearer of the ideal.

During his journalistic endeavors of 1842, however, Marx did not develop any comprehensive theory of the state, although he did attempt occasional reflections upon the state as an ideal. An interpreter can reconstruct Marx's inchoate understanding of the state based upon such reflections. Marx thought that philosophy had adequately grasped the nature of the ideal, namely human freedom. Thus Marx saw that the telos of politics was to make man a part of the state "by transforming the goals of the individual into universal goals, raw impulse into ethical inclination, and natural independence into spiritual freedom, and by the individual finding his satisfaction in the life of the whole and the whole in the disposition of the individual" (MEW, I, 95). In other words, the state is "the great organism in which legal, ethical, and political freedom has to receive its actualization and the individual citizen obeys in the laws of the state only the natural laws of his own reason, of human reason. *Sapienti sat*" (MEW, I, 104).

Marx has gained some theoretical clarity concerning what a political reconciliation between the ideal and real would entail. The state should be the embodiment of the ideal, the "secular deity" (Hegel). But this "secular deity" should not exist over and against the real and everyday life of its members. The life of the state must become daily life, and daily life must become ethical. Marx came to call the "daily" life of people the "real suppositions" of the state. This empirical life includes all nonpolitical activities, such as economic endeavors. Hegel had located the ethical life solely in political acts, not in the "real" (socioeconomic) activity of civil society. The state in a certain sense transcends the civil society in Hegel's thought, with the result that a vast area of particular acts (*e.g.* labor) was excluded from the transfiguring power of universal life. Marx was now insisting that *all* areas of social life should be penetrated by the ethical life of the state.

The salvific function of the state is clear. It is also clear that Marx felt that the real state is not ideal. The contradiction between the ought-to-be and as-is remains and infects the very life of the actual state. Man's life as a citizen is external to his socioeconomic life. In a letter to Arnold Ruge (1843) Marx notes: "As to what concerns actual life, the political state, particularly in all its modern forms, contains the demands of reason, even where it is not yet fully aware of socialistic demands. And it does not remain here. Everywhere it asserts reason as realized. However, everywhere it gets into contradiction between its ideal vocation and its real presuppositions." Resolutions can be obtained, not through further philosophizing in the idealistic manner, *i.e.* by deducing the ideal state of affairs from the concept of reason, but only by investigating the irrational nature of the actual state and its real presuppositions and then discovering the relationship of rationality and irrationality therein. "Social truth," writes Marx, "can be developed everywhere out of this conflict of the political state with itself. Just as *religion* is the table of contents of the theoretical struggles of mankind, the *political state* is that of the practical ones. The political state expresses within its form *sub specie rei publicae* all social struggles, needs, and truths" (MEW, I, 345). It should be noted that Marx does not speak now (1843) of pure philosophical truth, indeed, not even of political truth, but of social truth. In other words, the conflict between the ideal and real cannot be understood or resolved alone by means of the ontological categories of spirit but must be known within the terms of sociopolitical strife. Here we encounter an important shift in Marx's theorizing with his discovery of a new area from which to derive analytical paradigms. The question presents itself: How is the rational in the empirically irrational to be ascertained? "Reason has always existed, only not always in rational form. The critic, consequently, can catch hold of any form of theoretical and practical consciousness and develop out of the *special* forms of existing actuality true actuality as its ought [*Sollen*] and final goal" (MEW, I, 345). Once again the a priori, teleological, and poetic nature of Marxian rationality is evident. Reason exists empirically in the form of unreason and can be shown to constitute the ought-to-be goal of the irrational form of empirical experience. This is implicitly to insert the ironic process into the very structure of the real.

Marx now is in effect advising thinkers to seek a new starting point for critical analysis. This entails a reevaluation of the philosophical method of criticism. Marx had sought to translate philosophy into an ironic force. Inasmuch as the ironic philosopher possesses cognitive certainty of ideality, the real is criticized in the light of the ideal. In short, Marx's starting point in 1842 had been the ideal as constructed in and by thought. Philosophical activity had been accepted uncritically as an independent and autonomous process. But Marx's critical endeavors had led him to the belief that the conflict between the ideal and real had to be understood in the terms of social truth, of the "real presuppositions" of the state. If this is so, must not then the activity of the ideating philosopher be reevaluated? Philosophy must become critical of its own program. Philosophy has its origins, according to the idealistic tradition, in a more general and generic activity than cogitation alone. Man per se desires value, meaning, self-realization. In the subject-object terms of idealism, the cognizing self seeks to become aware of objectivity informed by subjectivity. Philosophy is the scientific consciousness of the unity of subject and object. If greater importance (if not primacy) is now granted to the social and "real" activities of man, then this ontological (and psychological) interpretation of the subject-object relationship must be revised. The subject-object relationship must be interpreted as a mode of real, *viz.* physical, activity. Philosophy will then be seen as a function of a value seeking, biological being. Marx himself writes:

But philosophers do not grow like mushrooms out of the earth; they are the fruit of their time, of their people, whose most subtle, precious, and invisible juices flow about in philosophical ideas. The same spirit builds philosophical systems in the brain of the philosophers that builds railroads by the hands of the workers. Philosophy does not stand outside the world, just as little as the brain is located outside of [man] because it is not situated in his stomach. But of course philosophy stands in the world with its brain before it stands on the ground with its feet, whereas many other human spheres have long been rooted with their feet in the earth and pluck with their hands the fruits of the world long before they have a notion that the "head," too, is of this world or that this world is the world of the head. (MEW, I, 97)

The pragmatic function of reason is evident in the last citation. Indeed, Marx is bordering on materialism. Theoretical thinking is rooted in this world and in man's physical needs for fulfillment in this world. Reason is, therefore, a function of bios, not of pure spirit. Theoretical thinking and economic activity are two aspects of the same bios. The task of philosophy, accordingly, is the investigation not of the metaphysical realm beyond the bio-physical, but rather the general nature of this world relative to the realization of absolute value. "Because every true philosophy is the spiritual quintessence of its time, the time must come when philosophy enters into contact and reciprocal activity with the actual world of its time, not only internally by its content but also externally through its appearance. Philosophy ceases, then, to be a determinate system relative to other determinate systems; it becomes philosophy per se against the world; it becomes the philosophy of the present world" (MEW, I, 97–98). Marx is on his way to relegating speculative philosophy to the realm of ideology and to limiting theoretical thinking (rationality) to the "real" laws of the social order. In other words, theoretical thinking must be analyzed in terms of a bio-social model. Here are the origins for Marx's shift from philosophical categories to social and economic ones. However, this shift does not entail a rejection of the ultimate goal—namely the reconciliation of the ideal and real. This salvational reconciliation is simply being interpreted within a new paradigm base. Furthermore, Marx's deflation of the creative role of philosophy (which is in part a return to a Hegelian concept of philosophy) does not mean he surrendered the notion of irony. Just as philosophical activity is to be explained in terms of real activity, irony too must be reinterpreted in real terms. Irony will have to put on a new character mask; the ironic philosopher will have to assume a new role. As we shall see, the new mask put on by the ironist is that of the proletariat.

1843: Critique of Hegel's Philosophy of the State

In order to ironize the gap between the ideal and the real, Marx began his critical career with a criticism of the actual state in the light of the ideal state. But examination of the real state soon led him to the conclusion that the failures of the real state are connected with the failures of its "real presuppositions." Hegel had conceived of the state as the locus of sacred power, as the visible hieroglyph of creative power. However, in actual procedure, Hegel, already having determined the structure of the state ideally, sought out corresponding features in the real political world. The recognition of the ideal embodied in the real was the reconciliation between the ideal and the real for Hegel. In other words, the very act of thinking the ideal in the real is the final phase of the real's becoming ideal. It was quite natural for Marx, still imbued with Hegelianism, to accept the state as the empirical locus of rationality and to criticize the existing order in this light. But in the course of 1842 and 1843 Marx's focus of theoretical interest shifted from the Hegelian Spirit to the empirical realm as the source for an explanation of the state. Perhaps the state, even as an ideal, is not the matrix of incarnation but a sign of alienation in the real itself? In other words, perhaps the contradiction between the "ought" and "is," between redemptive power and empirical existence, has its locus not in the opposition between the ideal state and the real state, but rather in the opposition of the real state and its "real presuppositions." But before Marx could embark along the lines just suggested, he had first to liberate himself from the systematic core of Hegel's philosophical approach to social reality. In his *Critique of Hegel's Philosophy of the State* Marx undertook a detailed criticism of Hegel's *Philosophy of Right*. Philosophy negated philosophy, philosophy ironized philosophy. Marx's philosophical annihilation of Hegelian philosophy can be conceived as a movement toward negativity. The "total" system of Hegel is reduced to theo-

retical chaos. But out of this decomposition of absolute totality
Marx forged the conceptual tools for a new round of creative positivity. Chaos (critique) follows system (totality) and is in turn followed by a new system. The romantic concept of philosophy is
evident in Marx's skepticism relative to Hegel's system. However,
Marx did *not* criticize the poetic imperative to achieve a reconciliation between the ideal and the real in man's empirical life! The Promethean value-imperative was simply given a new theoretical dress.
After all, the movement of romantic philosophy is caused by the constant urge to approach ever more closely the absolute. For Marx this
urge is identical with his desire to make philosophy worldly, and the
world philosophical. Let us now examine how Marx, the theoretical
ironist, criticizes Hegel, the systematizer.

In paragraph 262 of his *Philosophy of Right* Hegel contends that incarnate Spirit (the State) divides itself into two ideal spheres, namely
into the social institutions of the family and civil society, and thereby
mediates itself through such real moments in order to become ex-
plicit actual Spirit. Marx prosaically objects. "Actuality is not expressed as it is in itself but as another actuality. Ordinary empirical
method does not have its own rule but an alien one for its law"
(MEW, I, 206). The main thrust of Marx's objection is that the real
and empirical nature of the state is not revealed as it is but as a function of another entity, an alien causal system: "The family and civil
society are the [socioeconomic] presuppositions of the state; they
are really active elements; but in [Hegelian] speculation this is reversed. When the Idea is subjectivized, the actual subjects—civil society, family, circumstances, caprice, *etc .*—become *unactual*, objective
moments of the Idea that mean someting else" (MEW, I, 206). Thus
it becomes evident that Hegel's idealistic methodology entails a fundamental error from the very beginning. The State as a product of
real conditions (*i.e.* family and civil society) is viewed as a hyposta-
tized ideality that dirempts itself into the real conditions. "The condition is posited as the conditioned, the determining factor is posited
as determined, and the producing is posited as the product of its
product" (MEW, I, 207). In short, the effect is made into the cause.
However, this can only be done by viewing the state and civil soci-

ety not in their empirical reality but as embodiments of Hegelian ideality. The result is not only that Hegel misunderstands the actual causal relationships between social entities, but also that he uses his distorted perception of things as the theoretical grounds upon which to found an axiological justification of the way things are. Hegel does not read the rationality of the empirical *out of* empirical reality but rather *into* it, and thereby transforms it into something it is not. The state is reconciled with the real in thought only. "[Activities in the real] are *as such* not presented as rational; but they are presented as such, on the other hand, only in that they are presented as *apparent* mediation, in that they are left exactly as they are, while at the same time obtaining the meaning of a determination of the Idea, of a result, a product of the Idea. The distinction lies not in the content, but in the manner of observing or in the *manner of speaking*. There is a double history, an esoteric and exoteric one. The content is situated in the exoteric part. The interest of the esoteric part is to find again in the state the history of the logical concept. It is on the exoteric side that real development proceeds" (MEW, I, 206).

Following Feuerbach, Marx gives Hegel's error a logical formulation. "It is important that Hegel always turns the Idea into the subject and the real actual subject, such as 'political disposition,' into the predicate. But the development always takes place on the side of the predicate" (MEW, I, 209). In other words, the true causal development is explainable only in the terms of the laws of the real. Hegel treats the real not as an autonomous and self-determining subject but as the predicate (determinate effect) of another and ideal causal system. In short, Hegel's fundamental methodological error can be ontologically formulated as follows:

Hegel makes the predicates, the objects, independent but separated from their actual independence, from their subject. Subsequently the actual subject then appears as a result, while one should proceed from the actual subject and observe its objectivization. The mystical substance turns into the actual subject and the real subject appears as something else, as a moment of the mystical substance. Precisely because Hegel proceeds from the predicates of universal determination instead of from real *Ens* (*hüpokeimenon*, subject) and because there must be a bearer of these determinations, the mystical idea becomes this bearer. The dualism is that Hegel considers the universal not as the actual essence of the actual-finite, *i.e.* of the existing and determinate, or he considers the actual *Ens* not as the *true subject* of the infinite." (MEW, I, 224–25)

Hegel's false metaphysical premise makes it impossible to discover the true reason for the disparity between the actual and ideal state; indeed, such a false philosophizing must eventually result in false value judgments, or in a false construction of an ideal state (of affairs). The form of social organization, for instance, that conforms ideally to the exigencies of the (Promethean) nature of man should politically permit no (social) reality as having sovereignty (*i.e.* value determination) over all men. Yet through a series of sophisms Hegel presents the monarchical form of government of nineteenth-century Europe as the embodiment of absolute reason and freedom. Thus in actuality one man has de facto control over all other men, whereas philosophically the universal and collective will of Man conceived ideally and abstractly as the idea of sovereignty has the monarchy as its determination. Marx makes an interesting comparison:

The common Man:	*Hegel:*
The monarch has sovereign power, sovereignty.	The *sovereignty* of the state is *the* monarch.
Sovereignty does what it wants to do.	Sovereignty is "the abstract and to that degree the underground *self-determination* of the will, in which lies the ultimate basis of decision." (MEW, I, 226)

The common man, real man, biological man, experiences the sovereignty of the monarch as arbitrary power over his own individual and empirical reality, whereas the philosophical eyes of Hegelianism in a state of mystical ecstasy see nothing but the universal substance of the common man ruling himself.

The result of Marx's criticism of Hegel was that he gained a clearer grasp of the problem of the antinomy of the ideal and the real and the nature of critical irony. Sociopolitically expressed, such a metaphysical and mythopoetic antinomy shows itself as a division between man's political (species) life and his actual (individual-material) life. "Either, as in Greece, where the political state *qua* being political was the only true content of their life and will, the *res publica* is the actual private affair of the citizens, the actual content of the citizens, and the private individual is a slave or the political state is nothing other than the private arbitrariness of a particular individual, as it was in Asiatic despotism, where the political state, like the material one, was a slave" (MEW, I, 234). The long-run problem Marx had now to solve was how *real* man could reabsorb the state—the locus of the divine— back into his own "private" existence, which, of course, would mean a sublation of man's private life to the level of political universality. Marx's immediate task, however, was to ascertain more clearly the *real* reason for the division between the state and the individual in the first place.

With the completion of his first Hegel critique, Marx knew where he now had to look in order to formulate properly and in secular terms the mythic problem facing him, albeit Marx would not have admitted that his problem was mythic. In his *The Centralization Question* Marx writes: "True criticism . . . does not analyze the answers but the questions. Just as the solution to an algebraic equation is found as soon as the task has been put in its purest and sharpest relationship, so every question is answered as soon as it has become an *actual* question" (E, I, 379). In other words, criticism must begin with an investigation of the analytical principles or paradigms in terms of which an investigation of a specific real problem is undertaken. Once the generative ideas have been developed, adequate (*i.e.* answerable) questions can be formulated. Marx knew that the solution to the antinomy of the ideal and real could only be found by analyzing the real, and the real is biophysical man in a social and economic context. Socioeconomic man is the object to be investigated, not the metaphysical realm of pure spirit, if the rationality hidden in the unreason of human existence is to be comprehended. In other words, ontologically expressed, the being of the alienated actual world of man is a function of the essence of real, *i.e.* flesh and blood, man. The form (formal being) of human living must be derived from the (material) content of man. Irony as the form of theoretical consciousness must be viewed as an expression of the form of man's socioeconomic existence. The essence of man generates the irrationality of the social world, yet is also its inner rationality and will bring it to its teleological completion by annihilating the irrational. Marx's writings of the *Deutsch-Französiche Jahrbücher* (1843–1844), specifically his *On the Jewish Question* and *Toward the Critique of Hegel's Philosophy of Law: Introduction*, were concerned with deepening and concretizing the insights gained from his first critique of Hegel. Marx applied his basic insight, namely "for man the root is man himself," to an understanding of the conditions that would make the actual world philosophical, make an emancipatory revolution possible. Although Marx's analysis becomes markedly more anthropological, sociological, and even economic, the telos of his thinking remains the realization of Promethean mythos. His task was to give a "real" formulation to the mythic problem so that a "real" solution could be discovered. Science remained for Marx gnostic, *i.e.* concerned with salvational wisdom, though in a highly secular form.[3]

On the Jewish Question

It did not take long before Marx's critique of Hegel's theory of the state and methodology was to bear fruit. In 1843 Bruno Bauer, a leading young Hegelian and former comrade of Marx, published a pamphlet entitled *The Jewish Question*. Methodologically Bauer approached his problem in a manner similar to the method used by Marx during his journalism of 1842. Bauer was ostensibly interested in a political problem, but one with religious dimensions. Progressively throughout the nineteenth century Jews in Germany were pressing the Christian state of Prussia for political and civil emancipation. Bauer used this theme of political emancipation as a tool

3. In this connection see Topitsch, "Marxismus und Gnosis," 235–70.

with which to launch an attack upon Judaism in particular and religion in general. Underlying Bauer's position was the assumption that the only unity that could bind man together is the anthropological universal of being man. Jewish being is partial being insofar as Jews abstract themselves from the universal source of value, namely human being, for which science is the only theoretical expression. Furthermore, precisely because the German state is Christian, Germans too are not, according to Bauer, emancipated. Therefore, in order to emancipate the Jews, the state must be emancipated from religion, *i.e.* all religious qualifications should be totally abolished relative to political activity in the state. Religion should be relegated to the realm of private life. Marx summarized Bauer's conclusions: "Bauer thus demands on the one hand, that the Jew give up Judaism and man in general should give up religion in order to be emancipated *as a citizen*. On the other hand, he considers quite logically that the *political* abolition of religion is simply the abolition of religion" (MEW, I, 350).

Marx too was for the abolition of religion and the emancipation of the state from religion. But due to his critique of Hegelian philosophizing, he now views political emancipation in a different light. Marx must first pose a more fundamental question: "It does not suffice to examine: Who should emancipate? Who should be emancipated? Criticism has to do a third thing. It must ask: *What kind of emancipation?* What conditions are grounded in the essence of the demanded emancipation? Criticism of *political emancipation* itself was only the final criticism of the Jewish question and its true resolution into the *'universal question of the time'*" (MEW, I, 350). Marx is, in short, demanding that the question of emancipation (*i.e.* of Promethean redemption) be formulated "in the purest and sharpest" form. Bauer wanted man's emancipation, but he views the problem only from a political point of view without first ascertaining if such a viewpoint is an adequate one. Bauer simply assumes (as Marx had done in 1842) that a political criticism of the de facto state (*e.g.* the state as a Christian institution) in the light of the rational (*viz.* ideal) state is sufficient to point the way to emancipation. But this was now for Marx a questionable assumption. "So we find Bauer's error in the fact that he subjects *only* the 'Christian state,' not the 'state as such,' to criticism, that he does not investigate the *relation between political emancipation and human emancipation*, and hence he presents conditions that are only explainable from his uncritical confusion of political emancipation with universal human emancipation" (MEW, I, 350–51). Marx's interest in "universal human emancipation" is a sign of his essentially mythic interests in politics, his desire for a state of affairs that allows man to release the soul from its empirical limitations. Marx found that Bauer's "uncritical criticism" entails both factual and theoretical error.

Factually, Marx notes that various states in the world, such as the United States, have already freed themselves politically from religion, that is from confessional affiliation as a formal prerequisite for political participation in the life of the state. Yet, as is particularly the case with nineteenth-century North America, religions flourish. Thus factually it is evident that political emancipation does not generate human emancipation. "Political emancipation from religion is not the completed and consistent emancipation from religion because political emancipation is not the completed, the consistent way of human emancipation. The limits of political emancipation appear immediately in the fact that the *state* can free itself from its limits without man *actually* being free from it, in the fact that a state can be a *free state* without man being a *free man*" (MEW, I, 353). "*Political* emancipation is, to be sure, great progress; it is not the final form of human emancipation in general, but it is the final form of human emancipation *within* the world-order up to now" (MEW, I, 356).

If man is to become emancipated, free without restriction, the conditions of freedom must be understood in the terms of empirical man. Man is the root of man. This requires a radical theoretical comprehension of the essence of religion and its relationship to the state since the free state is compatible with man's alienated condition of religion.

Since the existence of religion is the existence of a defect, the source of this defect can be sought only in the *essence* of the state itself. We no longer consider religion to be the *ground*, only the *phenomenon* of secular narrowness.

Therefore, we explain religious limitation of free citizens on the basis of their worldly [secular] limitation. We do not maintain that they must do away with their religious limitation in order to do away with their secular limits. We do not maintain that they will do away with their religious limitation as soon as they have done away with their secular limits. We do not transform secular questions into theological ones; we transform theological questions into secular ones. . . . The question of the *relationship of political emancipation to religion* becomes for us a question of the *relationship of political emancipation to human emancipation.* . . . We humanize the contradiction between the state and a *determinate* religion such as *Judaism* as the contradiction between the state and *determinate secular* elements, the contradiction between the state and *religion in general,* as the contradiction of the state with its *presuppositions in general.* (MEW, I, 352)

Religion in the sense of belief in gods is not a primary phenomenon for Marx. It is causally a function of real or secular man's material struggles in a world in which there exists a contradiction between the state and civil society. Because real man does not find his fulfillment in this world, he projects his hopes into the next. Theologically, this is expressed as the belief in gods or in heaven. However, such a belief is but a specific form, and no longer the most primary form, of a more generic state of affairs. In other words, religion or religiosity refers ontologically to any *ought* existent "beyond" the reality of man's secular being. "The political state is related spiritually to civil society as heaven is to earth. [The state] stands in the same opposition to [civil society] and overcomes it in the same way as religion overcomes the limitation of the profane world, *i.e.* by having to acknowledge it, to reproduce it, and to allow itself to be dominated by it. Man in his closest actuality, in civil society, is a profane being" (MEW, I, 355). The "otherness" of the ought-existent, be it heaven or the state, is viewed as the source of man's perdition, or, as Marx expressed it in a fundamental criticism of the state: "It follows, finally that man, even when he proclaims himself an atheist through the medium of the state, *i.e.* when he proclaims the state to be atheistic, still remains religiously captive because he only recognizes himself in a roundabout way, through an intermediary. Religion is simply the recognition of man in a roundabout way. Through a mediator. The state is the mediator between man and the freedom of man. As Christ is the mediator upon whom man loads all his own divinity, his entire religious constraint, so is the state the mediator to which man transfers his entire unholiness, his entire *human unconstraint"* (MEW, I, 353). Once again we encounter the mythopoetic basis of Marxism. In the very act of rejecting Hegel's identification of the state and the (humanly) divine, Marx retains the belief in man's divinity. Marx does not ask whether divinity is possible for man, he only rejects the idea of a divine mediator outside of man. Man must be his own mediator, or rather his own object of worship. Since Marx was rejecting Hegelianism, he also was rejecting the identification of man's essence with theological reality. In the place of theological reality, Marx substituted Feuerbach's notion of species-being (*Gattungswesen*). The term *species* is the anthropological expression of the Promethean reality referred to in Hegelianism as God.[4] It is the collective, social power of man, now freed from strictly theological dress. The estrangement between the ideal and real is no longer between God and man but between human species-life and individual biophysical life. Marx describes the alienation of man in a politically religious state. "Here [*i.e.* in civil society], where [man] counts as an actual individual to himself and others, he is an *untrue* appearance. In the state, on the other hand, where he counts as a species-being, he is an imaginary member of an imagined sovereignty robbed of his actual individual life and filled with an unactual universality" (MEW, I, 355).

Religion as belief in gods or Christ as a mediator of value is a causal product of man's unredeemed secular (*viz.* material) condition. Thus these secular conditions themselves must be investigated if human emancipation is to be achieved. Man's secular life entails his living in and under a state. In the broad sense of religion it is evident that for Marx the state functions as a secular heaven. The state is therefore a theological entity. What is the source of religion in a bourgeois, democratic state? "The members of a political state are

---

4. For some historical background on the concept of species–being see Lobkowicz, *Theory and Practice*, 349–72.

religious through the dualism between individual and species life, between the life of civil society and political life, religious insofar as religion is here the spirit of civil society, the expression of the separation and distance of man from man" (MEW, I, 360). Once again, this time in a secular framework of Feuerbachian anthropology, the romantic antinomy of the ideal and real reoccurs in Marx's thinking. Marx has been able to reformulate such a mythopoetic antinomy in "real" terminology which, he believes, will ground the possibility of a real solution. The problem as to how philosophy could become worldly was being solved by Marx. Marx was showing how real man "becomes the plaything of alien powers" (MEW, I, 355). Marx even goes so far as to identify such "alien powers" with economic categories. "The question concerning the capability of the Jews for emancipation changes for us into the question, what specific *social* element is to be overcome in order to do away with Judaism? Indeed modern Jews' capacity for emancipation is the relation of Judaism to the emancipation of today's world" (MEW, I, 372). And what is this "*social* force"? "What is the worldly cult of the Jew? The *huckster*. What is his worldly god? *Money*. . . . An organization of society that would do away with the pre-conditions of the huckster and therefore of his possibility would have made the Jew impossible. His religious consciousness would dissolve like an insipid mist in the actual vital air of society" (MEW, I, 372). The social force which gives birth to Judaism is "a general, *contemporary antisocial* element, which was carried to its current high point by a historical development in which the Jews in this regard have cooperated—a high point at which it must necessarily be dissolved" (MEW, I, 372). Thus it is evident that Marx treats money and bargaining as elements of religious alienation. "Money is the jealous god of Israel before whom no other god may exist. Money degrades all the gods of man—and transforms them into commodities. Money is the universal, self-constituted *value* of everything. Therefore, it has robbed the whole world, the human world as well as nature, of its proper value. Money is the alienated essence of man's work and existence, and the alien essence dominates him as he worships it" (MEW, I, 374–75). Marx's condemnation of money is essentially mythic, indeed, a religious judgment. Marx does not approach economics as an autonomous science of empirical phenomena. Economic life is, like all human life, an objectification of man and as such it is a bearer of human categories, especially of man's pursuit of value. Money is the golden calf before whom "religious" people bow. Money is, in short, an economic correlative to the imaginative realm of religion. Thus the empirical meaning of economic categories rests for Marx upon a deeper mythopoetic paradigm, namely, the suffering Prometheus. Money is the "real" oppressor of Prometheus.

Finally, the question must be posed concerning the nature of human emancipation. The solution follows from the manner in which Marx formulated man's state of being lost, being alienated. "Only when the actual, individual man takes back into himself the abstract citizen and as an individual man has become a *species-being* in his empirical life, his individual work, and in his individual relationship, only when he has recognized and organized his *forces propres* as *social* powers and therefore social force is no longer separated from him as *political* power, only then is human emancipation accomplished" (MEW, I, 370). The almost magical quality of Marx's concept of redemption becomes apparent. Man possesses anthropological-ontological powers that can, quite literally, turn into other types of powers, that can, as Novalis said of absolute ego, charm themselves into becoming alien forces, an untrue otherness. Man's "own powers" must transform themselves into "social powers" which are creatively organized to reflect man's essential powers. However, man runs the risk of casting an evil spell upon himself and solidifying his own social powers as "political powers" which are external to his reality and which haunt him, oppress him, rule him. Man must reabsorb such political powers into his social powers (the locus of sacred power) and thereby live his social existence as a political (*viz.* universal) life and his political life as his social existence. Emancipation is complete only when there is nothing outside of man, nothing before which man feels limitation. This is a sociological version of Promethean psychology. But the question arises as to just how man's "social forces" can and necessarily will enact his *real* redemption, will ironize the existing order. In other words, what is the empirical force that will annihilate man's state of social alienation? This was the subject of Marx's second critique of Hegel.

Toward the Critique of Hegel's Philosophy of Law: Introduction

Marx began his second major critique of Hegel with the well-known thesis: "For Germany the criticism of religion is completed in essentials, and the criticism of religion is the premise of all criticism" (MEW, I, 378). The criticism of religion is for Marx, among other things, the criticism of Hegelianism, particularly as carried out by Ludwig Feuerbach. After all Hegel had considered religion to be a mode of absolute knowledge. According to Hegel, religion is not abolished by philosophy; rather its full and true content is expressed in philosophy. Hegelian philosophy is a theological philosophy. Accordingly, Hegel's definition of man, as Karl Löwith shows, is in the terms of absolute reality.[5] Only as the individual is subsumed under incarnate divinity—the ethical life of the community—does he receive eternal value. It is for this reason that socioeconomic categories for Hegel are reducible to metaphysical categories. Marx, following Feuerbach, sought to reverse Hegel. For Feuerbach and Marx man is a natural "flesh and blood" being. Therefore, naturalistic categories, not idealistic ones, should serve as the explanatory paradigms. But, and this is important, Feuerbach in his criticism of religion did not surrender Hegel's mythos, the *causa sui* project. Feuerbach was acutely aware that God is an extremely important concept for the understanding of man. God is simply "man's faith in the supernatural sublimity of his own being" projected out into reality.[6] The notion of God as world-conquering power was never rejected by Feuerbach; it was just radically identified with man: "God is essentially an idea, a model for man; its sole meaning and purpose is that man should become what the model represents; the model is simply the future man, personified and conceived of as an indepen-

5. Cf. Löwith, *From Hegel to Nietzsche*, 304–307.
6. Cf. Ludwig Feuerbach, *Lectures on the Essence of Religion*, trans. Ralph Mannheim (New York, 1967), 273–74.

dent being."[7] If God is simply the "supernatural sublimity" of man's essence, then must not man as God possess creative powers as his supreme value? "The idea of activity, of making, of creation," writes Feuerbach in his *Essence of Christianity*, "is in itself a divine idea; it is therefore unhesitatingly applied to God. In activity, man feels himself free, unlimited, happy; in passivity, limited, oppressed, unhappy. Activity is the positive sense of one's personality. . . . And the happiest the most blissful activity is that which is productive. To read is delightful, reading is passive activity; but to produce what is worthy to be read is more delightful still."[8] Here we have the Promethean mythos, the Apollonian imperative. Despite his apparent rejection of Hegelianism and his criticism of religion, Feuerbach shows himself to be a worshipper of creative power like Hegel. Instead of locating this power in a universal being, God, Feuerbach locates it in man as man's species-life. Awareness of divine nature "is in truth nothing else than feeling enraptured, in ecstasy with itself— feeling intoxicated with joy, blissful in its own plentitude."[9] Mythopoetically, the difference between Hegel and Feuerbach is negligible. If anything, Feuerbach is more radically Apollonian, and his criticism of religion is simply the total reduction of theology to anthropology, to a naturalistic model base.

The criticism of religion was not for Marx, as a follower of Feuerbach, a criticism of the Promethean *causa sui* project. Marx did not critically examine this mythos, nor did he question whether human self-consciousness could really be the highest divinity. The criticism of religion only criticized the theological vocabulary and conceptual framework in which the Promethean mythos had been previously expressed. But the exoteric criticism was not without profound consequences. What the criticism of religion did was to turn purely social categories into the highest categories of existence. "The foundation of irreligious criticism is: *man makes religion*, religion does not make man. . . . But *man* is no abstract being squatting outside of the

---

7. *Ibid.*, 270.
8. Ludwig Feuerbach, *The Essence of Christianity*, trans. George Eliot (New York, 1957), 217.
9. *Ibid.*, 9.

world. Man is *the world of men*, the state, society. This state, this society, produces religion, an *inverted consciousness of the world*, because
it is an *inverted world*" (MEW, I, 378). Otherwise expressed, Hegel
and/or theologians have been correct in seeking what religions seek,
namely salvation from suffering, endlessly abundant life, creative
power. But theologians have sought this plenitude in a reality beyond man, hence in mere appearance, in the nonhuman (*Unmensch*—
cf. MEW, I, 378). Therefore, false explanatory models, false ways of
redemption, have been proposed. All such models have led man beyond man. The criticism of religion has shown that there is no such
"beyond." Marx writes:

> Criticism plucked the imaginary flowers on the chain [of religion], not
> so that man will carry this chain without phantasy or consolation, but
> rather so that he will cast off the chain and break the living flower. The
> criticism of religion disillusions man so that he will think, act, and form his
> actuality like a disillusioned person who has come to reason, so that he will
> move around himself, his true sun. Religion is only the illusory sun around
> which man moves so long as he does not move about himself. (MEW, I,
> 379)

In short, the criticism of religion destroys any belief that there is
some power beyond man's being from which he needs succor. Marx
is often misunderstood by "modern" Christians in their rush to
prove that Christianity is not incompatible with Marxism "rightly
understood." But Marx was not just criticizing religion as a pretense
to do nothing in this world, to leave injustice untouched.[10] He was
claiming that religion per se in no way can offer anything to man
relative to his deepest needs. Man is his own sun; man's power alone
can illuminate the universe with a value that transfigures and justi-
fies all empirical existence. Since religion is no more than a surrogate
for what man does not have, the criticism of this illusion must force
man to become aware of the full negativity of his situation, that he
has no hope of salvation in the world as it is. Such a consciousness

---

10. In this see Delgaauw, *The Young Marx*. Delgaauw seems to have obtained no insight
into the "atheistic" basis of Marx's thought.

will generate in man the desire to think, to act, and to form his world in such a way that he can turn himself into his own god. This urge is essentially ironic. In other words, the criticism of religion turns man into a practical ironist.

In the previous section we noted that religion for Marx entailed more than the belief in the existence of gods. Whereas religion in the traditional sense is the acknowledgment that the ideal transcends the potential of the humanly real, Marx had come to conceive of the state (or political life) as a theological entity. Hegelianism had limited the divine to political existence. As a result, man's empirical existence remained unredeemed. Consequently, the criticism of religion is directed not only at the "holy" forms of human perdition but also at the "secular" forms. Marx writes: "It is, therefore, *the task of history*, after the *beyondness of truth* [*Jeneseits der Wahrheit*] has disappeared, to establish the truth of *this-sided-ness* [*i.e.* the empirical world—*Wahrheit des Diesseits*]. The first *task of philosophy* which stands in the service of history is to unmask self-alienation in its *unholy forms* after the *holy form* of human alienation has been unmasked. The criticism of heaven changes accordingly into the criticism of the earth, criticism *of religion* into *criticism of law, criticism of theology* into *criticism of politics*" (MEW, I, 379). Philosophical criticism has now become criticism of the empirical areas of human existence. Marx has raised social (and economic) categories to the highest explanatory principles. Marxism is becoming "scientific." But, the telos of all such scientific criticism is still mythopoetic. Because empirical actuality does not manifest to man consciousness of his divinity, the process of criticism is clearly mythopoetic for Marx and in that sense also religious. What changes is the vocabulary of criticism; what remains is the same gnostic and mythopoetic ideal. Let us focus a bit more on the function of criticism.

Even if for Marx the heart of philosophy is "world-conquering and absolutely free," the fact remains that the world stands over and against man, it does not "aesthetically" reflect his prideful power. Hence, the realization that philosophy is not actual led Marx to turn to criticism. Criticism is irony. The felt disparity between man's inner divinity and his outer finitude generates in him the urge to transcend the given by annihilating it. Irony does, of course, negate in order to re-create, but the initial impulse of irony is destructive, *i.e.* it volitionally seeks to annihilate the "is," to reduce the existing order to chaos. Total chaos is the prerequisite to total re-creation. And the philosophical form of irony was for Marx (as it was for Schlegel) criticism—the form which became for Marx an instrument for destroying the existing order of contemporary Germany. Marx writes:

> *War* on German conditions! To be sure! They are *below the level of history, beneath criticism,* but they remain an object of criticism. . . . Criticism in battle with [existing conditions] is not a passion of the head but the head of passion. It is not a scalpel, it is a weapon. Its object is its enemy, which it does not want to refute but *to annihilate* [*vernichten*]. . . . [Criticism] no longer presents itself as a *final goal* but simply as *means.* Its essential pathos is *indignation,* its essential work is *denunciation.* (MEW, I, 380)

Eric Voegelin has commented upon this passage: "Here the gnostic's will to murder speaks. The bond of reality is ripped to pieces. . . . Criticism is no longer argument. Judgment has been spoken, execution will follow."[11] Criticism is a passion to annihilate the enemy. Here is the same attitude of defiance, narcissism, and Promethean pride as found in "Human Pride" or in Oulanem's call to destroy the "marble-rock of Being." One can well speak of a madness of irony. There is no attempt to love, to reform, to improve—only the pathos of annihilation, pure and simple. I showed in my discussion of Schlegel's conception of ironic philosophy that philosophy must change from mere cognition into passion, from reason into will. Criticism, be it theoretical or practical, is a function of passion; indeed, criticism as the will to annihilation is the "head of passion," is pathos. Insofar as criticism can be described as pathos, it is a dramatic force, for pathos is the volitional dynamics of all great drama. Criticism is, indeed, a dramatic mask put on by the philosopher. It is the dramatic passion that impels the philosopher to enter into intrigues with the world, to war on the "is." Marx can still be seen as

---

11. Voegelin, *Wissenschaft, Politik und Gnosis,* 79–80.

following the romantic paradigm. Irony must reduce being to chaos; only then can pathos re-create things totally. Chaos is also a fundamental category of magic, for only if the objectivity which limits man can be shown to have no substance, to have no independence, *i.e.* to be chaotic, can the will of the magician act with unlimited causality. "In the womb of nothingness, in the limitless despair of sacrilege, man [as a magician] makes himself into an incarnate God."[12] This is, of course, the Promethean imperative and criticism unto annihilation is its magical instrument.

Marx's commitment to criticism would seem to involve him in a difficulty. The pathos of criticism is indignation, its work is denunciation. Indignation, is, of course, a psychological inclination that can result in concrete physical action. But denunciation as the content of criticism is only annihilation in thought. Philosophical criticism, no matter how negative, reveals itself to be no more than theoretical praxis. What is radicalized is man's theoretical will, not material reality. Given Marx's shift to a social paradigm base, praxis had to be given a real as well as an ideal meaning. "The criticism of speculative philosophy of law does not proceed in itself but in *tasks* for whose solution there is only one means: *praxis*" (MEW, I, 385). The philosophical ideal remains, but it must be injected into material form. This very act of actualization entails the abolition of philosophy simply as philosophical criticism.

Critical toward its counterpart, [the critical struggle of philosophy against the existing order] related itself uncritically to itself insofar as it proceeded from its own presuppositions of philosophy and either remained with its own given results or gave out demands and results gathered from elsewhere as direct demands and results of philosophy, although these latter— their justification being granted—are to be obtained, on the contrary, only by the *negation of previous philosophy*, of philosophy as philosophy. We intend a closer, detailed description of the [theoretical] party [which originated in philosophy]. Its main defect can be reduced to the following: *It believed, it could actualize philosophy without transcending [abolishing—aufheben] it.*" (MEW, I, 384)

12. Rony, *A History of Magic,* 147.

In short, philosophical criticism is not enough to effect a reconciliation between the ideal and real. Philosophical criticism itself must be annihilated to make way for real or material criticism.

Since man's alienation is grounded in the material conditions of his life, only a material force can annihilate the real locus of alienation. "The weapon of criticism cannot, to be sure, replace the criticism of weapons; material force must be toppled by material force" (MEW, I, 385). This statement by Marx must not be misunderstood. At this point Marx is not suggesting a conspiratorial theory of revolution. He is not yet concerned with such weapons as guns, terrorism, *etc.*, but with philosophy (*i.e.* the ideal) as a material force. In other words, man can alter the given sociopolitical order of things only by physically exerting himself. But action must have a motive and a telos. Marx was interested in how the "world-conquering and absolutely free heart" of philosophy could become not only the theoretical power of criticism but also a material force of revolution. How can ironic criticism become the form and principle of materially inspired action? The answer:

But theory turns into a material force as soon as it seizes the masses. Theory [*viz.* philosophy] is capable of seizing the masses as soon as it demonstrates *ad hominem*, and it demonstrates *ad hominem* as soon as it becomes radical. To be radical is to grasp things at the root. The root for man is, however, man himself. The evident proof for the radicalism of German theory, therefore, for practical energy, is its going out from the decisive *positive* transcendence [*Aufhebung*] of religion. The criticism of religion ends with the doctrine that man is the highest being for man and thus with the *categorical imperative to overthrow all conditions* in which man is a demeaned, enslaved, abandoned, contemptible being. (MEW, I, 385)

Ironic philosophy develops according to Romanticism in a series of alterations: system–chaos–system, reason–will–reason, and consciousness–volitional energy–consciousness. The skeptical or ironic phase of philosophizing is typified by the transformation of thought into practical energy, albeit such energy acts primarily as theoretical praxis. Marx had taken over this concept of philosophy as a creative or dialectical force as a way out of the Hegelian blind alley caused by

Hegel's nondialectical conception of philosophy. Marx's problem has been to translate theoretical (ideal) energy into practical (material) energy. The criticism of religion left man with no hopes in a beyond of any kind. Indeed, man is left with a full and undeniable awareness of his totally alienated condition. Indignation and denunciation are results of this awareness. But such dramatic and ironic pathos cannot become "practical energy" unless there is something radically wrong with the material root of man. Only then can there be a revolutionary, *viz.* salvational force. "Revolutions need a passive element, a material foundation. Theory is actualized in a people only insofar as it is the actualization of their needs. . . . It is not enough that thought strives toward [*drängt zu*] actualization; actuality must urge itself [*drängt sich*] toward thought" (MEW, I, 386). Empirical reality on its own, not at the urging of thought, must strive toward thought. But the content of thought is in this context the Promethean imperative that man becomes his own highest divinity. Man should be "the highest being for man." In short, Marx is demanding that material reality propel itself toward mythopoetic redemption. Man is, of course, a biophysical, economic being. This is the material root of his real life, and it is in this area of human existence that revolution must be rooted. Critical or ironic energy must be the form that directs the material activity of oppressed man toward revolution. In this way material force is subsumed under a dramatic causality, *i.e.* it becomes one of the masks that philosophy puts on in order to spin an efficacious intrigue with the world. Somehow, there must be something in the real, material, or economic life of the masses that will inspire not only material action, but material energy whose form is the categorical imperative to overthrow all conditions that oppress man. In other words, man as the root of man must contain in his anthropological heart a radical and mythic imperative to annihilate totally the existing order. There must be a class of individuals that possess "that breath of soul which identifies itself with the soul of the people [*Volksseele*], although only momentarily, that genius [*Genialität*] which inspires [*begeistert*] material power toward political power, that revolutionary boldness which hurls at the opponent the spiteful parole: *I am nothing, and I ought [müßte] to be every-*

thing" (MEW, I, 389). Let us examine this ironic imperative that follows from man's being the highest being for himself.

In previous chapters I have sought to show that the dynamics of romantic irony arise out of a contradiction situated in the very "heart" of man's being. According to Schlegel, man is composed of an *Ur-Ich* and *Ich*, divine potentiality and empirical actuality. Man's divine essence impels him to long for and to strive after an infinitely full experience of value, while his empirical self directs his psychic energies out into the world of finite objects. Man tries to gain psychological integrity by forming the objective world into an aesthetic representation of absolute, infinite value. But no given gestalt of the finite manifold can fully correspond to man's divine imperative. A contradiction must arise in man between what man is and what he ought to be, a contradiction between man's infinitude and finitude. This inner mythopoetic antinomy generates in man the infinite energy to annihilate the structure of the empirically given in order to pass on to higher levels of perfection. The contradiction between the is and the ought, when transformed into a negating-positing energy, is simply irony. Irony is, in short, the form (*viz.* directing principle) of human activity. Marx, however, deviated from Romanticism in that he accepted the Promethean imperative that man should become everything. Man is everything insofar as he dominates, controls, and forms his natural and social environment. This attitude is one of pride, indignation, defiance, and self-sufficiency. All these features are characteristic of the collegiate Marx's revolt against romantic dionysianism. Man's consciousness of himself as the highest being is the essence of the "ought-to-be-everything" imperative. This mythic ought can inspire man to total revolutionary (*viz.* dramatic) annihilation of the existing order only insofar as it is activated. And it is activated to the degree that man's Promethean divinity is demeaned, negated, or oppressed. Total negation must call forth total irony in response. Man's essential urge is to be everything; his de facto reality is that he is nothing. It may well be, as Ernest Becker claims, that this contradiction is a sign of "boundless megalomania."[13] This categorical imperative is, nevertheless, the form

13. Cf. Becker, *The Denial of Death*, 265.

of material energy and hence the reason it will strive toward thought. This categorical imperative is nothing else but critical irony having become real. Irony as the form of philosophy has become the form of man's material life.

It is readily evident that the basis of Marx's belief in the efficacy of revolution is grounded in a mythopoetic model, namely in Promethean psychology. One will look in vain in Marx's writing for any empirical studies proving that man not only has the urge but also the power to be everything, to be absolute value. Fichte once claimed that as a man wills so too will he philosophize. Marx willed that man should become God. So he theorized! Marx's theorizing is a function of his Promethean complex.[14] He did not dispassionately approach the human condition. On the contrary, his thinking is informed by an a priori value judgment. Theory is but the way in which Marx sought to realize the untouchable, indisputable mythos of the *causa sui* project. Theory is simply the exoterics of Marx's thinking. The purpose of theory was, in my judgment, to enable Marx to continue his dreams of human divinity. Let us now focus more intently upon the mythic if not magical core of Marx's discovery of the proletariat as the "the soul of the people."

Society is a functional totality, a whole, but within society each class has particular material needs and interests. Indeed, only through particular needs are the members of the class real human beings. But to the degree that individuals are real they must abstract themselves from universality, from society as a whole; *i.e.* they become mired in the purely empirical, sensuous, and finite. In short, they take up a partial perspective. In Kantian terms,[15] each class is heteronomously

14. Lewis S. Feuer has written a devastating psychological profile of Marx and related it to his theorizing. What emerges is a conceited and megalomaniac personality that can stand no opposition, no conflict. See "The Character and Thought of Karl Marx: The Promethean Complex and Historical Materialism."

15. I have introduced Kant for two reasons. First of all Marx as quoted above makes reference to the "categorical imperative to overthrow all conditions" that oppress men. This is a reference to Kant. The categorical imperative is a demand to realize absolute value in and by human activity. Secondly, a Marxist such as William Ash recognizes that morality entails an "ought," rather than mere descriptive assertions. In this context, Ash refers approvingly to Kant. See *Marxism and Moral Concepts* (New York, 1964), 13–16. Kant was concerned with the connection between universal value and particular need. As such his method can cast some light upon the problem facing Marx.

determined by a series of specific needs and objects. Each class enters into specific material relationships to determinate objects that satisfy biophysical wants. Activity, real life per se, is only possible as specific, material-physical needs motivate the members of a class to "labor" for specific and defined goals. But as Kant noted in his explanation of the moral act, a concrete act of itself, because it is finite, can never be morally productive of universality, except when it is carried out in the name of universal reason. The ultimate maxim determining and forming human choice must be universal rationality. Kant called this axiological power the categorical imperative—a term acquired by Marx. The source of this power is not the individual but mankind. Therefore, the individual can only act morally, freely, and with redemptive dignity, if he acts not *qua* his individuality, but as a representative of humanity. Marx, following Hegel, rejected Kant's moral formalism, and his belief in a noumenal realm beyond time and space; he did, like Hegel, retain the belief in Kant's Promethean ideal. There is a categorical imperative in man to realize absolute value in human society, and mankind is this absolute value. For Marx, the phenomenal realm, empirical reality itself, must contain immanent in itself the grounds for the universalization of man's concrete acts. Man cannot be radically emancipated for Marx except through the causal activity of a real class of individuals. Only concrete individuals with concrete needs can act. Indeed, this is the definition of material force. However, biophysical needs imply partiality, self-interest, abstraction from the interests of the whole. Just as the concrete and heteronomously motivated acts of the individual become redemptive for Kant only if they are simultaneously representative of mankind as a whole, of sacred power, so too can the material interests of a class and the ensuing actions become a universal "social force" only on the condition that the specific class concerned represents (*i.e.* re-presents) the exigencies of "the whole of society."

Marx himself writes that no class can attempt to realize "*universal human emancipation.* . . . without calling forth a moment of enthusiasm [*Enthusiasmus*] in itself and in the masses, a moment in which it fraternizes and flows together with society in general, in which it is confused with [society] and is felt and acknowledged as [society's] *general representative*, a moment in which its claims and rights are in truth the rights and claims of society itself, in which it is actually the social head and the social heart" (MEW, I, 388). It is interesting to note that Marx turns to a life or psychological model in order to elucidate his notion of general representation. Only if a group (at least in intention) flows together with society can it represent society as a whole, can it function as the heart and head of society. Such a fusion with society as a whole will generate a feeling of "enthusiasm." The term literally means "being-in-God." If a class is to redeem society it must "be in God," *i.e.* be infused with divine energy. We have here a repeat in anthropological terms of what the romantics sought in cosmological terms, namely the absorption of individuality by absolute creative power—only the "heart" and "head" of society have replaced God as the locus of infinitude.

Marx's notion of "representation" or "standing for" has two levels of meaning. On the empirical level it means that the opposition between what ought to be and what is, between the state and civil society, between classes in civil society, comes to a head in the material suffering of an empirically identifiable class of humans. The universal as a material force can only enter into a class of men *qua* their concrete wants and sufferings. However, suffering per se, although the necessary prerequisite for an emancipatory revolution, is not the sufficient cause. Many classes in history have suffered, rebelled, and taken power without really achieving *"universal human emancipation."* Revolution as radical emancipation is possible only if the real suffering of the class concerned represents mythic value, *i.e.* incorporates the demands of universality in its particularity. A class's concretely motivated desires to alter society to its material self-interest must at the same time manifest the categorical imperative: "I am nothing, and I ought to be everything." The categorical imperative to be everything as an energizing principle transforms particular and materially motivated actions into redemptive acts. A class whose concrete real needs represent the demands of mankind to be "the highest being" will function as a savior. Representation thus also has an ideal meaning, a mythopoetic significance. The categorical imperative as a motivating impetus to activity is, essentially, pathos. But pathos is not merely physical activity but a mental attitude, a direction of the will. But that which makes the rebellion of one special class (namely the proletariat) *sui generis* is the ironic intentionality of the will. The ideal pathos of the will transforms physical activity into a dramatic intrigue with the world. The intent of the will is the decisive factor! This geniality impels material force toward thought. A primary feature of magic is the power of the will to alter things simply by intention. Whatever the "material" origins of the categorical imperative might be, once awakened, the divine will of man will of itself transform mere physical effort into redemptive power. This will is nothing less than the "soul of the people" having become energy.

In order to represent the social totality, a particular class must possess "that breath of soul which identifies itself with the soul of the people [*Volksseele*], although only momentarily, that genius [*Genialität*] which inspires [*begeistert*] material power toward political power" (MEW, I, 389). It is most amazing that, when Marx seeks to explain "scientifically" and "materialistically" the dynamics of a real emancipatory revolution, he utilizes a pneumatological model, *i.e.* he must refer to a "soul," to the ancient idea of a pneuma. Even if one were to assume that Marx was only talking exoterically or "poetically" at this point, the fact remains that his explanatory metaphor is a mythic, religious, and spiritual category. A mythic analogy is used to impart meaning to socioeconomic concepts.

In my opinion, Marx's choice of a soul-category was an excellent one. Ernst Topitsch in many writings has shown that the constellations of ideas entailed in the soul are grounded in man's very real experience of physical suffering, guilt, and death.[16] The pressure of empirical reality oppresses man and threatens his life. Ontologically, the soul has been considered (and still is) to be that "stuff" in man which is superior to the oppressive environment. As Otto Rank wrote: "Thus the facts of death and of the individual's denial of death brought the idea of the soul into being."[17] The soul's independence from the material environment is the ontological guarantee

16. Cf. Ernst Topitsch, "Seelenvorstellungen in Mythos und Metaphysik," in *Mythos, Philosophie, Politik, Zur Naturgeschichte der Illusion* (Freiburg, 1969), 61–78.
17. Cf. Otto Rank, *Psychology and the Soul*, trans. William D. Turner (New York, 1961), 14.

that man is in some sense immortal. The soul as the "true self" must be nourished above all as it offers the possibility of salvation. The soul, as G. van der Leeuw writes, "was always, and in all its most widely contrasting structures, numinous in its type and a means of indicating the sacred in man." [18] Although the soul is man's bridge to immortality, a divine soul must infuse, inform, and imbue the human soul with sacred power. Spirit (*Geist*) alone can mediate immortality to spirit. Human longing no longer remains mere finite energy but becomes inspired or, literally, "breathed into by holy fire," by a holy spirit. "In Gnosticism," writes van der Leeuw, "also for St. Paul, the *pneuma* is the life principle of man together with *psyche* and divine Power, which penetrates man from without and transforms him into a 'pneumatized' or 'spiritual' man." [19] The divine soul is a supra-individual, universal, and mental energy that, once infused into the finite individual, raises individual life to divine Life.

In accordance with his monism, Hegel immanentized the divine "soul-stuff." It became for Hegel the *anima mundi*.[20] As such, the soul for Hegel is the undifferentiated and universal mental-substance out of which particular individuals arise. This soul-stuff comes to pulsate in the manifold of the individuals as their one Life. "Soul is the *substance* or 'absolute' basis of all the particularity and individualizing of mind; it is in soul that mind finds the material on which its character is wrought and soul remains the pervading, identical ideality of it all." [21] "The soul universal, described, it may be, as an *anima mundi*, a world-soul, must not be fixed on that accord as a single subject; it is rather the universal *substance* which has its actual truth only in individual subjects." [22] Soul is thus the principle of Absolute Spirit in all things, the foundation of immortality.

The soul for Hegel is absolute power, the mental-stuff that di-

---

18. G. van der Leeuw, *Religion in Essence and Manifestation*, trans. J. E. Turner (2 vols.; New York, 1963), I, 275.

19. *Ibid.*, I, 34.

20. For a discussion of Hegel's concept of the soul see Murray Greene, *Hegel on the Soul: A Speculative Anthropology* (The Hague, 1972).

21. Hegel, *Philosophy of Mind*, 29.

22. *Ibid.*, 35–36.

rempts itself into the many only to return to itself as spirit by forming the many into an image of itself. The highest development of
soul-spirit is the life of the community. More specifically, the collective sociality, the oneness of social labor, is the anthropological locus
of the *anima mundi*. Social power is, consequently, the highest form
of dynamic "soul-stuff." Marx accepted Hegel's deification of sociality, although he rejected the theological basis. There was no longer
any spirit, or *anima mundi*, for Marx other than man himself. All that
exists is the *Volk*—*i.e.* the social collectivity, subjectively as com-
munity-spirit and objectively as culture. Here is where Marx sought
immortality. Culture is the visible and hence aesthetic proof of man's
divine creativity. Jules Monnerot has shown that thinkers such as
Marx sought immortality in the social collectivity. "What most ap-
peals to men who long, consciously, or unconsciously, to forget human insufficiency and to transcend their personal limitations, is the
promise of social solidarity and collective euphoria. . . . It is as though
an attempt were being made to compensate for the failure of [indi-
vidual] immortality by turning to the durable and long-lived, to the
permanent character stamped in flesh and soil, of this or that variety
of the human species."²³

Marx very aptly describes the transforming causality of the social
collectivity upon an individual class in mental, mythic, and religious
terms. In doing so, he ceased talking the exoterics of material causality and started talking the esoterics of mental causality. The soul
of the people is equated with *Genialität*— *i.e.* mental power, genius.
"Since we can assume no other reality than spiritual," writes Schlegel, "everything is ingenious [*genialisch*, mental]" (KA, XXII, 105).
Reality for idealism is mind-like, mind-stuff. Causality is, therefore,
also mind-like. The genius, as a *mind* of extraordinary creative power,
be it poetic or intellectual, is able to put the imprint of mind upon
material things. Marx juxtaposes the "soul of the poeple" with genius. The soul of the people has, therefore, a mental power, a genius,
that enables it to inspire [*begeistern*] material power toward the sei-
zure of social power. This is clearly an act of poetic creation. The

23. Cf. Jules Monnerot, *Sociology and Psychology of Communism*, trans. Jane Degras and
Richard Rees (Boston, 1953), 269–70.

German term Marx used for "to inspire" is *be-geist-ern*. The root *Geist* is in the verb. *Geist* originally meant "excitement" or "agitation." That is, it referred to an intense volitional and motivational experience. The term came plausibly to be associated with the subject of emotion, namely with consciousness, mind, spirit, or soul. *Begeistern* means literally "to infuse with mind-like qualities," *i.e.* to excite. And what is the content of the *Geist* infused into material force? Nothing less than the imperative "I should be everything." An individual class infused with such a *Geist* will experience the emotional energy and impulse to actualize the categorical imperative. When the antithetical poles of "I ought to be everything" and "I am nothing" coincide as a dramatic tension in a given limited class of individuals, the material reality and energy of this class are transubstantiated into the "head" and "heart" of the social "soul" of the people. A fragment of society is thereby transformed into a pneumatized class, a representative of society as a whole. Remove the soul from the people and there would be no emancipatory revolution, just the hopeless ragings of mere biological animals. Marx was able to discover that material force is revolutionary because he had already projected a pneumatological structure into it.

Marx's pneumatology is simply overwhelming. Marx, the arch-materialist, had to explain the causality of revolution in mythopoetic terms, and the mythopoetic foundation of Marx's materialism shows itself to be a pneumatology. But how can a class identify itself with the "soul of the people"? What is the nexus of union? Let us again consider the mythopoetic notion of representation and examine Marx's version of the "incarnation." In this way we will be able to grasp the very being of the proletariat.

The ontological absolute of Christianity, namely God, is absolutely realized from eternity unto eternity. God's potentiality is from *illo tempore* actualized reality. This makes God the parent of all things. The Promethean absolute of Marx (as it was for idealism) is in *illo tempore* only radical potentiality. The absolute of dialectical thinking, as noted previously, lacks "in the beginning" all actuality. It is absolute essence without any existence, though it is an essential urge to achieve absolute existence. This fundamental difference in absolutes results in different theories of incarnation. The Christian God becomes freely incarnate in one human reality. Not mankind but this man—Jesus—is incarnated God. Jesus is truly man and truly God. God exists in and as Jesus as a realized positivity. Jesus Christ—a single, finite, and positive individual raised to (united with) the infinite—can for the Christian redemptively represent all men because Christ is truly man (and hence shares the interests of man), truly God (hence shares the interests of absolute value), and totally innocent (not stained by that which separates man from absolute value). Thus the sufferings of Christ can have redemptive significance and causal efficacy (two sides of the same coin) since they are committed by pure man and pure God for impure man. That which joins Christ with man is not physical causality, but a symbolic and mythic analogy. Christ's very representation (symbolization) of man constitutes the causality of his redemptive act. The Marxist absolute, on the other hand, since it is only perfect at the "end of history" when the classless society has been achieved, can only appear beforehand in a negative manner. The members of the redemptive class are, to be sure, positive entities, but only *qua* their finitude, *qua* their concrete interests. They become representatives of the whole society, not under the form of positivity but under negativity. The "soul of the people" exists in the class of perdition as the energizing principle only as a loss, as an unrealized potentiality, whose essence is defined by radical negativity (*i.e.* it is not what it ought be, namely everything).

Only as absolute negation, *i.e.* as abstraction from *all* positivity, does a limited and hence all too human class transcend its finite status and become a living universal, a soteriological force, or one with "the soul of the people." The Promethean absolute first comes to self-consciousness, *i.e.* begins to exist in man, as a suffering consciousness caused by the absolute and irreconcilable antinomy between essence and existence. This necessary dialectical connection between being nothing (existence) and becoming everything (essence) is the mythopoetic prerequisite for an emacipatory revolution in the real.

Because it experiences unqualified negation, the proletariat pos-

sesses unqualified innocence and hence it can become the redeemer
of humanity as a negative incarnation by dialectically negating the
negation of humanity. Without *unqualified* (mythopoetic) suffering
the proletariat could never function as the savior. Suffering alone is
insufficient; only mythic suffering is salvationally efficacious. Mythic
suffering is not simply a physical and hence irrational given; it is the
result of the evil done by an empirical class. Mircea Eliade comments
upon the attitude of archaic man to the reality of suffering: "Every
moment of the magico-religious treatment of suffering most clearly
illustrates its meaning: suffering proceeds from the magical action
of an enemy, from breaking a taboo, from entering a baneful zone,
from the anger of a god. . . . The primitive—and not the primitive
alone . . . cannot conceive of an unprovoked suffering. . . . There is
always a fault at the bottom of it. . . . Individual or a collective suffering always has its explanation. And consequently, it is, it can be,
tolerable."[24] The source of fault for Marx is the capitalist; the instrument of offense is private property; and the innocent victim is the
proletariat. The suffering of the proletariat is tolerable (provision-
ally) as it is of a special type, namely it is redemptive, *i.e.* possesses
dramatic efficacy. Only the dramatic can overcome the dramatic.
Marx himself writes in *The Holy Family* (1845):

> Because man is lost in [the proletariat] while at the same time he has not
> only won a theoretical consciousness of that loss but has also been forced
> into revolt against this inhumanity immediately by an absolutely imperious
> need . . . the proletariat can and must liberate itself. . . . It is not a question
> of what this or that proletarian or the entire proletariat *imagines* as its goal.
> It is a question of *what it is* and what it will be historically compelled to do
> in accordance with this being. (MEW, II, 38)

And just what constitutes the "being" of such an emancipatory
class? What ontological properties must a particular and hence limited group of individuals possess if its actions are to generate an
emancipatory revolution? The being of such a class is its being uni-

24. Cf. Mircea Eliade, *Cosmos and History: The Myth of the Eternal Return*, trans. Willard
R. Trask (New York, 1959), 97–100.

versally wronged, *i.e.* such a class must function as society's negative representative, as the innocent victim of all the evil produced by society. Marx writes in his critique of Hegel:

> In order for the *revolution of the people* to coincide with the *emancipation of a particular class* of society, in order for an estate to stand for [represent—*gelten*] the estate of the entire society, all the defects of society must conversely be concentrated in another class; a particular class must be the estate of general offense, the incorporation of general limitation; a particular social sphere must stand for [represent—*gelten*] the *notorious crime* of the entire society, so that the liberation of this sphere appears as general self-liberation. In order for *one* estate to be par excellence the estate of liberation, another estate must conversely be the obvious estate of enslavement. (MEW, I, 388)

Suffering is not, according to Marx, a brute given. Suffering for Marx as for any magico-religious thinker is "provoked." Suffering has an explanation: it is undeserved and hence redeemable. In other words, moral innocence, victim-being, is the negative form of reality assumed by the social soul in an emancipatory class. Once again the question is asked, in just what is the positive foundation of emancipation grounded in modern Germany? Marx answers:

> In the formation of a class with radical chains, of a class of civil society which is not a class of civil society, of an estate which is the dissolution of all estates, of a sphere which possesses a universal character through its universal suffering, which claims no *particular right* [*besondres Recht*], but rather *wrong pure and simple* [or unqualified wrong—*Unrecht schlechthin*] has been committed against it, [a class] which can no longer invoke a *historical* but only a *human* [*i.e.* universal] title, which does not stand in a one-sided opposition to the consequences of the German political system but [stands] in a complete opposition to its presuppositions; [in the formation] of a sphere, finally, which cannot emancipate itself without emancipating itself from all the remaining spheres of society and thereby emancipating all the remaining spheres of society, which in one word is the *complete loss* [*völlige Verlust*] of man and thus can only win itself through the *complete rewinning of man* [*völlige Widergewinnung des Menschen*]. This dissolution of society as a particular estate is the *proletariat*. (MEW, I, 390)

In this last quotation Marx formally and for the first time identifies the proletariat as the class of universal emancipation. The proletariat is such a class precisely because it possesses symbolic or representative value. Marx appears to be talking about material conditions, but what empirical meaning can designations such as "general offense," "unqualified wrong," "notorious crime," "no particular wrong," "the complete loss of man," "universal suffering," *etc.* have? It is important to determine the meaning of such designations because they constitute the being of the proletariat and are that which will compel the proletariat to fulfill its historical mission.

In my opinion, such designations have no concrete or empirical meaning. To be sure, one can point to a particular instance of suffering. This suffering may be made possible because of a certain set of social arrangements. All this can be an example of injustice. But that is not what Marx is claiming. In good Hegelian fashion, Marx does not see this or that particular injust act but rather the essence—"unqualified wrong" (as the German has been translated). Particular and individual acts are viewed as appearances of the social Wrong per se. Therefore, the condition of the proletariat, its essential being, is described in the nonempirical but religious terms of "complete loss." Such a description has meaning only in a mythopoetic framework. Humanity—an essence—is lost in the proletariat—a particular. Humanity as the locus of sacred power is incarnate as a negative and suffering God, *i.e.* incorporated as a "complete loss" of value in a given group of individuals. Universal essence has become concrete in the empirical form of the proletariat. Or, conversely, a set of empirical features and events (*e.g.* the working class of the nineteenth century and its acts of labor) are identified as mythopoetic representatives of the social soul in a state of absolute negation. Such an identification, which is one of symbolism, imparts to the empirical group a qualitatively new causal power, namely a mythopoetic efficacy. A revolutionary act in the empirical order becomes a poetic act of creating a socioempirical embodiment of absolute value, *i.e.* a social poem. In other words, a dramatic causality is thereby introduced into the otherwise mechanistically regulated process of material events. The real thereby becomes soteriological, *i.e.* strives toward thought.

It must be stressed that the nexus between the limited group and the universal soul is one of representation, of symbolization. Only when a class is physically negated to the point that it is spiritually and hence unqualifiedly insulted, does the class become a representative of universality. The notions of "unqualified" and "wrong" are essentially religious and symbolic concepts. No empirical act of oppression—since all empirical acts are finite and hence "qualified"—can be absolute. But if the "essence" of the one who suffers is absolute, *i.e.* contains the unqualified, then that essence becomes "insulted" or wronged to an "unqualified" degree if the act of oppression is not deserved. If a class is totally innocent, and if its physical existence is threatened with total negation, then its claims to be everything—the contents of its dignity—are obviously wronged. A similarity, an analogy, or a sympathy arises between the existence of the limited class and the exigencies of the universal social self. This similarity or representative nexus between material reality and ideality is simultaneously a causal link. Marx borders on using what James G. Frazer has called "sympathetic magic" or "homeopathic magic"; that is to say a causal connection is generated between two entities because of their similarity.[25] The very symbolic function of the proletariat quite magically imparts the causal efficacy of ideality to its material activity. As Mircea Eliade has written, "A symbol always reveals the basic oneness of several zones of the real . . . by transforming things into *something other* than what they appear to profane experience to be."[26] Because of its symbolic function, the proletariat ceases on the profane level to be a mere empirical class and is transformed into something else, namely the whole of sacred power. "A thing that becomes a symbol tends to become one with the Whole."[27] More than that: "Magico-religious experience makes it possible for man himself to be transformed into a symbol."[28] The proletariat is the real, physical symbol—the living hierophany—of the "soul of the people." Indeed, the being of the proletariat is its sym-

25. Cf. James G. Frazer, "Sympathetic Magic," reprinted in part from *The Golden Bough* in Williams A. Lesser and Evon Z. Vogt (eds.), *Reader in Comparative Religion: An Anthropological Approach* (Evanston, 1958), 247–67.
26. Eliade, *Patterns in Comparative Religion*, 452.
27. *Ibid.*
28. *Ibid.*, 455.

bol-existence and this is nothing less than magic. Charged with sympathetic energy, a class of individuals becomes the creative movement of desire, of the Promethean imperative. Nothing can stand before the magical desire of the social self. Nature and society must submit to the magical will of the soul of the people.[29]

Marx himself once seemed to have been vaguely aware that he was demanding magic in a universe structured by sympathetic attraction (and magic is only possible within such a cosmic order).[30] In a letter to Ludwig Feuerbach (August 11, 1844) Marx extolled the proletariat as the "practical element for emancipation." The French workers seem to please Marx the most. At any rate, Marx continues on to contrast the "French character" with the "German character" in a manner favorable to the French. German theorists are too inclined to verbal criticism, not to action. German thought does not seem to become the passion of action. In this connection Marx cites some French passages from the French utopian critic and Fourierist, Edouard de Pompery, as examples of what he means and comments:

> "L'*homme* est tout entier dans ses *passions.*" "Avez-vous jamais rencontré un homme qui *pensât pour penser*, qui se *ressouvint pour se ressouvenir*, qui *imaginât pour imaginer*? cela vous-est-il jamais arrivé à vous meme? . . . non, evidement non!"[31]

The main dynamic force]*Hauptmobil*] of nature as well as of society is consequently the magical [*magische*], the *passionate*, the non*reflecting attraction* and

> "tout être, homme, plante, animal ou globe a reçu une somme des forces en rapport avec sa mission dans l'ordre universel."[32]

---

29. Concerning such features of the magical self see Rony, *A History of Magic*, 142–46.

30. Concerning the sympathetic structure of a magical universe see Rony, *A History of Magic*, 29–38. Rony writes: "This rhythm of vital attraction—which sees the whole world as if it were a beating heart—seems to be the foundation of all magical practice—as the theoreticians of magic have indeed always claimed" (p. 29).

31. "Man shows himself entirely in his passions." "Have you ever met a man who thought in order to think, who remembered in order to remember, who wanted something in order to want, who imagined in order to imagine? Has that ever happened to you? . . . No, evidently not."

32. "Every being, human, plant, animal or planet has received a sum of forces in accordance with its mission within this universal order."

It follows from that:

"les *attractions* sont proportionelles aux *destinées*."[33]

(MEW, XXVII, 426)

A universe in which every distinct entity possesses an amount of power corresponding to its universal destiny is a universe whose "gravity" is sympathy or magic. Such sympathy constitutes a continuum between inanimate, animate, and human reality. All parts of the cosmos become manifestations of the one cosmic law of sympathy (attraction). Marx could not have found a more accurate designation for such a universe than magic. And the social form of magic is *passion*—the very passion that transforms the proletariat into "the practical element for emancipation" and thereby enables the proletariat to fulfill its "mission" within the universal order. Such magical passion is a direct socioeconomic descendant of the ironic passion of the Magical Idealism of German Romanticism. Irony was a magical force for romantics in the form of an all-transforming passion.

How the World Becomes Philosophical

Let us recall Marx's problem as formulated in his dissertation. How is philosophy to become worldly and how is the world to become philosophical? This double question requires a material and a formal answer. There must be a particular empirical entity whose root entails philosophical demands. This entity is the proletariat. "Just as philosophy finds its *material* weapons in the proletariat, so the proletariat finds its *intellectual* [or spiritual—*geistig*] weapons in philosophy, and as soon as the lightning of thought has thoroughly entered into the naïve soil of the people [*Volksboden*], the emancipaton of Germany into men will complete itself" (MEW, I, 391). Philosophy, with its "world-conquering and absolutely free heart," entails the absolute demand of human subjectivity to know itself as the highest divinity. This imperative is an ideal and its ideality constitutes the essence of philosophy. But this ideal cannot change empirical, material reality simply by so wishing. Only material force (or weapons)

---

33. "The attractive forces are proportional to [their] *destinies*." Marx cited Pompery's *Exposition de la science sociale, constituée par C. Fourier* (Paris, 1840), 13 and 29.

can do that. This material force is biophysically grounded in man's real being. But the real being of man contains *de potentia* the Promethean imperative. When man's physical being is threatened with real negation, so too is man's mythopoetic being totally and symbolically wronged. The opposition between the ought and is is thereby driven to its absolute limit. A dramatic, as opposed to a merely physical, tension arises. The "character mask" for this mythic tension is the proletariat. The proletariat is the union of particularlity and universality, is and ought, existence and essence in an absolute state of opposition. At this point, the spiritual-intellectual content of philosophy acquires real material efficacy and, conversely, material force gains a "soul"—the soul of mankind. The proletariat as the pneumatized class thereby becomes the real heart of philosophy. "The *head* of this emancipation is *philosophy*, its *heart* is the *proletariat*" (MEW, I, 391). The proletariat as the heart of philosophy simultaneously gains a theoretical, critical, or ironic head.

Marx has now answered his question. He has translated the ideal of Hegelianism into real terms. He has also mythologized the real! Marx had contended that philosophy cannot become real without abolishing (transcending) itself. Through the revolution of the proletariat this prophecy becomes an empirical act. "Philosophy cannot actualize itself without abolishing the proletariat and the proletariat cannot abolish itself without the actualization of philosophy" (MEW, I, 391). And lo, the day of reconciliation—the ideal and real totally reconciled—is at hand! And what better designation for this day is there than "resurrection." "When all the inner conditions have been fulfilled the *German day of resurrection will be proclaimed by the crowning of the gallic rooster*" (MEW, I, 391). Marx was referring to the French Revolution as a prophecy of the German "resurrection."[34] Once again Marx utilized mythopoetic terminology to express his longed-for redemption. The total union of sacred power and empirical existence is, indeed, a resurrection—and that is precisely the meaning of the term in Christian theology. As Eliade recalls: "Mythical drama re-

34. For comments upon the relationship of "resurrection" to Marx's thought see E. A. Olssen, "Marx and Resurrection," *Journal of the History of Ideas*, XXIX (1968), 131–40. Resurrection is the rhythm of Marx's thought.

mind[s] men that suffering is never final; that death is always followed by resurrection; that every defeat is annulled and transcended by final victory."[35]

Summary

Science is paradigmatic.[36] Marx sought to understand reality in a scientific manner, but his approach to reality rests upon the belief that the empirical realm can and must come to manifest absolute Promethean value. This commitment to Promethean mythos as the heart of philosophy meant that he had to discover the dramatic logic of mythopoetic salvation in empirical reality. As a scientist Marx analyzed humanized nature, *i.e.* social life, in conceptual terms derived from empirical observation. This universe consisted of civil society, classes, money, commodities, physical suffering, political powers, *etc.* Marx believed that he was simply enunciating the natural laws immanent to human society, but it is evident that these laws also reflect a mythopoetic core. Once a set of empirical events has been raised to the representation of mythic values, a new causal efficacy pertains to it, namely the dramatic causality of a soteriological "tale." Real causality loses its mechanistic blindness and becomes dramatically ordered. For example, on the one hand, an empirical entity, *e.g.* the proletariat, is treated as a "material force" and, on the other hand, Marx seeks to show that material force will ultimately pursue ideal goals. Thus Marx must continually be read on two levels of causality, natural causality and dramatic causality. Material causality is evident as a series of semimechanistic systems that, however, are imbedded in and ordered by the teleological rationality of the mythic whole. Thus the proletariat empirically suffers; yet empirical suffering, when it represents universality, has redemptive meaning. Marx selects, evaluates, and interprets the empirical entities of society in the light of the exigencies of his basic mythopoetic paradigm of prometheanism. The dramatic exigencies of Promethean self-salvation

---

35. Eliade, *Cosmos and History*, 101.
36. In this connection see Thomas S. Kuhn, *The Structure of Scientific Revolutions* (2nd ed.; Chicago, 1970).

become the parameters, the structural skeleton in terms of which empirical evidence is evaluated and organized.

If the proletariat is viewed functionally relative to its soteriological role in the story of salvation it appears to possess features of the child-god archetype described by Carl G. Jung.[37] Jung emphasizes that the child-god archetype is not an empirical image based upon a real model but a mythological idea symbolizing universal human needs. For example, the child-god symbolizes, among many things, an innocence, absence of evil and frustration. The child image points to the future, intends futurity, the promise of a better life. The child-god is a savior because in his naïveté he represents a psychic unity, a wholeness of personality that reconciles the centrifugal forces to which the conscious psyche is exposed. The child-god is of a special origin, often announced by virgin birth, and possesses miraculous powers. The child-god is often exposed to unusual dangers, *e.g.* is abandoned, symbolizing his separation from the evils of contemporary social existence. But he is also invincible precisely because of his divine powers. He embodies hope and certainty of renewal. It takes little imagination to recognize such features in Marx's proletariat. The proletariat is total innocence, the last born of history, and under unusual circumstances, is a total outcast, yet offers promise of a better time—redemption in the future. The proletariat possesses universal and hence divine power and this power grounds its redemptive efficacy. Most importantly the proletariat promises innocence, reconciliation, wholeness, oneness of man with himself, escape from the dangers and sufferings of contemporary society, of empirical existence per se. One is almost tempted to speculate that Marx unconsciously projected the rationality of a salvational archetype as a dramatic principle into history, society, and man and thereby came to interpret empirical entities in the terms of dramatic causality. Whatever the unconscious forces were that might have been active in Marx's abstract theorizing, it is certain that Marx had the indis-

---

37. Cf. "The Psychology of the Child-Archetype," in C. G. Jung and C. Kerenyi, *Essays on a Science of Mythology*, trans. R. F. C. Hull (New York, 1949), 95–118. The proletariat can easily be seen to be one of the hero's thousand faces. Cf. Joseph Campbell's discussion of the hero as he develops from psychology to metaphysics in *The Hero with a Thousand Faces* (2nd ed.; Princeton, 1973), 255–60.

putable dramatic genius for casting the material forces of real man within a mythic script of human salvation. Mircea Eliade has written: "An adequate analysis of the diffuse mythologies of the modern world would run into volumes: for myths and mythological images are to be found everywhere, laicized, degraded or disguised; one only needs to be able to recognize them."[38] One can readily recognise in Marx's proletariat a "mythological image," albeit one that is laicised, degraded, and disguised.

---

38. Cf. Mircea Eliade, *Myths, Dreams, and Mysteries: The Encounter Between Contemporary Faiths and Archaic Realities*, trans. Philip Moiret (New York, 1960), 33.

VI
Epilogue:
Marxism as a Vital Lie

The Problem of Paradigms

*M*arxists can find no higher praise for Marx's mature theories than to call them "scientific." Marx, it is held, rejected the position that mind is primary and sought to explain things materialistically. Rejection of his idealist past for materialism allegedly enabled him to grasp scientifically the historical development of mankind. There is, according to this position, a deep hiatus between the scientific Marx and the philosophical idealist, particularly Hegel. Herbert Marcuse has clearly presented this thesis. "The transition from Hegel to Marx is, in all respects, a transition to an essentially different order of truth, not to be interpreted in terms of philosophy. . . . Every single concept in the Marxian theory has a materially different foundation, just as the new theory has a new conceptual structure and framework that cannot be derived from the preceding theories."[1]

I deny Marcuse's thesis, as is obvious from my analysis of the proletariat. Marcuse has, in my judgment, uncritically accepted a shift in exoterics for one in esoterics. The most fundamental of Hegel's

---

1. Cf. Marcuse, *Reason and Revolution*, 258.

concepts, the *causa sui* project, informs the whole of Marx's materialism (as Garaudy has noted in different terms). To be sure, Marx ceased speaking the language of Hegelian idealism and started speaking the language of historical materialism, but he continued on to tell the same "old" mythos. I do not mean to imply that the shift in exoterics was a mere verbalism, that it had no theoretical significance. In fact, it is the reason why Marxism is alive today and Hegelianism has evaporated. Marx, and here we have the greatness of his poetic genius, reconstituted the poetics of the human condition in language acceptable to the "rational" mind of a materialistic age. As such, Marx offered a program, a dramatic plan, for critical activity, be it theoretical or practical. The telos of this program is nothing less than the erection of the mythic "Golden Age." O. V. Kuuisinen and other Soviet materialists have written in their collective exposition of Marxist fundamentals: "The ideal of communism goes back deep into history, into the very depths of the lives of millions of the working people. Dreams of this ideal can already be found in folk tales about the 'Golden Age' that were composed at the dawn of time."[2] Marxism is indeed the stuff folk tales are made of! How, then, does materialism further the pursuit of "dreams"? "Materialism is imbued with the utmost faith in the human intellect, in the power of knowledge, in man's ability to fathom all secrets of the world around him, and to create a social system based on reason and justice."[3] And what is the content of the "Golden Age"? "The supreme goal of communism is to ensure *full freedom of development of the human personality*, to create conditions for the boundless development of the individual, for the physical and spiritual perfection of man."[4] The "Golden Age" will be a time of boundless development, which is to say the limitations of empirical existence will be overcome. And who is to realize this "dream"? Man, for man possesses the cognitive power to fathom all the secrets of the universe and to transform dream into reality. As Novalis said in his *Astralis* poem: "The world becomes a dream, and dream becomes a world, / And what one be-

---

2. O. V. Kuuisinen, *et al.*, *Fundamentals of Marxism-Leninism* (Moscow, 1963), 714.
3. *Ibid.*, 25.
4. *Ibid.*, 709.

lieved, it has happened" (S, I, 319). This is the romantic version of Marx's thesis that the world must become philosophical and philosophy worldly. The Soviet writers have embraced the Promethean myth of the *causa sui* project. And what is the "scientific" guaranty that such dreams will come true? The rational answer of materialism is: *faith!*

With their faith in materialism's promise to make dream a reality, it is easy to fathom why Marxists do not consider communism to be utopian. Faith does work wonders. Marcuse himself—and let us not forget that he claims Hegelianism and Marxism are "essentially different"—speaks of total liberation. "It [liberation] has been the great, real transcending force, the '*idée neuve*,' in the first powerful rebellion against the whole of the existing society, the rebellion for the total transvaluation of value, for qualitatively different ways of life."[5] Marcuse's *idée neuve* is the old *idée fixe* of the *causa sui* project. At most it is an updating of romantic irony—that desire to annihilate all in order to re-create it.

I have spent some time with the "dreams" of Marxian materialism because they reveal an esoteric core, namely, religious and poetic longing. In contrasting Marx to Hegel Marcuse speaks of "an essentially different order of truth." I do not see any such essential difference. Marxism like Hegelianism is imbued with Promethean mythos. The essence of sacred power for both Hegel and Marx is the creative domination of objectivity, of nature. Sacred power is the technological eros.[6] Furthermore, the locus of sacred power for both is the social bond or labor between individuals, *i.e.* the "species" character of man. By transforming objectivity into a manifestation of his universal and social will, man comes to see his own creativity actualized, to see himself as a creator. The *causa sui* project is thereby realized. In the *Economic and Philosophic Manuscripts* (1844) Marx writes: "Production is [man's] species-life. By means of it nature appears as *his* work and his actuality. The object of work is therefore

5. Herbert Marcuse, *An Essay on Liberation* (Boston, 1969), 22.
6. For an excellent study of the technological form that prometheanism assumes in Hegel and Marx, also in Heidegger, see Jakob Hommes, *Krise der Freiheit: Hegel-Marx-Heidegger* (Regensburg, 1958). Hommes's study is one of the best I have read. It lacks only the reduction of technological eros to Promethean mythos.

the *objectification of man's species-life*: . . . he sees himself in a world created by himself" (E, I, 517). Elsewhere Marx writes: "The universality [*i.e.* creative power] of man appears in practice exactly in the universality which makes the whole of nature into his *inorganic* body. . . . Nature is the *inorganic* body of man" (E, I, 515–16). This is idealism, albeit expressed in anthropological and economic categories. The whole of nature—the objective manifold—loses its autonomy and is, so to speak, ingressed into man as his extended body. There is only one cosmic organism and man is its soul, its life. Insofar as the whole of nature is the body of man, it has been permeated and informed by "spiritual" power. This is nothing less than the poetization of nature. Man knows himself as the truth of things. Furthermore, man's relationship to nature is not Dionysian but Apollonian; nature is the medium in and through which man totally individualizes his species-self. In short, if the object of human labor is but an objectification of man's species-life, if man sees himself in what he makes, and if the whole of nature is his inorganic body, then man must inevitably see himself as a cosmic creator, as, in the words of "Human Pride," equal to the creator. Man's creative powers must indeed be unlimited, for they encompass nothing less than the totality of all existence. Nature or objectivity has thereby been subjectivized insofar as it has been sublated into man's body. The subjectification of objectivity is, of course, the imperative of idealism, be it romantic or Hegelian. Under the surface of scientific rationality lurks the selfsame mythos of Hegelianism. Following Eric Fromm, we can plausibly say that the ideal of Marxism is nothing less than extreme narcissism. The narcissistic psychotic, according to Fromm, conceives himself as the entire world, as both subject and object. Marx simply transforms narcissism into a collective ideal, into a social psychosis. Such are the poetics of Marxism.

There are other similarities between Marx and Hegel. The world is rational for Hegel only if it fully embodies the ideal. The reconciliation of the ideal and real, the secular and the divine, is an absolute imperative in the thought of Marx as well as of Hegel. The Promethean dream must become reality. The union of the world with spirit (or of nature with species-life) constitutes the essence of rationality for both thinkers. Rationality is not simply a consistent and systematic ordering of facts. Value is the main criterion of rationality. For Marx, if rationality is equated with goodness (salvation), and if the world is (or should be) rational, then science must quite obviously be the theoretical explanation of this equation. This can be designated the transcendental foundation of Marxian theory.[7] In short, scientific categories are not just "social and economic categories" as Marcuse claims, but essentially value or mythic categories. Social and economic categories receive their ultimate intelligibility from the mythopoetic story they must tell. As a consequence, the mechanistic explanations of science are sublated into the dramatic exigencies of Promethean mythos. And the scientific name for this drama is dialectics. Mythos and science, drama and economics are, accordingly, integrally linked in Marx's theorizing.

However, beginning around 1842 and intensifying thereafter, Marx theorizes in a socioeconomic vocabulary. Certainly by 1845 or 1846 (cf. *The German Ideology*) Marx was consciously seeking to understand the human condition in terms of socioeconomic categories. The ultimate fruition of this analysis was, of course, *Das Kapital* (the first volume printed in 1867). It is nevertheless false, in my judgment, to conclude that the mythopoetic core of Marx's thinking disappeared as he increased his economic knowledge. On the contrary, mythopoetic structures determined the theoretic meaning of the key economic concepts. Marx's genius consists in recasting mythopoetic, theological, and, indeed, even magical paradigms as socioeconomic concepts. Esoterically, Marx's economic theories retell a very "old" mythopoetic "folktale" about how the "Golden Age" is to come.

I cannot hope to substantiate my thesis in this investigation that the mature Marx's "scientific" theorizing is essentially mythopoetic. However, because my thesis is important for my evaluation of Marx's thinking, I shall seek to illustrate my contention with a rather striking quotation from the "mature" Marx. In June of 1865 Marx delivered an address to the General Council of the First International in London. This address has been posthumously published as *Value,*

7. For an interpretation of Marx's economics as a type of "transcendental philosophy" see Klaus Hartmann, *Marxens "Kapital" in transzendentalphilosophischer Sicht* (Bonn, 1968).

Price and Profit. The anonymous editor of an English translation states: "A study of this pamphlet is still the best introduction to Marx's *Capital.*"[8] In other words, the pamphlet manifests the "mature" Marx. Indeed, it contains *in nuce* Marx's economics. In one section Marx notes the curious fact that the economic system of capitalism consists of those who possess the machinery, raw material, in short, the means of production (capitalists) and those who have nothing to sell but their laboring power (workers). The nexus between the groups is the market. Marx notes in effect that division between the means of production and labor is a historical fact, meaning it has its origins in a historical development. Concerning the general outline and future direction of such a historical development Marx writes:

The investigation of this question would be an investigation of what economists call *"Previous, or Original Accumulation,"* but which should be called *Original Expropriation.* We would find that this so-called *Original Accumulation* means nothing other than a series of historical processes which result in a *Decomposition of the Original Union* existing between the worker and his means of work. Such an investigation, however, lies beyond the parameters of my present theme. As soon as the *Separation* between the man of labor and the means of labor is once established, this situation will maintain itself and reproduce itself upon a constantly growing scale, until a fundamental revolution in the mode of production overturns it again and restores the original unity in a new historical form. (MEW, XVI, 131)[9]

In economic vocabulary Marx has summarized in effect his conception of historical development. The aware reader, however, does not have to exercise his imagination in order to catch a glimpse of a neoplatonic theological model. M. H. Abrams in a book on German and British Romanticism has traced this model from Plotinus into its Christian versions and finally into the theoretical paradigms of German Idealism.[10] Concerning this model Abrams writes: "The theological design . . . is an extraordinarily complex, but nonetheless

8. Karl Marx, *Value, Price and Profit,* ed. Eleanor Marx Aveling (New York, 1969), 7.
9. The German title of the work is *Lohn, Preis und Profit.*
10. M. H. Abrams, *Natural Supernaturalism: Tradition and Revolution in Romantic Literature* (New York, 1971), 141–96.

recognizable, version of the great circle of neoplatonic Christianity, according to which the process of emanation ends its beginning, and the beginning and ending are the One."[11] In other words, Marx conceives history as triadically structured: (1) an original Oneness, (2) a decomposition of primal unity into an antinomic antithesis, and (3) a reversal of decomposition resulting in a reunion on a higher level. Marx strings out, so to speak, the economic categories of history on this mythopoetic line of oneness-duality-higher oneness. Schlegel's theory concerning the evolution of consciousness in the terms of *Ur-Ich*, opposition between subject and object, and romantic annihilation was in effect but a romantic version of this neoplatonic model. This same mythopoetic and theological model reoccurs as *the* structure of historical development for Marx! At this point I can do no more than make the assertion. Nevertheless, I contend that *every* major economic concept in Marx's *Kapital* has its source and meaning in the neoplatonic mythos of being's circuitous journey unto salvation. Marx's socioeconomic vocabulary allowed him to theorize about truly economic phenomena, while his mythopoetic paradigm enabled him to order such phenomena according to a mythopoetic structure. Marx's economic categories have accordingly a twofold reference. They refer, first of all, to empirical phenomena and, secondly, to salvational models. The proletariat, for instance, is supposed to designate an empirically identifiable group of individuals. But the economic identity of this group arises out of its mythopoetic function within the historical development of oneness-duality-higher oneness. The proletariat occurs at the moment of optimal antithesis and therefore has the soteriological task of totally reversing duality and initiating a higher unity. And the power to destroy the structure of the decompositional phase of history in order to begin the new integrational phase is, as shown in the last chapter, irony. Romanticism and economics, mythopoetics and science coalesce to create the great Marxian folktale of the Golden Age. This self-same "folktale" is also the structural heart of Marx's economic theory.

11. *Ibid.,* 179.

I have discussed the relationship between mythopoetics and rationality in Marx's theorizing for several reasons. First of all, before bringing my exposition of the romantic origins of the proletariat to a close, I wanted to summarize and explicate my thesis concerning the mythopoetic essence of Marxism. I have noted Marx's shift from idealistic esoterics to socioeconomic exoterics. But I want to communicate forcefully my thesis that a Promethean mythopoetics remains the constant model in Marx's thought. I have outlined his relationship to Romanticism and Hegelianism in some detail. My purpose has been to show that the inspiration behind the young Marx's speculations is religious. Marx, the heir to Hegelianism and Romanticism, was imbued with the need for salvation within man's empirical existence. Like all idealists, he was concerned with the problem of human finitude. The more "advanced" Marx's thought became, the less explicitly he referred to man's salvational plight in unambiguous terms. Hegel freely utilized theological terminology. For this reason it is easy to reveal the mythopoetic core of Hegelian rationality. But Marx came to speak in "materialistic" language. This language does not immediately convey a theological content; hence the poetic core of Marxism must be uncovered by patient work. An interpreter has to learn to "see through" the socioeconomic content of Marx's concepts if he is to grasp the inner dramatic causality informing and forming the empirical-material causality suggested by materialistic language. I have felt obligated to conclude my investigation of Marx by showing that, despite their scientism, Marx and Marxists do occasionally reveal the theological essence motivating their thinking. Garaudy, Marcuse, the Soviet writers, and even Marx were all seeking a "transvaluation of value," a realization of the "Golden Age."

But modern man, as Jules Monnerot has pointed out, must express his beliefs in scientific terms.[12] Since Marxists, in my judgment (and also many of their critics), are oblivious to the mythopoetic core of Marxism, I believe that my summary exposition of this fact

---

12. Cf. Monnerot, *Sociology and Psychology of Communism*, 140. Monnerot writes: "In a society where science is supreme no system of illusions can be acceptable unless it wears a scientific livery."

had to be undertaken, if for no other reason than to provoke thought. Discussions about Marxism, pro and con, are often conducted on an inadequate level of discourse. Marxism's scientific claims are accepted at their face value and then proven or refuted. But a critique of the inadequacies of Marxian economics is simply a useless exercise if the aim is to convince the Marxist of his scientific errors. Empirical evidence against the validity of Marx's thesis is of secondary importance because the Marxist's "scientific" belief is grounded in the psychological exigencies of faith—faith in the *causa sui* myth, in man's redemptive powers. For instance, Agnes Heller, a Hungarian Marxist, confesses her belief: "We swear our loyalty . . . to the invincibility of the human substance. Our hope in this invincibility is not separable from Marxism. We say 'Hope.' As long as alienation exists, as long as the alternative of the alienated society (indeed, of further alienation), in one word, as long as the alternative of the accumulation of non-values perdures, there is and remains only hope. But it is *not separable* from Marxism, since it *is inseparable from the perspective of communism, from the standpoint of the proletariat, of new materialism.* Should it turn out that our hope for the construction of value is not fulfillable, Marxism would lose its validity. As Marxists, who have made the decision for communism . . . we rely, however, upon the invincibility of the human substance."[13] Once an individual has "made a decision for" communism (simply substitute Christ for communism and Billy Graham would be happy), for hope, no empirical evidence can disprove the decision, because the decision is grounded in hope, not knowledge. In short, Marxism is first and foremost a function of hope for salvation, not of science. Marxism is gnosticism.

The real reason for the acceptance of Marxism today is the attraction of the Promethean way of redemption. Marxism has its strongest appeal because it offers a "scientifically" palatable path of redemption—a secular poetics. Marxism offers a secular redemption first; reasons follow. *Credo quia absurdum.* A proper analysis and criticism of Marxism should begin with an examination of the Prome-

13. Cf. Agnes Heller, *Hypothese über eine marxistische Theorie der Werte* (Frankfurt, 1972), 85.

thean myth itself. A critic should carry out a mythic criticism of myth. In other words, does Marxian heroism, psychologically viewed, offer a plausible myth that could, if true, answer the predicament of the human condition? I think that the answer is an unequivocal no. Ernest Becker, who at one time shared Marx's belief in man's unlimited power to achieve freedom, has recently shown that not only is narcissistic heroism (my terminology for the myth of human creativity) psychologically self-defeating, but that man's very attempt to do away with the evil, to conquer finitude here on earth, has been the single greatest cause of evil.[14] Marxism predictably will not and cannot enact a total reconciliation of finitude and infinitude, the real and the ideal. In the Marxist's poetic attempt to ironize the "is" through revolution he will negate and has already negated the real existence of countless millions. I would like briefly to outline why I consider the Promethean inspiration to be an inadequate myth, indeed, to be a vital lie.

Marxism and the Art of Mythopoetic Deceit

What is it that man wants with his myths, at least with the most profound ones? The Soviet authors already answered the question. Man wants the "Golden Age." A. M. Hocart, an anthropologist of considerable talents, has formulated the answer quite succinctly. According to Hocart, "myth itself confers, or helps to confer, the object of man's desire—life."[15] We should not let ourselves be lead astray by the term *life*. Life does include physical existence, the maintenance of biological being, but human life entails much more. Albert Camus, philosopher of the absurd, informs us: "The mind's deepest desire . . . is an insistence upon familiarity, an appetite for clarity. Understanding the world for man is reducing it to the human, stamping it with his seal. . . . If man realized that the universe like him can love and suffer, he would be reconciled. . . . That nostalgia for unity, that

---

14. Cf. Ernest Becker, *Escape from Evil* (New York, 1975). See particularly Chapters 7 and 8, "The Basic Dynamic of Human Evil" and "The Nature of Social Evil," 91–127.
15. Cf. A. M. Hocart, *The Life-Giving Myth and Other Essays*, ed Lord Reglan (London, 1970), 16.

appetite for the absolute illustrates the essential impulse of the human drama."[16] Friedrich Nietzsche, the atheist's atheist, put the matter most poignantly in his "Drunken Song" towards the end of *Thus Spoke Zarathustra*. What does human joy want? "All joy wants eternity, / Wants deep, deep eternity." And Saint Augustine wrote in his *De libero arbitrio*: "The more you love being, the more you will yearn for eternal life." Perhaps we can sum it all up in the terms of Friedrich Schlegel. Man longs for infinite fullness of being. This is life.

I do not wish to attempt to suggest what the content of "eternal life" might be. This is the function of myth, namely to hint at the ineffable, at transcendence. For the moment I wish only to call to mind the psychological similarity between such diverse thinkers as Augustine, Camus, Nietzsche, Schlegel, and Hegel. Whatever the content of "eternal life" might be, functionally it represents sacred power and hence the triumph over suffering, death, and insignificance. The individual who has delved into the absolute has transcended his finitude, has become one with a lasting and therefore transcending ground of meaning. This linkage manifests itself in the empirico-historical flow of the individual's life by transforming his life into a mythopoetic expression.[17] Myth mediates to man an aesthetic confirmation of the meaningfulness of his particular life. In order to forestall any misunderstanding I should like to stress that I do not consider the mythopoetic to be per se false. Mythos is equivalent to the dramatic and I see no a priori grounds for excluding the dramatic from existence as myopic positivists are wont to do. On the other hand, not all myths are of equal value. Indeed, if an individual seeks existential security in too narrow a focus, he will find not psychological liberation but a constriction of his life. The artificial inflation of a small area of existence is what is psychologically known as fetishization. To fetishize is to organize the aesthetics of meaning around a too restricted theme. Because of the narrowness of the fetish, the individual develops character armor that he uses to

16. Albert Camus, *The Myth of Sisyphus and Other Essays*, trans. Justin O'Brien (New York, 1961), 13.

17. Robert Jay Lifton and Eric Olson have written penetratingly about the individual's need to "master" history by conceiving it as a vehicle of immortality. See *Living and Dying* (New York, 1975), 75–96.

defend himself against the horror and anxiety of existence. But such armor does not open him toward the truth of his condition; rather it hides it from him. The mythopoetics of the individual's character becomes thereby a vital life, *i.e.* he can only live with "hope" at the price of lying to himself.

Ernest Becker has written a fascinating and horrifying chapter entitled "Human Character as a Vital Lie" in his magnificient *Denial of Death*.[18] I do not wish to repeat in detail that which Becker has said in his incomparable manner. I only intend to focus upon his main thesis. Mankind does not empirically exist. Men do. Society does not have independent life. Individuals do. Sociality does not die, the individual does. The being of man's physical finitude is crushing and negating. Given the vastness and magnificence of nature—galaxy after galaxy—how small, fragile, and transitory is human existence in the vast reaches of time and space. The individual needs to experience a fullness of being, an absolute. But this need is always opposed by nature's eternal weapon—death and transitoriness. Man's highest hopes, his greatest cultural achievements, conceived as acts imprinted upon nature, appear one and all to be condemned to final annihilation. A contradiction exists between the infinitude of human wants and the finitude of his existence. This is the romantic antinomy. Camus has expressed succinctly the essential plight of the individual. "I can negate everything of that part of me that lives on vague nostalgias except this desire for unity, this longing to solve, this need for clarity and cohesion. . . . And these two certainties— my appetite for the absolute . . . and the impossibility of reducing the world to a rational and reasonable principle—I also know that I cannot reconcile."[19] By rationality Camus means an intelligible ordering of the universe around man's need for absolute value.

Man stands before an abyss of annihilation, of negation, and is afraid, ridden with anxiety. Mortality, be it biological or cultural, speaks to man in everything he does or perceives. This is why the body—the very vehicle of biological mortality—is the repository of so much horror and repression as psychoanalysis has revealed. In

18. Becker, *Denial of Death*, 47–66.
19. Camus, *The Myth of Sisyphus*, 38.

short, the individual from childhood to old age must experience the anxiety of losing support and certainty that all is all right. In order to defend himself from the chilling truth of his creatureliness, from the weakness of his being, the individual builds defenses that permit him to feel he controls his destiny and hence his death. The individual focuses upon something human—social role, sexuality, money, professional success, a cause, or an ideology—in short, the individual fetishizes his existence by convincing himself he is somebody, not just a whim of nature. This is the "vital lie." The individual puts on a character mask in order to hide one thing from himself, namely that he is not the self-sufficient center of his existence. The individual must do this if he is to suppress and repress the existential anxiety which would inhibit him from living.

The mythopoetic ground of Marxism is the Promethean *causa sui* project. Human self-consciousness is to be the highest divinity; man is the highest being for man; man is his own sun; nature is the inorganic body of man—these are but some of the ways Marx formulated his basic myth. The young and romantic Marx revolted against the sufferings, limitations, and destructiveness of life. And well he might. Such a revolt (or escape from evil) grounds all religious myths. But—and this is the legacy of Romanticism—Marxism demanded the experience of sacred power *fully* incarnate in empirical form. The real and the ideal must be made to coincide. Since Marx could no longer seek succor from nature, that is relate himself passively and Dionysian-like to the absolute, he had no choice but to appropriate the absolute as man's own power to annihilate evil and to re-create chaos in his own image. That which man is to perceive as death-conquering power is his own collective self. Man has the sacred power to create lasting value. The Promethean commitment connects Marx with idealism. Once Marx began to transform the Hegelian version of the *causa sui* project into purely socioeconomic terms, he had to find a limited, empirical locus of evil—a socioeconomic fetish. This fetish was and still is the capitalist. The ironic power of annihilation—the new savior—is the proletariat.

But can the revolution really usher in the total reconciliation of the ideal and real, of the social collectivity and the individual life? In the *Economic and Philosophical Manuscripts* (1844), Marx describes communism as the true resolution "of the conflict between man and nature . . . freedom and necessity, individual and species" (E, I, 536). But the ultimate conflict between man and nature is centered in the ineluctible fact of death and transitoriness. Can communism really resolve this conflict? If the ideal and real are to become indissolubly one, must not the individual become immortal? Marxists universally deny personal immortality. How then does Marx deal with death, for surely death annihilates the unity of species-life and individual being? Marx answers: "Death seems to be a harsh victory of the species over the determinate [particular] individual and to contradict their unity [oneness]; but the determinate individual is only a determinate species-being, and as such is mortal" (E, I, 539). That is the entire corpus of Marx's discussion of death, the *full* profundity of his thoughts on the matter! In my judgment, it is also a confession of the utter failure of Marx's version of the *causa sui* project. Death is indeed a harsh victory over the individual—more than that, it is not the resolution between, but the dissolution of species-life and individual existence. It reintroduces the very contradiction Marx found in Hegel's adulation of the state, *i.e.* sacred power does not coincide with the individual's *real* existence. What can the individual say to his own annihilation? He can hurl a "but" and "only" at the nature. He can say: "*But* I am *only* mortal and, well, that is that!" This is no solution but the avoidance of the problem.

What has Marx done? He has located sacred power in the social collectivity. A contradiction arises here. Duration, perdurance through time, pertains to the species, to social institutions. But consciousness belongs only to the individual. The individual *qua* his individuality is alone conscious. But it is precisely the finitude of his consciousness that is mortal. Insofar as Marx can, with so much apparent indifference, discount the particularity of the individual as merely mortal, he reduces individuality to a vehicle for the species. Marx is in effect seeking to deprive individual consciousness of any legitimacy. In other words, any individual aspirations or hopes simply do not count, having no meaning. The individual is seen then to have one transcending function, *i.e.* to be the instrument through which the species lives. But the species is not a subject, has no consciousness. This is Marxian immortality.[20] It is clear that immortality is outside the individual in the same way that the Hegelian state is outside the individual. Marx's valid objections to Hegel's deification of the state can, in my opinion, be leveled against Marx's deification of the species. For whether the species or the state be divine or not, both idealities are abstractions from the real individual and his real destruction. But it is precisely the ideology of the species that Marxism must protect, around which it must construct a vital lie. The individual must be persuaded to forget his individuality by sinking it in the allegedly sacred collectivity.

I contend that one can find ramifications of this vital lie in the thinking of many Marxists. Marxism is an ideology of immortality grounded in the *causa sui* project. Marxists must defend themselves from the untruth of this Promethean myth by cutting themselves off from the possibility of refutation, by concocting a clearly magical image of man, and by resorting to science fiction when confronted with truth. In the interest of this thesis I would like to conclude with three brief examples of the vital lie of Marxism: Georg Lukács, Leon Trotsky, and Roger Garaudy, all outstanding minds.

Theory as Vital Lie (Lukács)

Georg Lukács reveals the real subordination of truth-seeking to myth-rationalization that takes place in Marxism. In an essay entitled "What is Orthodox Marxism?" Lukács is willing to grant as a hypothesis that "recent research has disposed once and for all every one of Marx's individual theses." Nevertheless, the "orthodox" Marxist "would still be able to accept such findings without reservation and hence dismiss all of Marx's theses *in toto* without having to renounce his orthodoxy for a single moment." How can a Marxist savant remain orthodox if he has no empirical confirmation of Marx's theories? The answer: "Orthodox refers exclusively to

20. For an excellent discussion of the function of species-life in Marxism see Monnerot, *Sociology and Psychology of Communism*, 264–85.

method. It is the scientific conviction that dialectical materialism is the road to truth."[21] Karl Popper has rather laboriously shown that any "scientific" theory which, on principle, cannot be falsified by empirical evidence is a pseudo-theory, an act of faith, an assertion of subjectivity.[22] Lukács' dialectical materialism *cannot* be falsified because he is simply unwilling to accept any such empirical evidence *in toto*. It is quite impossible to "refute" Lukács in an argument because his dialectical method is, despite his verbal claims to "scientific conviction," a matter of dogmatic faith. Here is the last refuge of Marxian irony. Irony annihilates scientific evidence in order to affirm itself as scientific.

However, the most important point to ponder is why an intellectual giant like Lukács would accept a method as scientific that cannot be scientifically checked. I suggest the answer lies in the structure of the method. The method is *dialectical*. If my thesis is correct, dialectics is esoteric psychology and Apollonian myth translated into rational categories. The structural origins of dialectical materialism are not scientific but psychological and mythic. No wonder mere "objective" facts cannot disconfirm Lukács' orthodoxy. Should Lukács admit the scientific vacuity of Marxism, he would be stepping out of a salvational umbrella and casting himself into an abyss of existential absurdity. He would be faced with the "ought-is" contradiction without his theoretical character armor. Better a cognitive lie than truth with despair. Luckács' theoretical vital lie indicates why it is so important to grasp the mythopoetic faith inspiring Marxism. Marxian rationality builds upon this faith, but it does not ground it. Lukács differs from the religious believer only as he hides "belief" from himself. When the theoretical foundation of this faith is questioned it is the duty of Marxian reason to envelop the irra-

---

21. Cf. Georg Lukács, *History and Class Consciousness: Studies in Marxist Dialectics*, trans. Rodney Livingstone (Cambridge, 1971), 1.
22. Cf. Karl Popper, *The Logic of Scientific Discovery* (New York, 1965), 27–111. Popper emphatically writes: "[I]t must be possible for an empirical scientific system to be refuted by experience" (p. 41). It is impossible on Lukács' terms to refute Marx's method even if his empirical theses *in toto* have been falsified. Ergo: Marx's theory is not an empirical scientific system!

tionality of faith in an aura of "scientific conviction." But a Marxist such as Lukács was first and foremost seeking "to convince" not the non-Marxist but himself. A vital lie is always self-directed.

Vital Lie as Magical Idealism (Trotsky)

In 1924 Leon Trotsky published his fiery *Literature and Revolution*. In the last chapter he attempted to outline the nature of socialist art in an emancipated society. According to Trotsky, "the liberated passions [of socialist man] will be channelized into technique, into construction which also includes art. Art then will become . . . the most perfect method of the progressive building of life in every field. . . . All forms of life . . . will vitally engross all and everybody." In short, the collective power of society will be both a technological and artistic force, indeed, the synthesis of both. The collective act of creating and the creation will constitute everybody's experience of vitality. What will be the spiritual content of this new techno-poetic creation? "The wall will fall . . . between art and nature."[23] Nature will become art and art become nature. Nature will become art because every aspect of nature will be dominated by man. In other words, nature will become the poetics of man's inner self, his Promethean urge to view himself as the All in all things. For instance, Trotsky claims:

The present distribution of mountains and rivers, of fields, of meadows, of steppes, of forests, and of seashores, cannot be considered final. . . . Faith merely promises to move mountains; but technology, which takes nothing "on faith," is actually able to cut down mountains and move them. . . . In the future this will be done in an immeasurably larger scale, according to a general industrial and artistic plan. Man will occupy himself with re-registering mountains and rivers. . . . In the end he will have rebuilt the earth, if not in his own image, at least according to his own taste. . . . Through the machine, man in Socialist society will command nature in its entirety. . . . He will point out places for mountains and for passes. He will change the

23. Cf. Leon Trotsky, *Literature and Revolution*, trans. Rose Strunsky (Ann Arbor, 1971), 230–31, 250.

course of rivers, and he will lay down rules for the oceans. . . . Most likely, thickets and forests and grouse and tigers will remain, but only where man commands them to remain. . . . The machine is the instrument of modern man in every field of life. . . . The passive enjoyment of nature will disappear from art. Technique will become more powerful inspiration for artistic work.[24]

Not since Jehovah brought forth the earth and heavens in six days has nature been so completely created. Trotsky replaces the infinite God of the Judeo-Christian tradition with the "endless collective creativeness"[25] of socialist man. This is technological megalomania! But at the same time it is a theoretical necessity. If the species-life is to be the carrier of immortality, then man's species-life as social power must be able to take command of all that can oppose and destroy man—namely, all of nature. There cannot be a speck of nature free from man's domination or the possibility of man's demise can never be done away with. Nature via the magic of the machine will become nothing but an extension of "the revolutionary man,"[26] of the machine-using will. All passive or Dionysian enjoyment of nature will be banished. How can Promethean man aesthetically and artistically enjoy nature as it is, as a reality beyond him, since nature as it is does not reflect the power of the machine and hence of man's technological will to power? Nature in itself is highly unpoetical, it is mere "stuff" awaiting the Promethean power of collective man. Here we have the vital lie of the Promethean complex, albeit dressed up in industrial language. Man can only feel his collective creativeness and hence his collective superiority over the destructiveness of nature when he can literally "command nature in its entirety." This is wanton and industrial narcissism. It is also idealism, in that the human self "will lay down the rules" for nature. Anything less than the total domination of nature will leave man faced with a "fate" he cannot control. By constructing a "scientific" vision of the Golden Age Trotsky is able to disguise man's limitations vis-à-vis nature, a

24. *Ibid.*, 251–53.
25. *Ibid.*, 253.
26. *Ibid.*, 229

limitation that the current ecological crisis has taught man. Nature cannot be entirely at the command of man.

But the control of "emancipated man" extends, according to Trotsky, not only over objective nature, but also over subjective nature. Trotsky writes: "[Man] will try to master first the semi-consciousness and then the sub-conscious processes in his own organism, such as breathing, the circulation of the blood, digestion, reproduction, and within necessary limits, he will try to subordinate them to the control of reason and will."[27] But this is not all. Not only will man bring his biological functions under the control of his consciousness, he will delve even deeper:

> Man will make it his purpose to master his own feelings, to raise his instincts to the heights of consciousness, to make them transparent, to extend the wires of his will into hidden recesses, and thereby to raise himself to a new plane, to create a higher social biologic type, or, if you please, a superman. . . . Man will become immeasurably stronger, wiser, and subtler; his body will become more harmonized, his movements more rhythmic, his voice more musical. The forms of life will become dynamically dramatic.[28]

This is adulterated idealism, but idealism nevertheless. Man's biological processes, his instincts, his feelings, hidden recesses of his being, in short, his physical self will be raised to "the heights of consciousness," *i.e.* put under the control of consciousness. This is nothing else but the goal of Magical Idealism. Novalis sought total control of mind over matter, will over reality. And this is what Trotsky, the archatheist, is now affirming as the content of socialist society. "The world shall be as I will it" (S, II, 554). So wrote Novalis. The world as a manifestation of the will is the essence of magic. The magician is the one who changes things by his will. Trotsky simply adds a technological "wire" to the human will and it reaches into the deepest recesses of biological being and controls it. The will extends itself outward through the "wire" of industry and controls objective nature. The result is that not only is nature poetized but man's physi-

27. *Ibid.*, 254.
28. *Ibid.*, 254–55.

cal being will become musical, rhythmic, harmonized.[29] This is romantic lyricism in an industrial form. It is also a vital lie.

There is a more ominous note in Trotsky's scientific poetry. How will man achieve self-mastery and mastery of the world? "The human species, the coagulated *homo sapiens*, will once more enter into a state of radical transformation, and in his own hands, will become an object of the most complicated methods of artificial selection and psycho-physical training."[30] Trotsky's almost humorous reference to homo sapiens as "coagulated" suggests once again the anti-individualistic tendency of Marxism. In order to achieve a new form of coagulation, socialist society (read: specific members of the new ruling class) will use artificial selection and psycho-physical training. In short, socialist society will bring forth a new biological type, a Superman. As Eric Voegelin writes: "The new man [of Marxism] is thus in fact like Nietzsche's Superman, the man who has made himself into God."[31] But there is a difference. Whereas in recent years scholars such as Walter Kaufmann have shown that Nietzsche's superman was not so much a biological type as a spiritual type, Trotsky's superman is clearly a product of biology—*i.e.* is a new species, a master race. Trotsky differs from Nazis in that he does not identify any given race existing now as the master race. The master race is the race of the future—it is a race in which the human reason and will shall command physical and biological nature. But, nevertheless, the Marxist dream of conquering the world culminates in a racist theory. Trotsky does not consider what the relationship of the "old" man will be to that of the "new" man. But judging from other writings, if the "old" man does not submit to the imperatives of "collective creativeness," Trotsky would not hesitate to use force, terror, and murder. Such are the poetic exigencies of Marxist prometheanism.

29. In this context it would be enlightening to compare Trotsky's version of the socialistic superman with Mircea Eliade's discussion of archaic man's conception of man's pristine life in paradise. When the "scientific" trappings are discarded, it becomes obvious that Trotsky has not advanced the conception of perfected man at all. Cf. Eliade, *Myths, Dreams, and Mysteries,* 23–98.
30. Cf. Trotsky, *Literature and Revolution,* 254–55.
31. Voegelin, *Wissenschaft, Politik und Gnosis,* 78.

222 Karl Marx, Romantic Irony, and the Proletariat

Vital Lie as Science Fiction (Garaudy)

According to Trotsky's image of socialist society, collective man
will eventually command nature. But what if nature were to retain
some power independent of man? In specific, science teaches that the
solar system of which the earth is a part will eventually be destroyed. Would not the impending solar doom also doom man's
command of nature and hence show that "endless collective creativeness" is quite finite and hence mortal. Roger Garaudy has faced
this problem and claims that once socialist society has been set up,
"then the infinite dialectics of history will fully unfold."[32] Garaudy
goes on to give a "scientific" explication of this claim.

In the first place, man's conquest of nature will persist. In the endless
laboratories of the triple infinity—the microscopic, the large and the complex—man has the perspective of exertions without end. . . . To master the
elements, to change climates, to achieve better controls in biology than
those our own century has achieved over inert matter—these are among the
vistas that open before us. From these researches and these discoveries in
science, we contemplate unlimited powers.[33]

Garaudy uses the language of science, but his content is theological.
The "triple infinity" of science (Garaudy's version of the Trinity)
will bestow upon man "unlimited powers." Quite literally, there
will be nothing man cannot do. Garaudy, like Trotsky, has visions
of controlling climate, biology, etc., but what appears to be scientific
is really theological and mythic. Man's "unlimited powers" will
produce eternal life. Although Garaudy does not use the term *eternal
life*, it is clear from the following lines he has that in mind. The locus
of death-conquering power is for Marxists the social collectivity.
This is what is worshipped. But will not this collectivity be annihilated in the solar cataclysm? Garaudy calmly contemplates:

The chilling thoughts of those who go so far as to touch upon the death of

32. Cf. Garaudy, *Karl Marx: The Evolution of His Thought*, 205.
33. *Ibid.*, 108.

man and the human species, envisaging, for example, the thermic death of the universe; the first advance of man into the infinite which opens the perspectives of cosmic migrations. And if the power to split the atom for now only makes the annihilation of the earth possible, might not the social uses of atomic energy, the utilization of the internal energy of matter, enable a united humanity to concentrate its powers in such a manner that it might be able to change the orbit of the earth, as has been accomplished with artificial satellites?[34]

This quotation is inexhaustible in its mythic implications. Why is the thought of the "death" of man and the human species so "chilling"? I would suggest that it destroys the Promethean myth that man has unlimited powers. Garaudy, like any other individual, needs to feel himself part of something that transcends time, destruction, and death. Instead of turning to divine energy, Garaudy turns to "internal energy." This energy is not indifferent to man; it can be used by man to further his species existence, indeed, to immortalize it. Garaudy feels comfortable in this world as long as man can tap "internal energy." But Garaudy offers no proof that this energy will be eternally kind. Indeed, science tells us this internal energy is leading to the thermic death of the universe, and hence of the human species. Here Garaudy turns science into fiction, into science fiction. Why, man could well—some day in the distant future when he has enough knowledge—transform the earth into a spaceship and fly away to another solar system when his old one dies. Presumably this flight can be indefinitely repeated. From a purely imaginative point of view, such a flight is thinkable, is possible. And that is precisely the heart of the matter. Garaudy grasps hold of a mere possibility— and that is all that it is for the forseeable future. As long as science has indefinite possibilities that cannot now be empirically falsified, Garaudy can select any one he chooses in order to avoid considering the "chilling" thought that man will be snuffed out by the universe and that therefore his species powers are not unlimited, that man is not "an untroubled god." In other words, not only is the individual mor-

34. *Ibid.*

tal, but so too the cultural vehicle of immortality. Garaudy is able to lie to himself and his readers by turning science into fiction and fiction into science. On the surface, Garaudy's attempt to answer the problem of death and insignificance with the notion of spaceship earth is ludicrous, almost stupid. But the surface stupidity manifests a deep anxiety, a fear of meaninglessness. When a thinker of the depth of Garaudy has to grasp at science fiction in order to ward off the fear of human mortality, then it is clear that his underlying ideology has miserably failed in its poetic function, namely to mediate to man a sense of existential security.

Summary

Lukács, Trotsky, and Garaudy are but a few examples of a dishonesty endemic to Marxist thinking. They all reveal a fear of truth. And this truth is nothing less than the failure of the *causa sui* project. Marxism is a poetic interpretation of reality. But because Marxism does not calm man's basic fear it has to turn its poetics into a vital lie. The believing Marxist can, indeed, live, die, and kill with mythopoetic certainty, but not with consciousness of truth. Perhaps this is the ultimate refutation of Marxism, namely that it is a "bad" aesthetics. Its poetry is not that of life and openness but that of ideological paranoia. The Marxist is able to forget the inadequacy of the human condition, to repress truth, by holding on to and hating his socioeconomic fetish—the capitalist. In order to maintain "scientific" respectability for his ideological paranoia, the Marxist must create a fictional image of man functioning as God and then construct a theoretical apparatus in order to deny any empirical disconfirmation. In the process the Marxist turns the poetics of the human condition into a vital lie. Rational argument, detente, international cooperation, all the tools used by Western politicians in dealing with communism will, in my judgment, fail to alter the dynamics of the believing communist, because none of these penetrate the mythopoetic armor of the Marxist. I have reluctantly concluded that in the long run only mythos can conquer over mythos. And mythos appears to be lacking in the West.

Appendix
Marx's Romantic Poems

POEMS OF ONENESS

Widmung An den Vater

I

Schöpfung

Ferne zog auf leichten Wellen
Unerschaff'ner Schöpfergeist,
Welten wogen, Leben quellen,
Ewigkeit sein Auge kreist.
Seiner Blicke Allbeseelend Walten
Brennt sich magischfester in Gestalten.

Räume heben, Zeiten wallen,
Betend um sein Antlitz hin,
Fluten branden, Sphären schallen,
Und die gold'nen Sterne ziehn.
Segnend winkt sein Vaterhaupt Gewährung,
Liebend zieht sich um das All Verklärung.

Leis in selbstempfund'nen Schranken
Drängt sich Ew'ges sinnend fort,
Bis die heil'gen Urgedanken
Form verhüllt und Dichtungswort.
Da ertönt's, wie fern von Donnerleiern,
Wie ein ahndungsvolles Schöpferfeiern:

"Sterne ziehn und strahlen milder,
Welten ruhn in Urbergs Last,
Meines Geistes sel'ge Bilder,
Seid vom Geiste neu erfaßt.
Wenn die Busen wogend zu euch schlagen,
Sollt ihr liebend-fromm die Deutung sagen.

Dedication to my Father

I

Creation

In the distance moved on light waves
  An uncreated creator-spirit.
Worlds billow, life gushes forth,
  His eye circles eternity.
The all-animating rule of his glances
Burns itself with more firm magic into forms.

Spaces undulate, times roll gently,
  Praying to his countenance;
Floods rage, spheres resound,
  And the golden stars move on.
With blessings his father-heart indicates approval;
Lovingly transfiguration draws itself around the All.·

Softly in self-felt limits
  The eternal throngs reflectingly on,
Until the holy primeval thoughts are
  Veiled by form and poetic word.
Then there resounds, as if afar from thunder-lyres,
Like a prescient celebration of the creator:

"Stars move and beam more mildly;
  Worlds rest in the primordial mountain's weight.
My spirit's holy images,
  You are newly embraced by the spirit.
When my heaving breasts beat for you,
You shall say the meaning with loving piety.

"Nur der Liebe seid erschlossen,
Ihr des Ew'gen ew'ger Sitz,
Wie ich mild in euch ergossen,
Schlag' aus euch mein Seelenblitz."
"Harmonie kann nur das Gleiche finden,
Seelen können nur die Seele binden."

"Aus mir brannten eure Geister,
Zu Gebilden deutungshehr,
Rückwärts kehrt ihr zu dem Meister,
Seid nun keine Bilder mehr,
Von des Menschen Liebblick hei_ umfangen,
Ihr in ihm und er in mir vergangen!"

II

Dichtung

Schöpersohnlich strömten Flammen
Rieselnd mir aus Deiner Brust,
Hochweit schlugen sie zusammen,
Und ich nährt' sie in der Brust.
Strahlend stand Dein Bild, wie Aeolsklingen
Deckt die Gluten sanft mit Liebesschwingen.

Rauschen hört' ich's, sah es blinken,
Ferne Himmel zogen hin,
Tauchten auf, hinabzusinken,
Sanken, höher aufzufliehn.
Als der inn're Kampf sich nun geschlichtet,
Blickt' ich Schmerz und Lust im Lied verdichtet.

Schmiegend an der Formen Milde,
Steht die Seele festgebannt,
Aus Dir waren sie entbrannt.
Geistig lösen sie die Liebesglieder,
Sprühn sie voll im Schöpferbusen wieder.
(MEGA, I¹, 622–23)

"Be only unlocked to love,
　　You, stars, eternal seat of the eternal,
As I mildly pour myself into you,
　　May my soul's light strike out of yourselves.
"Harmony can only find its equal,
Only souls can bind souls."

"Out of me burned your spirits;
　　To structures with sublime meaning,
You return again to the master.
　　You are no longer.
By man's look of love hotly embraced
You vanished in him and he in me."

II

Poetry

Similar to a creator flames streamed
　　Rippling to me out of your breast;
High and wide they beat together,
　　And I nourished them in my breast.
Beaming stood your image, like Aeolus-sounds,
Covers softly the fire with love's wings.

I heard rustling, I saw it gleam,
　　Distant heavens moved onward,
Rose up, to sink down,
　　Sunk down, to fly even higher.
As the inner battle now quieted itself,
I saw pain and joy condensed in song.

Nestling next to the mildness of the forms,
　　The soul stands firmly bound;
Image swelled out of me,
　　Out of you they were kindled.
They spiritually set love's limbs free,
They sparkle again fully in the Creator's breast .

Erwachen

I

Bricht dein strahlendes Auge
Entzückt und bebend,
Wie wallender Saitenton,
Der gebannt an der Lyra
Sinnend geschlummert,
Empor durch den Schleier
Urheiliger Nacht,
Dann blitzen von oben
Ewige Sterne
Liebend hinein.

II

Du versinkest bebend,
Es klopft dein Busen,
Du schaust unendliche
Ewige Welten,
Ueber Dir, unter Dir,
Unerfaßbar, unendbar,
Schwebend im Reihentanz
Rastloser Ewigkeit,
Und ein Atom
Versinkst du im Weltall.

III

Dein Erwachen
Ist unendliches Aufgehn,
Dein Aufgehn
Ewiger Fall.

IV

Schlägt Deiner Seele
Rieselnde Flamme
In die eigene Tiefe,
In den Busen zurück,
Dann taucht unabgrenzbar,
Von Geistern gehoben,

The Awakening

I

If your beaming eye breaks
Transported and trembling,
Like the undulating tone of strings,
Which, bound to the lyre,
Musingly has slumbered,
Upwards through the veil,
Of primeval night,
Then flash from above
Eternal stars
Lovingly inwards.

II

You sink tremblingly,
Your breast beats,
You view unending
Eternal worlds,
Above you, under you
Incomprehensible, unending,
Hovering in dancelike rows
Restless eternity,
And an atom
You sink in the World-All.

III

Your Awakening
Is endless rising,
Your rising,
Eternal fall.

IV

If your soul's
Rippling flame
Strikes into its own depths,
Back into its breast,
Then comes forth unbounded,
Lifted by spirits,

Getragen von süssem
Schwellendem Zauberton,
Der Seele Geheimnis
Empor aus der Seele
Dämonischem Abgrund.

V

Dein Untersinken
Ist unendliches Aufgehn,
Dein unendliches Aufgehn,
Ist mit bebenden Lippen,
Vom Aether geröteter,
Flammender, ewiger
Liebkuß der Gottheit.
(MEGA, I¹ , 639–40)

Carried by a sweet,
Swelling magical tone,
The soul's secret
Upwards out of the soul toward
Daemonic abyss.

V

Your sinking under
Is endless rising,
Your endless rising,
Is with quivering lips
Reddened by ether,
Flaming, eternal
Lovekiss of divinity.

POEMS OF ALIENATION

Zauberharfe

Ballade

Es zieht gar seltsam sein Ohr entlang
Wie Harfenlust, wie Saitenklang,
    Ruft wach den Sängermeister;
"Wie klopft die Brust so hoch, so bang,
Was schallt herüber für Gesang,
    Als klagten Stern' und Geister?"

Er rafft sich auf, er springt empor,
Streckt aus sein Haupt in Schattenflor,
    Da sieht er's golden streifen;
"Folg' Sänger, Stufen auf und ab,
Hoch aus der Luft, tief in das Grab,
    Kannst keine Saite greifen!"

Der Sänger sieht, wie' groß sich rankt,
Dem Sänger tief die Seele schwankt,
    Da hört er's voller rauschen;
Er folget nach, es zieht ihn mit,
Trepp' auf, Trepp' ab, wie Gesitesschritt,
    Muß oft die Wege tauschen.

Da hält er still, da springt ein Thor,
Und brausend stürzt Gesang hervor,
    Scheint ihn hinwegzutragen;
'ne Leier spielt in gold'ner Pracht,
Als klängen aus ihr Tag und Nacht,
    Von keinem angeschlagen.

Magic Harp

Ballad

It draws so strangely along his ears
Like the joy of harps, the sound of strings,
   It awakens the master singer;
"How my breast beats lively, so fearfully,
What kind of song echoes over this way,
   As if stars and spirits were complaining?"

He pulls himself together, he jumps up,
Sticks out his head into the shadowy blossom,
   Then he sees it roam goldenly;
"Follow, singer, up and down steps,
High out of the air, deep into the grave,
   You can grasp no string."

The singer sees how it glows greatly,
The soul of the singer reels deeply,
   Then he hears it rush more fully;
He follows after, it draws him along,
Up steps, down steps, like the gate of spirits
   He must often change paths.

Then he stops still, a door bursts open,
And a song rushes roaringly forth,
   It appears to carry him away;
A lyre plays in golden magnificence,
As if day and night were resounding out of it,
   Played by no one.

Es greift ihn an, wie Weh, wie Lust,
Es schwillt ihm hoch, es klopft die Brust,
  Nicht länger kann er's hehlen;
"Die Zyther spielt mein eigen Herz,
Das bin ich selbst, das ist mein Schmerz,
  Das hallt aus meiner Seelen."

Und trunken faßt er Ton und Griff,
's klingt hoch, wie Quell von Felsenriff,
  's klingt tief, wie Abgrundsbrausen.
Sein Blut tanzt wild, weit rauscht sein Sang,
Ihn faßt's so selten Wehmutsbang,
  Sah nie mehr Licht da draussen.
        (MEGA, 1^1, 624–25)

Sehnsucht

"Was seufzt die Brust, was glüht der Blick,
  Was brennen all' die Venen,
Als drückt' dich Nacht, als peitscht' Geschick,
  Hinab in Sturm dein Sehnen?"

" "Zeig' mir das Aug', wie Glockenklang,
  Gefaßt in Regenbogen,
Wo's strömt wie Gluth, wo perlt Gesang,
  Wo Stern' herüberwogen!

" "Mir träumt' davon, mir träumt' so schwer,
  Kannst nimmer wohl es deuten,
Mein Kopf ist hohl, mein Herz ist leer,
  Will mir ein Grab bereiten!" "

"Was träumst du her, was träumst du hin,
  Was zieht's nach fernen Landen?
Hier braust die Flut, hier wogt Gewinn,
  Hier glüht's in Liebesbanden."

" "Hier wogt es nicht, hier glüht es nicht,
  Schon seh' ich's fernher blinken,

It grasps him, like woe, like joy,
He swells up, his breast beats,
    He cannot conceal it any longer;
"My own heart plays the lyre,
That I am myself, that is my pain,
    That echoes out of my soul."

And drunken he grasps tone and grip,
It resounds high, like a spring from a craggy reef,
    It resounds deeply, like the raging abyss.
His blood dances wildly, his song rushes far,
It grasps him so strangely fearful of melancholy,
    He saw the light outside no longer.

Longing

"Why does your breast sigh, why does your look glow?
    Why do all your veins burn,
As if night were pressing, as if fate were flogging,
    Your yearning down into the storm?"

"Show me my eye, like the sound of bells,
    Held in rainbows,
Where it streams like a glow, where song is bubbling,
    Where stars passed.

"I dreamed about it, I dreamed so heavily,
    You can, indeed, never interpret it,
My head is hollow, my heart is empty,
    I want to prepare myself a grave."

"What are you dreaming here, what are you dreaming there,
    What draws the eye to distant lands?
Here the tide rages, here gain surges,
    Here it glows in bands of love."

"Here it does not surge, here it does not glow,
    I see it already flash from afar;

Mich brennt die Lust, mich blendet Licht,
Muß schier heruntersinken." "

Hoch blickt' er, bis das Aug' ersprüht,
Da zucken alle Glieder,
Die Sehnen schwelln, das Herz erglüht,
Entgeistert sinkt er nieder.

(MEGA, 1^1, 625)

Spielmann

Spielmann streicht die Geigen,
Die Lichtbraun Haare neigen,
Trägt einen Säbel an der Seit',
Trägt ein zerrissen gefaltet Kleid.

"Spielmann, Spielmann, was streichst du so sehr,
Spielmann, was blickst du so wild umher,
Was kreist sich das Blut, was springen die Wogen,
Zerreißt dir ja deinen Bogen."

" "Was geig' ich Mensch! was brausen Wellen,
Daß donnernd sie am Fels zerschellen,
Daß's Auge erblind't, daß der Busen springt,
Daß die Seele hinab zur Hölle klingt!" "

"Spielmann, zerreibst dir's Herz mit Spott,
Die Kunst, die lieh dir ein lichter Gott,
Sollst ziehn, sollst sprühn auf Klangeswellen,
Zum Sternentanz hinanzuschwellen!"

" "Was, was! Ich stech', stech' ohne Fehle,
Blutschwarz den Säbel in deine Seele,
Fort aus dem Haus, fort aus dem Blick,
Willst Kindlein spielen um dein Genick?

" "Got kennt sie nicht, Gott acht't nicht die Kunst,
Die stieß in den Kopf aus Höllendunst,
Bis das Hirn vernarrt, bis das Herz verwandelt,
Die hab' ich lebendig vom Schwarzen erhandelt!

Desire burns within me, light blinds me,
  I must almost sink under."

He looks up, until his eye sparkles,
  Then all his limbs twitch.
His sinews swell, his heart glows brightly—
  Thunderstruck he sinks down.

The Player

The player strikes his fiddle;
  His light brown hair hangs down.
He wears a saber at his side,
Wears a tattered, pleated garment.

"Player, player, how you strike so hard,
  Player, how you look around so wildly,
How your blood circulates, how the waves leap.
You'll rip your bow to pieces."

"How I fiddle, man! How the waves roar,
  So that they shatter thunderingly against the cliff,
So that my eye goes blind, my breast leaps
So that my soul resounds down to hell."

"Player, you are pulverizing your heart with scorn.
  A luminous God lent you Art;
You should draw, should flash on waves of tone,
To swell on to the dance of stars!"

"What, what! I'll stick, I'll stick without fail
  Blood-black the saber into your soul.
Away out of the house, out of view,
Do you want, child, to play for your neck?

"God knows it not, honors not art;
  It rose into my head from the mist of hell,
Until my brain goes mad, until my heart changes.
I purchased it from the Dark One!

" " Der schlägt mir den Takt, der kreidet die Zeichen,
Muß voller, toller den Todmarsch streichen,
Muß spielen dunkel, muß spielen licht,
Bis Herz durch Sait' und Bogen bricht." "

    Spielmann streicht die Geigen,
    Die lichtbraun Haare neigen,
Trägt einen Säbel an der Seit',
Trägt ein zerrissen gefaltet Kleid.
      (MEGA, 1^1, 670–71)

Lied an die Sterne

Es tanzen eure Reigen
    In Schimmer und in Strahl,
Und eure Bilder steigen,
    Und schwellen ohne Zahl.

Hier bricht die schönste Seele,
    Hier springt das vollste Herz,
Und gleich 'nem Goldjuwele
    Umfaßt es Todtesschmerz.

Es hebt zu euch die Augen,
    Mit dunkler Allgewalt,
Und will da Hoffnung saugen
    Und Ewigkeitsgehalt.

Doch ach! ihr glänzt nur immer,
    In ruh'gem Ätherschein,
Und Götter werfen nimmer
    Die Gluth in euch hinein.

Ihr seid nur Truggebilde,
    Von Strahlen flammt's Gesicht,
Doch Herzensglut und Milde,
    Und Seele habt ihr nicht.

Und euer Schein ist Höhnen.

"He strikes for me the beat, he draws the signs,
He must more fully, madly strike the march of death,
Must play darkly, must play lightly
Until the heart breaks from the bow and strings."

The player strikes the fiddle;
His light brown hair hangs down.
He wears a saber at his side,
Wears a tattered, pleated garment.

Song to the Stars

You are dancing around
    In glimmer and in rays,
And your images ascend
    And swell without number.

Here the most beautiful soul breaks,
    Here bursts the fullest heart,
And similar to a jewel set in gold,
    The pain of death encompasses it.

The heart raises its eyes to you,
    With dark all-powerfulness,
And wants to suck in hope,
    And Eternity's substance.

But, alas, you only glitter,
    In a quiet ethereal illusion;
The gods never cast
    Their glow into you.

You are only phantom visions,
    Your face flames from the rays;
Yet heart's glow and mildness
    And soul you do not have.

And your radiance is mocking,

Für Tat und Schmerz und Drang,
An euch zerschellt das Sehnen,
Und Busens Flammensang.

Wir müssen Leid ergrauen,
    Verzweiflend untergehn,
Und dann zum Hohne schauen,
    Daß Erd' und Himmel stehn.

Daß, wenn wir auch zersplittern
    'Ne Welt in uns ertrinkt,
Kein Baumstamm muß zersplittern,
    Kein Stern herunter sinkt.

Sonst lägt ihr all' begraben
    Im tiefen blauen Meer,
Würd't keine Strahlen haben,
    Und längst kein Feuer mehr.

Dann sprächt ihr stumm die Wahrheit,
    Und lögt nicht todte Pracht,
Und prangtet nicht in Klarheit,
    Und rigsum wär' es Nacht.
                (MEGA, 1^1, 529–30)

Der Wassergreis

Ballade

1

Wasser rauscht so seltsam dort,
    Kreist sich in Wellen fort,
Glaubt wohl! es fühle nicht,
Wie sich die Woge bricht,
    Kalt sei's im Herzen, kalt in dem Sinn,
    Rausche nur, rausche nur hin.

For deed and pain and urge,
On you is shattered longing,
  And the breast's song of fire.

We must turn grey from pain,
  Despairingly go under,
And then look to the mockery,
  That earth and heaven remain,

That, even if we burst,
  A world drowns in us.
No tree must split to pieces,
  No star sink under.

Otherwise you all would lie buried
  In the deep blue sea;
You would have no rays,
  And long ago no more fire.

Then you would speak silently the truth,
  And would not lie with dead splendor,
And would not shine in clarity,
  And all around would be night.

The Old Man of the Water

A Ballad

1

Water rushes so strangely there,
  Circles on its waves,
Believe well! It does not feel
As the wave breaks,
  It is cold in its heart, cold in its mind,
  Rush only, rush only onward!

2

Doch in den Wellen, im Abgrund heiß,
Sitzt gar ein alternder Greis,
Tanzt auf, tanzt ab, wenn der Mond sich zeigt,
Wenn Sternlein aus Wolken steigt.
   Springt gar seltsam und ringt gar sehr,
   Will trinken das Bächlein leer.

3

Wellen sind ja die Mörder sein,
Zehren und nagen des Alten Gebein,
Grinzt ihm eisig durch Mark und Glied,
Wenn er die Wogen so springen sieht,
   Schneid't gar ein bängliches Wehgesicht,
   Bis Sonnenglanz Mondtanz verbricht.

4

Wasser rauscht dann so seltsam dort,
Kreist sich in Wellen fort,
   Glaubt wohl, es fühle nicht,
   Wie sich die Woge bricht,
Kalt sei's im Herzen, kalt in dem Sinn,
Rausche nur, rausche nur hin.

          (MEGA, 1¹, 627)

Menschenleben

Stürmisch entfliehet
   Der Augenblick;
Was er entziehet,
   Kehrt nicht zurück.

Tod ist das Leben
   Ein ewiger Tod;
Menschenbestreben
   Beherrscht die Noth:

2

> Yet in the waves, in the abyss so hot
> Sits indeed an aging old man,
> Dances up, dances away, whenever the moon shows itself,
> Whenever a little star ascends out of the clouds,
>> He leaps very strangely and wrestles so hard,
>> Wants to drink the little stream empty.

3

> Waves are indeed his murderers,
>> They consume and gnaw the old one's bones,
> It grins at him icily through marrow and limb,
> Whenever he sees the waves thusly leap,
>> He cuts an anxious face of woe,
>> Until the sun's beaming breaks off the moon's dance.

4

> Water rushes so strangely there,
> Circles on its waves,
>> Believe indeed! It does not feel,
>> As the wave breaks,
> It is cold in its heart, cold in its mind,
> Rush only, rush only onward.

Human Life

> The moment
>> Flees stormily away;
> Whatever it takes away
>> Does not return.

> Life is death,
>> An eternal death;
> Distress dominates
>> Human striving.

Und er verhallet
    In Nichts dahin;
Und es verschallet
    Sein Thun und Glühn.

Geister verhöhnen
    Ihm seine That;
Stürmisches Sehnen,
    Und dunkler Pfad;

Ewiges Reuen
    Nach eit'ler Lust;
Ewiges Breuen
    In tiefer Brust;

Gierig Bestreben
    Und elend Ziel
Das ist sein Leben,
    Der Lüfte Spiel.

Groß es zu wähnen
    Doch niemals groß,
Selbst sich zu höhnen,
    Das ist sein Loos.
                    (MEGA, 1^1, 759–60)

Oulanem

Dritte Szene

Oulanem. Verfall'n! Die Stunde, sie ist abgelaufen,
    Die Horen stehn, der Zwergbau stürzt zusammen!
    Bald preß' ich Ewigkeit ans Herz und heule
    Der Menschheit Riesenfluch in sie hinein.
    Ha, Ewigkeit! das ist ein ew'ger Schmerz,
    Ein unaussprechlich unermeß'ner Tod!
    Schnöd' Kunstwerk, uns zum Hohn ersonnen,
    Wir Uhrwerk, blindmechanisch aufgezogen,

And it echoes ever fainter
  Into nothing;
And its doing and glowing
  Echoes away.

Spirits scorn
  Its deed;
Stormy longing,
  And dark paths;

Eternal regretting
  After vain desire;
Eternal repenting
  In the depth of the bosom;

Greedy striving
  And miserable goal
That is its life,
  The play of breezes.

To imagine it great,
  Yet never great,
To mock itself,
  That is its lot.

Oulanem

Scene 3

Ruined! The hour, it is gone,
The hours stand still. The pigmy universe collapses.
Soon I shall press Eternity to my heart and howl
Humanity's gigantic curse into it.
Ha, Eternity! That is an eternal pain,
An inexpressible, immeasurable death!
Vile work of art, device for your dismay,
We are clockwork, blind-mechanically wound up

Des Zeitenraums' Kalendernarr zu sein,
Zu sein, damit doch irgendwas geschieht,
Zerfall'n, damit doch irgendwas zerfällt!
Ein Ding mußt' sein, das für die Welten fehlt,
Des Schmerzes stumme Pein, der sie umklaustert,
Mit seiner Seele Riesenmacht in Lüfte wälzt,
Lebendig wird der Tod, trägt Strümpf und Schuhe,
Der Pflanze Leid, des Steines dumpf Vergehn,
Der Vogel, der umsonst die Töne sucht,
Zu klagen, was sein luftig Leben kränkt,
Das Alles blinder Zwist und Kampf, zu schütteln,
Sich von sich selbst, im Zank sich aufzureiben,
Das alles steht nun auf und hat zwei Beine
Und eine Brust, den Lebensfluch zu fassen!
Ha! flechten muß ich mich ans Flammenrad,
Im Kreis der Ewigkeiten Lust zu tanzen!
Gäb's ausser ihr ein Etwas, das verschlänge,
Ich spräng' hinein, müßt' ich 'ne Welt zertrümmern,
Die zwischen ihr und mir sich aufgethürmt!
Zerschelln müßt' sie am langgedehnten Fluche,
Die Arme schlüg' ich um das harte Sein,
Und mich umarmend müßt' es stumm vergehn,
Und dann hinab, versinken in dem Nichts,
Ganz untergehn, nicht sein, es wäre Leben,
Doch so gewälzt hoch auf dem Strom der Ewigkeit,
Wohnmelodie zu brausen für den Schöpfer,
Hohn auf der Stirn! Brennt ihn die Sonne weg?
Vermeß'ner Fluch in zwanggebannter Seele!
Vernichtung jauchzt der Blick in gift'gen Strahlen,
Wälzt er die plumben Welten fort, die binden?
Gebunden, ewig, bang, zersplittert, leer,
Gebunden an dem Marmorklotz des Seins,
Gebunden, ewig angebunden, ewig!
Die Welten fassen's und sie roll'n dahin,
Und heulen ihren eig'nen Totensang,
Und wir, wir Affen eines kalten Gottes,
Wir hegen noch die Natter üppig warm,
Mit toller Müh' an voller Liebesbrust,
Daß sie zur Allgestalt hinauf sich denkt,

To be the calendar-fool of time's space,
To be, so that nevertheless something happens,
Decayed, so that nevertheless something decays.
A thing had to be which was lacking for the worlds,
The mute agony of pain, which encloses them.
With his soul's giant power, whirling in the air,
Death becomes alive, wears stockings and shoes—
The plant's suffering, the stone's musty perishing,
The bird, which in vain seeks tones
To lament what hurts its airy life,
That all is blind discord and battle, shaking
Itself out of itself, wearing itself out in quarrels—
All that stands up now and has two legs
And a breast to grasp life's curse!
Ha! I must bind myself to the wheel of flame,
To dance with joy in the circle of eternity!
Were there besides joy a Something which might devour,
I would jump in, even if I had to smash a world,
Which had towered up between it and me!
It would have to shatter on the long drawn-out curse,
I would sling my arms around hard Being
And, embracing me, it must mutely perish,
And then downward, to become immersed in Nothingness,
Only to go under, not to be, it would be life,
Yet whirled along high on the storm of eternity,
To thunder the melody of woe for the creator,
Scorn on the brow! Does the sun burn it away?
Vile curse in a soul held in compulsion,
The glance exudes annihilation in poisonous rays,
Does it whirl forth the ponderous worlds which bind?
Bound, eternally, fearfully, splintered, empty,
Bound to the marble-block of Being,
Bound, eternally fastened, eternally!
The worlds grasp it and roll on,
And howl their eternal song of death,
And we, we apes of a cold God,
We harbor still the viper sumptuously warm
With insane effort upon our loving breast,
That it expands itself out to universal form

Von ihrem Gipfel aus uns anzugrinzen!
Und ewig braust die überdrüß'ge Welle,
Den Ekel zu erschöpfen, in das Ohr!
Jetzt schnell—das Los geworfen—alles fertig,
Zerstört, was Lügendichtung nur ersann,
Mit Fluch vollendet, was der Fluch begann.

(MEGA, 1¹, 660–61)

Das bleiche Mädchen

Ballade

Das Mägdlein steht da so bleich,
    So still und verschlossen,
Die Seele, engelweich,
    Ist trüb und verdrossen.

Da blitzt kein Strahl hinein,
    Da treiben die Wogen,
Da spielen Liebe und Pein,
    Die sich wechselnd betrogen.

Sie war so fromm, so mild,
    Dem Himmel ergeben,
Der Unschuld seliges Bild,
    Das Grazien weben.

Da kam ein Ritter hehr,
    Auf prunkendem Rosse,
Im Auge ein Liebemeer,
    Und Gluthgeschosse.

Das traf so tief in die Brust,
    Doch er zog von dannen,
Hinstürmend in Kriegeslust,
    Nichts mag ihn zu bannen.

Und die stille Ruhe geflohn,
    Der Himmel gesunken,

From its peak to grin out at us!
The tired waves roar eternally on
To exhaust disgust, into our ear!
Now quickly!—the lot is cast—everything ready,
Destroy, what poetry's lie devised,
Finish with a curse what a curse began.

The Pale Maiden

A Ballad

The maiden stands there so pale
   So quiet and reserved,
Her soul, angel-soft,
   Is somber and vexed.

No ray flashes therein,
   Waves urge on,
Love and agony play there,
   Which have alternatively deceived each other.

She was so pious, so mild,
   Surrendered to heaven,
Holy image of innocence,
   Which the graces weave.

Then came a knight bold,
   On a splendorous charger,
In his eyes a sea of love,
   And a glowing thrust.

It struck so deeply in her breast
   Yet he went away,
Storming away in battle's thirst,
   Nothing captivated him.

The still quietude is flown,
   Heaven has sunk;

Das Herz des Jammers Thron,
Und sehnsuchtstrunken.

Und wie es ein Abend ist,
Da wirft sie sich nieder,
Hin vor den heiligen Christ,
Und betet wieder.

Doch zwischen seine Gestalt
Ein and'rer sich dränget,
Der faßt sie mit Allgewalt,
Wie sie's Herz auch zwänget.

"Bist doch das Liebchen mein,
Und für stets mir eigen,
Dem Himmel magst du zum Schein,
Die Seele zeigen."

Da ergreift es sie graus,
Wie Eisesbeben,
Sie stürmt entsetzt hinaus,
Von Dunkel umgeben.

Sie ringt die Lilienhand,
Und bricht in Tränen:
"So ist die Brust entbrannt,
Und das Herz voll Sehnen!

"So ist der Himmel geraubt,
So bin ich verloren,
Der Geist, der an Gott geglaubt,
Ist der Hölle erkoren.

"Doch ach! er war so groß,
So gottgestaltig,
Das Auge so bodenlos,
So tief und gewaltig.

"Und hat mich nicht gesehn,
Keinen Blick mir gespendet,
Und läß mich trostlos vergehn,
Bis die Seele endet."

Her heart is the throne of sorrow,
  And drunk with longing.

And as it is evening,
  She throws herself down,
Before the holy Christ
  And prays again.

Between Christ's figure
  Another pushes itself,
He seizes her with all-powerfulness,
  However much she tries to control her heart.

"You are my darling love,
  And always you will be my own,
You may show your soul to Heaven
  For the sake of appearances."

Terror grips her,
  Like icy quivering;
She storms out horrified,
  Surrounded by darkness.

She wrings her lily-hands,
  And breaks into tears:
"Thus my breast is set afire
  And my heart full of desire!

"Thus is heaven taken from me
  Thus I am lost,
The spirit that believed in God
  Is chosen for hell.

"Yet, alas, he was so great,
  So of divine form,
His eyes so fathomless,
  So deep and powerful.

"And he never saw me,
  Never imparted to me a glance,
And lets me disconsolately perish
  Until my soul ends.

'ne andre umschlingt sein Arm,
    Und darf ihn pressen,
Und ahnt nicht meinen Harm,
    So unermessen.

"Wie gern gäb' ich Seelenheil,
    Und all mein Hoffen,
Würd' mir sein Blick zu Teil,
    Wär' sein Herz mir offen!

"Wie kalt muß der Himmel sein,
    Den er nicht durchsprühet,
Ein Land voll Leid und Pein,
    Und schmerzdurchglühet.

"Hier rauschet Welle und Flut,
    Die mögen kühlen,
Des Herzens rasende Gluth,
    Und des Busens Fühlen."

Und sie wirft sich mit Macht
    In die sprudelnden Wogen,
Und in düstere, kalte Nacht
    Wird sie fortgezogen.

Und das Herz, das so heiß empfand,
    Darf nicht weiter pochen,
Und der Blick, ein Glutenland,
    Ist stumm und gebrochen.

Und die Lippe, so süß und mild,
    Ist entfärbt und geleichet,
Und ihr schlankes Ãetherbild,
    Im Nichts entweichet.

Und es fällt kein wundes Laub
    Von den Zweigen nieder,
Die Erde, der Himmel sind taub,
    Erwecken nicht wieder.

Und die Welle rauscht ruhig fort,
    Durch Tal und Klippen,

"His arms may embrace another,
    Another may squeeze him,
And is not aware of my distress,
    So immeasurable.

"How gladly would I give my soul's salvation
    And all my hopes;
Would that his glance fall upon me,
    Were his heart open to me!

"How cold must heaven be,
    Through which he has not sparkled,
A land full of pain and agony,
    Inflamed with pain.

"Here rushes wave and tide;
    They may cool
The heart's raging glow,
    And the bosom's feeling."

And she hurls herself with force
    Into the bubbling waves,
And into the dark, cold night
    She is drawn away.

And her heart, which so hotly felt,
    May not further beat,
And her look, a land of glowing,
    Is mute and broken.

And her lips, so sweet and mild,
    Are discolored and pale,
And her slim ethereal image
    Evaporates into Nothingness.

And no withered foliage falls
    Down from the branches;
Earth, heaven are deaf.
    They do not awaken again.

And the wave rushes quietly on,
    Through valley and cliffs,

Am harten, felsigen Ort
Zerschmettern die Rippen.

Und den Ritter, hehr und groß,
'ne Buhle umschlinget,
Und von Glück und Liebesloos
Die Zither klinget!
(MEGA, 1¹ , 494–96)

On the hard, rocky place
  Her ribs smash to pieces.

And the knight, bold and great,
  Is embraced by a mistress,
And the zither resounds
  About fate and the plight of love.

POEMS OF REVOLT

Empfindungen

Nimmer kann ich ruhig treiben,
  Was die Seele stark erfaßt,
Nimmer still behaglich bleiben,
  Und ich stürme ohne Rast.

And're mögen nur sich freuen,
  Wenn's so recht zufreiden geht,
Mögen Glück wunsch sich erneuen,
  Beten nur ihr Dankgebet.

Mich umwogt ein ewig Drängen,
  Ew'ges Brausen, ew'ge Gluth,
Kann sich nicht in's Leben zwängen,
  Will nicht ziehn in glatter Fluth.

Himmel such' ich zu erfassen,
  Und die Welt in mich zu ziehn,
Und in Lieben und in Hassen
  Möcht' ich bebend weitersprühn.

Alles möcht' ich mir erringen,
  Jede schönste Göttergunst,
Und in Wissen wagend dringen,
  Und erfassen Sang und Kunst;

Welten selber stark zerstören,
  Weil ich keine schaffen kann,
Weil sie meinem Ruf nicht hören,
  Stummgekreist im Zauberbann.

Ach! die todten, stummen gaffen
  Uns're Thaten höhnend an,

Feelings

Never can I carry out in peace
    What has seized my soul so intensely,
Never remain comfortably quiet,
    And I storm without rest.

Others may enjoy themselves only,
    When everything goes quite peacefully,
May renew their congratulations,
    Praying only their thanksgivings.

An eternal urging smothered me;
    Eternal roaring, an eternal glow,
Cannot force itself into life,
    Will not move in a smooth flow.

I seek to grasp the heavens,
    And draw the world into me,
And in loving and hating
    I would like to spray sparks tremblingly.

I would like to achieve everything for myself,
    Each beautiful blessing of the gods,
And to penetrate boldly into knowledge,
    And to grasp song and art;

To destroy worlds forcefully myself,
    Because I cannot create any,
Because they do not listen to my cry,
    Having mutely circled in the enchanted spell.

Alas, the dead, mute stars gape
    With scorn at our deeds,

Wir zerfalln und unser Schaffen,
  Und sie wandeln ihre Bahn.

Doch ich möcht' ihr Loos nicht tauschen,
  Von der Fluth dahingejagt,
Ewig fort im Nichts zu rauschen,
  Pracht, die stets sich selbst beklagt.

Denn die Mauern und die Hallen,
  Alles stürzt im raschen Lauf,
Kaum sind sie im Nichts zerfallen,
  Und ein neues Reich steigt auf.

Und so schwankt es durch die Jahre,
  Von dem Nichts bis zu dem All,
Von der Wiege bis zur Bahre,
  Ew'ges Steigen, ew'ger Fall.

Und so treiben tief die Geister,
  Bis sie selbst sich aufgezehrt,
Bis sie ihren Herrn und Meister
  Selber schonungslos verheert.

Darum laßt den Kreis durcheilen,
  Den ein Gott uns herrschend zog,
Laß uns Lust und Leiden theilen,
  Wie die Schicksalswage wog.

Darum laßt uns alles wagen,
  Nimmer rasten, nimmer ruhn;
Nur nicht dumpf so gar nichts sagen,
  Und so gar nichts woll'n und thun.

Nur nicht brütend hingegangen,
  Aengstlich in dem niedern Joch,
Denn das Sehnen und Verlangen,
  Und die That, sie blieb uns doch.
        (MEGA, 1^1, 535–36)

We and our activity decay,
   And they wander in their course.

Yet I would not like to exchange their fate,
   Chased on by the floodtide,
To roar eternally onward in the void,
   Magnificence which is always complaining.

For the walls and the halls,
   Everything plunges in the swift course,
Hardly are they decayed in the void,
   And a new empire arises.

And so it reels on through the years,
   From the void up to the all,
From the cradle to the bier,
   Eternal ascension, eternal fall.

And so the spirits carry on deeply,
   Until they have consumed themselves,
Until they themselves devastated
   Their lord and master without pity.

Therefore, let us transverse the circle,
   Which God drew so commandingly for us,
Let us share joy and pain,
   As the scales of fortune sway.

Therefore, let us dare everything,
   Never rest, never cease;
Only not dankly say nothing at all,
   And want and do nothing at all.

Only not having broodingly gone on,
   Fearfully in the lower yoke,
For yearning and longing
   And deed, they remain nevertheless for us.

Sirenensang

Ballade

Die Welle rauscht gelinde,
Und spielet mit dem Winde,
    Und hüpfet hoch hinauf;
Da sieht man's beben, schweben,
Sich neigen und sich heben,
    Das ist Sirenenlauf.

Sie schlagen voll die Leier,
In hehrer Himmelsfeier,
    In süßen Melodien;
Sie wissen alle Ferne,
Die Erde und die Sterne
    In ihren Sang zu ziehn.

Er faßt so tief, so selten,
Man kann den Ton nicht schelten,
    Der Gluten weiterhaucht,
Als suchten Allgewalten,
Den Lauscher fest zu halten,
    Bis Flut ihn untertaucht.

Es scheint zu schwelln, zu spriessen,
'Ne Welt aus Wogen fliessen,
    Geheimnisvoll und hehr,
Wie wenn in Wassertiefen
Die Götter alle schliefen,
    Im dunkel blauen Meer.

Da naht auf Kahn und Wellen,
Die wonnig um ihn schwellen,
    Ein Sänger hoch und mild.
Er blickt so frei, so offen,
Wie Liebe und wie Hoffen
    Verklärt sich Sang und Bild.

Die Leier herrscht die Tiefen,
    Najaden, die da schliefen,

Siren Song

A Ballad

The wave murmurs softly
And plays with the wind,
   And leaps up high:
There one sees it tremble, hover,
Slope down and rise up.
   That is the path of the sirens.

They play the lyre perfectly,
In exalted heavenly celebration,
   In sweet melodies;
They know how to draw
All distance, earth and stars,
Into their song.

It grasps so deeply, so exquisitely,
One cannot chide the tone,
   Which breathes forth flames,
As if cosmic forms sought
To hold fast the listener,
   Until the flood submerges him.

It seems to swell and bud,
A world flowing out of waves,
   Secretly and loftily
As if in the water's depths
The gods all were sleeping
   In the dark-blue sea.

There approaches on a boat and waves
Which blissfully swell around him,
   A singer lofty and mild.
He looks so free, so open,
Like love and hope,
   Song and glance are transfigured.

The lyre rules the depths;
Naiads, which sleep there,

Sie leihn ihr trunken Ohr,
Und alle Wogen klingen
Vor seinem Spiel und Singen,
    Und tanzen hoch empor.

Und horch', da hallt's gleich Sehnen,
Gleich fernen Zaubertönen
    Von der Sirenen Sang;
Den Jüngling zu bestricken,
Die Göttlichen sich schmücken,
    In Schönheit und in Klang:

"Jüngling, schwebe und spiele,
    Herrsche das horchende Meer,
Treibt dich wohl nach hohem Ziele,
    Busen schwillt dir hehr!

"Hier, in üpp'gen Wasserhallen
    Tönt allein der Sang.
Wie die Fluthen niederfallen,
    Hebet sich der Klang;

"Tragen ihn spielend und treiben ihn weiter,
    Daß er wirbelnd flieht,
Blick verklärt sich sehnendheiter,
    Himmel niederzieht.

"Komm in unsre Geisterkränze,
    Zauber lernt dein Herz.
Horch nur auf die Wogentänze,
    Klingt wie Liebesschmerz.

"Welten sind der Fluth entstiegen,
    Geister trug das Meer,
Durfte schon die Hohen wiegen,
    Und das All war leer.

"Wie die Himmel niederschauen,
    Und der Sterne Glanz,
In die Wogen, in die blauen,
    In der Welle Tanz;

Lend their intoxicated ears,
And all waves resound
From his playing and singing
   And dance up high into the air.

And listen, there echoes like longing,
Like distant magic tones
   From the songs of the sirens;
To bedazzle the youth,
The goddesses adorn themselves
   In beauty and in sound.

"You, hover and play,
   Master the listening sea,
It drives you on indeed toward the highest goal,
   Your bosom swells elatedly!

"Here, in sumptuous water-halls
   The song alone rings.
As the flood tides fall,
   The sound rises!

"The tides bear it and drive it onward
   So that it flees swirlingly;
The view is transfigured into gay longing,
   Draws down the heavens.

"Come into our spirit's wreaths,
   Your heart shall learn magic.
Hearken only to the dance of the waves,
   It resounds like the pain of love.

"Worlds arose out of the flood,
   The sea bore spirits,
Dared to cradle the High Ones,
   And the All was void.

"As the heavens look down,
   And the beaming of the stars,
Into the waves, into the blue ones,
   Into the dance of the waves,

"Wie die Tropfen zitternd beben,
 Welten stolz umhülln,
So entsteigt der Geister Leben,
 Die die Wogen fülln.

"Treibt es dich das All zu kennen,
 Auszuglühn Gesang,
In dem Himmelsschein zu brennen,
 Rührt dich Saitenklang;

"Steige nur zu uns hernieder,
 Reich uns deine Hand,
Geistig werden deine Glieder,
 Blickst das tiefe Land."

Sie heben sich, sie steigen,
Die Locke wallt in Reigen,
 Das Haupt auf Aether ruht,
Und ihre Blicke glühen,
Und ihre Leiern sprühen
 Und brennen durch die Fluth.

Den Jüngling faßt's, wie Wähnen,
Es stürzen ihm die Tränen,
 Es klopft die volle Brust;
Er kann den Blick nicht trennen,
Er muß für sie entbrennen,
 Vergehn in heißer Lust.

Tief scheinet sein Herz zu sinnen,
Will Fassung sich gewinnen,
 Dann hebt es sich empor,
Blickt auf in stolzer Haltung,
In kühner Gottgestaltung,
 Und laut erklingt's zum Ohr:

"In euren kalten Gründen
Kann Hohes sich nicht künden,
 Da brennt kein ew'ger Gott;
Ihr prangt, mich zu bestricken,
Wollt nimmer mich beglücken,
 Und euer Sang ist Spott.

"As droplets shiveringly quiver,
   Enfold worlds proudly,
So emerges the life of spirits
   Which fill the waves.

"It drives you on to know the All,
   To burn within the song,
To burn in heaven's appearance,
   The strings' sound touches you.

"Descend down to us,
   Extend to us your hand,
Your limbs will become spiritual,
   When you see the deep land."

They rise up, they ascend,
Their locks move in their dance,
   Their heads rest upon the ether,
And their glances glow,
And their lyres bud,
   And burn through the flood.

It seizes the youth like a delusion,
Tears fall precipitously,
   His full breast beats.
He cannot tear his glance away,
He is inflamed by them,
   Perishes in hot desire.

His heart appears to brood,
It wants to gain composure,
   Then it rises up,
Looks around in a proud attitude,
In a bold godly form,
   And loudly it rings out to the sirens' ears.

"In your cold depths
Nothing that is high can make itself known,
   There burns no eternal God,
You make a show to bedazzle me,
You never want to make me happy,
   And your song is scorn.

"Es fehlt euch Busens Pochen,
Des Herzens heisses Kochen,
    Der Seele hoher Flug;
In meiner Brust, da walten,
Die Götter all' und schalten,
    Und Nimmer sinn' ich Trug.

"Mich könnt ihr nimmer fassen,
Mein Lieben nicht, mein Hassen,
    Und meine Sehnsuchtsglut;
Sie schlägt wie Blitz nach oben,
Von zarter Kraft gehoben,
    In Melodienfluth."

Und die Sirenen sinken,
Vor seinem Drohn und Blinken,
    In lichten Tränenquelln;
Es zieht sie mit von dannen,
Doch ach! die Fluten bannen,
    Und hüllen sie in Welln.

                    (MEGA, 1,¹, 586–90)

Schluß-Sonett an Jenny

Eines muß ich Dir, mein Kind, noch sagen,
    Fröhlich schließt mein Abschiedssang den Reihn,
Denn die letzten Silberwellen schlagen,
    Sich in Jenny's Hauche Klang zu leihn
So wird kühn durch Felsensprung und Ragen,
    Lauf durch Flutenfall und Hain,
Fort der Stundenlauf des Lebens schlagen,
    Zur Vollendung sich in Dir zu weihn.

Kühn gehüllt in weiten Gluthgewanden,
    Lichtverklärt das stolzegehob'ne Herz,
Herrschend losgesagt von Zwang und Banden,
Tret' ich festen Schritt's durch weite Räume,
    Schmett're vor Dein Anlitz hin den Schmerz,
Und zum Lebensbaum entsprühn die Träume!

                    (MEGA, 1¹, 680–81)

"You lack the bosom's beat
The hot brewing of the heart,
   The soul's high flight,
In my breast there
   The gods rule
And never do I sense deceit.

"You can never seize me,
Not my love, nor my hate,
   Nor my longing's glow;
It fires like lightning upward,
Raised by a tender power,
   Into the flood of melodies."

And the sirens sink,
Before his threats and glances,
   In light springs of tears;
It summons them away.
But alas! The floods banish
   And enfold them in waves.

Concluding Sonnet to Jenny

I must tell you one thing yet, my child,
   Happily my farewell song closes the dance,
For the last silver-waves beat,
   Lend themselves music in Jenny's breath.
Thusly, through the cliff's abyss and pinnacles,
   This course through cascade and grove,
Life's course of hours will beat on,
   To dedicate itself to perfection in You.

Boldly clothed in broad glowing cloaks,
   Light-transfigured the proudly lifted heart,
Dominatingly, freed from compulsion and bonds,
   I walk a firm step through wide spaces,
Smash before your countenance pain,
   And dreams flash out to the Tree of Life.

Zwei Lieder an Jenny

Gesucht

Macht' auf mich, ließ nicht länger binden;
"Wo willst du hin?" " "ne Welt zu finden!" "
"Gibts hier nicht schwanke Fluren viel,
Hier unten Wogen, droben Sternenspiel? "

" "Glaub' Thor, nicht jenseits führt mein Wallen,
Ob schlagen Fels, ob Aether hallen,
Sie binden stumm den kecken Fuß,
Zur Fessel Wird ihr Liebegruß.

" "Die Welt soll aus mir selbst entsteigen,
Zu meiner Brust, aus ihr sich neigen,
Ihr Fluthensprung mein Lebensstrom,
Mein Seelenhauch ihr Aetherdom." "

Wohl wallt' ich fern, wohl kehrt' ich wieder,
Wohl trug ich Welten auf und nieder,
Wohl sprangen Stern' und Sonne drein,
Da zuckte Blitz, sie sanken ein.

Gefunden

Was schlingt das Buschwerk Wirbeltänze,
Was walln zur Ferse Maienkränze,
Was wölbt der Himmel seinen Saal,
Was strebt zum Wolkenberg das Thal?

Rausch' ich entgegen mein Gefieder,
Verhallend schlägt's am Felsen nieder,
Vermählt sich Aug' und Sternenlicht?
Ich wälz' den Blick, er bebt, er bricht.

So rollt denn fort, ihr Lebenswogen,
Stürzt weiter, reisset ein die Bogen,
Von Freiheit golden angehaucht,
Wenn ihr in's Nichts entgeistert taucht.

Noch einmal zuckt der Blick vermessen,

Two Songs to Jenny

Sought

I got up, let myself no longer be bound;
"To where do you want to go?" "To find a world!"
  "Are there not many wavering fields here,
  Here below waves, there above the play of stars?"

"Believe, fool, my wandering does not lead beyond,
Whether rocks fall or ether sounds,
  They bind so mutely the bold foot,
  Their love's greeting becomes a chain.

"The world shall arise out of myself,
Incline itself out of itself to my breast,
  Its wellsprings are my life's flow,
  My soul's breath, their ether-dome."

I wandered far, I returned again,
I carried worlds up and down;
  Stars and sun leaped within,
  Then lightning flashed, they sank down.

Found

Why do the bushes spin whirling dances,
Why do the May-wreaths stay to heel,
  Why does the heaven arch its vault,
  Why does the valley strive to the cloudy mountain?

If I rush on toward my plumage,
Echoing it beats down against the cliff,
  Do eye and starlight wed?
  I turn about my glance, it trembles, it breaks.

So roll on, you waves of life,
Hurtle further, tear down the arches,
  Inspired by golden freedom,
  When you plunge thunderstruck, into Nothingness.

  Once again the glance jolts arrogantly,

Er blitzt, sich selig zu vergessen,
    Wo hätt'er Welten suchen solln?
Er war in dir zur Welt geschwolln.
    (MEGA, 1^1, 679–80)

Des Verzweiflenden Gebet

"Hat ein Gott mir alles hingerissen,
    Fortgewälzt in Schicksalsfluch und Joch,
Seine Welten—alles—alles missen!
    Eins blieb, die Rache blieb mir doch!

"An mir selber will ich stolz mich rächen,
    An dem Wesen, das da oben thront,
Meine Kraft sei Flickwerk nur von Schwächen,
    Und mein Gutes selbst sei unbelohnt!

"Einen Thron will ich mir auferbauen,
    Kalt und riesig soll sein Gipfel sein,
Bollwerk sei ihm übermenschlich Grauen,
    Und sein Marschall sei die düst're Pein!

"Wer hinaufschaut mit gesundem Auge,
    Kehre totenbleich und stumm zurück,
Angepackt von blindem Todteshauche,
    Grabe selbst die Grube sich sein Glück.

"Und des Höchsten Blitze sollen prallen
    Von dem hohen, eisernen Gebäu,
Bricht er meine Mauern, meine Hallen,
    Trotzend baut die Ewigkeit sie neu."
        (MEGA, 1^1, 640–41)

Lied eines Schiffers auf der See

"Ihr möget spielen, ihr möget schlagen,
    Und hüpfen um meinen Kahn,
Ihr müßt ihn zum Ziele tragen,
    Ihr seid mir untertan!

It flashes, to forget itself blissfully,
    Where should it have sought worlds?
    It had grown to be a world in You.

The Prayer of One Who Despairs

"So a God has snatched all from me,
    Rolled on into fate's curse and yoke,
His worlds lack all—all!
    One thing remained, revenge remained yet to me!

"I will avenge myself proudly on myself,
    On that being, which is enthroned above;
Let my power be a patchwork only of weaknesses
    And let my goodness itself be unrewarded!

"I will build up for myself a throne,
    Cold and gigantic shall its summit be;
As a bulwark let be my superhuman dread,
    And let dark pain be its marshall!

"Whoever looks up with a healthy eye,
    Let him return deathly pale and mute,
Siezed hold of by the blind breath of death;
    Let the pit itself dig itself its fate.

"And the highest One's lightning shall rebound
    From the high, iron edifice;
If He breaks my walls, my halls,
    Eternity defiantly will build them anew."

The Song of a Sailor at Sea

"You may play, you may beat,
    And skip about my skiff;
You must carry it to the goal,
    You are subject to me!

"Da unten ihr blauen Wogen,
  Da ruht mein Bruder klein,
Ihr habt ihn hinabgezogen,
  Und zehrt nun sein Gebein.

"Ich selber war noch ein Knabe,
  Verwegen löst er das Schiff,
Greift nach dem Ruderstabe,
  Und sank vom sandigen Riff.

"Da schwur ich tief im Herzen,
  Bei den Wellen blau und naß,
An euch zu rächen die Schmerzen,
  Euch zu peitschen ohn' Unterlaß.

"Und treulich hab' ich gehalten
  Der Seele Schwur und Wort,
Ich geiß'le euch stets, ihr Kalten,
  Bin selten am trockenen Ort.

"So oft die Tiefe erbrauset,
  Die Glocke zittert vom Turm,
Und dumpf Orkan ersauset,
  Und es rast in Wut der Sturm;

"Dann treibt's mich weg vom Bette,
  Von meinem sichern Sitz,
Von der still und warmen Stätte,
  Zu segeln in Sturm und Blitz.

"Und ich kämpfe mit Winde und Wellen,
  Und bete zu Gott, dem Herrn,
Und laß die Segel schwellen,
  Und halt' mich an sichern Stern.

"Dann sammeln sich die Kräfte,
  Voll Feuer und kühner Lust,
Und in dem Todteschäfte,
  Ertönt der Sang aus der Brust:

"Ihr möget spielen, ihr möget schlagen,
  Und hüpfen um meinen Kahn,

"There below your blue waves,
  There rests my small brother;
You have drawn him under,
  And now gnaw at his bones.

"I myself was yet a lad—
  Boldly he casts off his ship,
Grasps for the oar
  And sinks on the sand reef.

"Then I swore deeply in my heart,
  By the waves blue and wet,
To revenge the pain on you,
  To beat you without relent.

"And faithfully I've kept
  My soul's oath and word;
I lash you continually, you cold ones,
  Am seldom at a dry spot.

"So often the depths thunder,
  The ball trembles from the tower,
A disagreeable hurricane blows,
  And the storm hastens on in rage.

"Then it drives me from bed,
  From my safe seat,
From the quiet and warm abode,
  To sail in storm and lightning.

"And I fight with wind and waves,
  And pray to God, the Lord,
And let the sail swell
  And hold myself to a sure star.

"Then the powers gather
  Full of fire and bold joy,
And in death's business,
  Resounds the song out of my breast.

"You may play, you may beat,
  And skip about my skiff;

Ihr müßt ihn zum Ziele tragen,
Ihr seid mir untertan."
(MEGA, 1¹ , 542–44)

Menschenstolz
An Jenny

Als ich diese stolzen Hallen
    Schaute und der Häuser Riesenlast,
Und der Menschen stürmisch Wallen,
    Und die unruhvolle Fieberhast;

Fühlte ich der Pulse Schlagen,
    Und der Seele stolze Riesengluth,
Sollen dich die Wellen tragen,
    Hin ins Leben und in Meeresfluth?

Soll ich staunen vor den Massen,
    Die zum Himmel keck sich aufgethürmt?
Soll mich dieses Leben fassen,
    Das dem Ungefähr entgegenstürmt?

Nein! ihr armen Zwerggiganten,
    Und du kaltes steinern Ungetüm,
Schaut den Blick, den Weggewandten,
    Ihn durchglüht der Seele Ungestüm!

Er durcheilet rings die Kreise,
    Flieht durch sie mit raschem Forschersinn,
Und die Sehnsucht klingt, die heisse,
    Höhnend durch die weiten Hallen hin.

Wenn ihr alle stürzet, sinket,
    Giebt's nur eine Scherbenwelt,
Ob die kalte Pracht uns blinket,
    Ob Ruin sich dumpf entgegenstellt!

Keine Grenze ist gezogen,
    Keine harte, arme Scholle bannt,
Und wir segeln durch die Wogen,
    Und wir wallen fort in fern'res Land.

You must carry it to the goal,
    You are subject to me."

Human Pride
To Jenny

When I viewed these proud halls
    And the gigantic burden of these houses,
And man's stormy undulating,
    And the feverish haste full of unrest,

I felt the throbbing of the pulse
    And the proud giant flow of the soul.
Shall the waves bear you, my soul,
    Onward into life and into the sea's flood?

Shall I stand amazed before the masses
    Which have piled themselves up impudently to the heavens?
Shall this life take hold of me,
    Which storms toward chance?

No! You poor pigmy-giants,
    And you cold, stone monster,
See the glance, the one turned away,
    The fury of the soul glows through it!

It hastens around the circles,
    Flees through them with the quick sense of the explorer,
And longing resounds, hot,
    Mockingly through the wide halls.

If you all plunge, sink,
    There is only a world of fragments,
Although cold magnificence blinks at us,
    Although decay opposes disagreeably!

No boundary is drawn,
    No hard, poor clod stops us
And we sail through the waves,
    And we surge forth into foreign land.

Keines mag uns festzuhalten,
  Schliesset unser Hoffen ein,
Es enteilen die Gestalten,
  Und es bleibt des Busens Lust und Pein.

Diese weiten Ungeheuer
  Sind nur ängstlich aufgerafft,
Fühlen nie das Liebesfeuer,
  Das aus leerem Nichts sie schafft.

Keine Riesensäule hebet
  Aus sich selbst in eins sich siegend auf,
Dürftig Stein an Stein gewebet,
  Formen arm den bangen Schneckenlauf.

Doch die Seele fasset Alle,
  Ist nur eine hohe Riesengluth,
Selber noch in ihrem Falle,
  Reißt sie Sonnen in Vernichtungsfluth.

Aus sich selber hebt sie siegend
  Auf sich zu des Himmels Sitz,
Götter in der Tiefe wiegend,
  Und in ihrem Auge Donn'rers Blitz.

Und ihr schwindelt nicht vor Stegen,
  Wo der Gottgedanke geht,
Wagt ihn an der Brust zu pflegen,
  Eig'ne Grösse ist ihr Hochgebet.

Muß sie in sich selbst verzehren,
  In der eig'nen Grösse untergehn,
Dann tönt's, wie Vulkanengähren,
  Und Dämonen weinend um sie stehn.

Trotzend will sie unterliegen,
  Einen Thron erbaun für Riesenhohn,
Und ihr Fallen selbst ist Siegen,
  Und ihr stolz Verschmähen Heldenlohn.

Doch, wenn Wechselglut sich bindet,
  Wenn zwei Seelen ineinanderwehn,

Nothing, no land, can stop us,
   Nothing locks in our hoping;
Forms hasten away,
   And the breast's joy and pain remain.

These vast monsters
   Are only fearfully piled up together;
They never feel the fire of love,
   Which creates them out of empty nothingness.

No giant column raises itself up
   Out of itself victoriously into one,
Stone woven into stone deficiently,
   Shape poorly the snail's course.

Yet the soul embraces all;
   It is only a high giant glow.
Even still in its fall,
   It drags suns into annihilation's flood.

Out of itself it rises victoriously
   Upon itself to heaven's seat,
Rocking gods gently in its depths,
   And in its eye the flash of thunder.

And it does not grow dizzy before paths,
   Where the God-thought goes,
Dares to care for it on its breast;
   Its own greatness is its lofty prayer.

It must consume it in itself,
   Go down in its own greatness;
Then it resounds where volcanoes seethe,
   And demons weepingly stand around it.

With defiance it will succumb,
   Construct a throne for gigantic scorn,
And its falling itself is conquering
   And its proud disdaining is a hero's reward.

Yet when exchanged glow binds itself,
   When two souls flow into one another,

Eine leis der andern kündet,
   Nicht so einsam mehr durch's All zu gehn;

Hört man's laut durch Welten tönen,
   Mild wie voller Aeolsharfenklang:
Hoch im Strahl des Ewigschönen
   Glühn zusammen Wunsch und Seelendrang.

Jenny! Darf ich kühn es sagen,
   Daß die Seelen liebend wir getauscht,
Daß in eins sie glühend schlagen,
   Daß ein Strom durch ihre Wellen rauscht,

Dann werf' ich den Handschuh höhend
   Einer Welt ins breite Angesicht,
Und die Riesenzwergin stürze stöhnend,
   Meine Glut erdrückt ihr Trümmer nicht.

Götterähnlich darf ich wandeln,
   Siegreich ziehn durch ihr Ruinenreich,
Jedes Wort ist Gluth und Handeln,
   Meine Brust dem Schöpferbusen gleich.
        (MEGA, 1^1, 487–89)

One quietly announces to the other,
   To go, no longer so lonesome through the All,

One hears it loudly resound through worlds,
   Mildly as the aeolian harp's tone;
Solemnly in the ray of the eternally-beautiful,
   Wish and the soul's desire glow together.

Jenny! May I boldly say it,
   That we have lovingly exchanged souls,
That they beat glowingly as one,
   That a storm roars through their waves.

Then I'll hurl the glove scornfully
   Into the world's broad countenance,
And let the gigantic she-dwarf plunge with groans.
   Her debris will not crush my glow.

Similar to gods I dare roam,
   March triumphantly through the realm of ruins;
Every word is flame and acting
   My breast equal to the creator's bosom.

LIST OF ABBREVIATIONS FOR
WORKS FREQUENTLY CITED

Source	Abbreviation and Volume
Die deutschen Romantiker. Ed. Gerhard Stenzel. 2 vols.	*DR*, I
Salzburg / Stuttgart: Verlag "Bergland-Buch," n.d.	*DR*, II
Fichte, Johann Gottlieb. *Sämmtliche Werke.* Ed.	
J. H. Fichte. 15 vols. Berlin: Verlag von Veit und Comp.,	
1845ff.	
Band I: *Erste Abteilung. Zur theoretischen Philosophie*	*SW*, I
Band II: *Erste Abteilung. Zur theoretischen Philosophie.*	*SW*, II
Marx, Karl. *Karl Marx–Friedrich Engels Werke.* 41 vols.	
Ed. Institut für Marxismus-Leninismus beim ZK der	
SED. Berlin: Dietz Verlag, 1960ff.	
Band I: 1839 bis 1844	*MEW*, I
Band II: 1844 bis 1846	*MEW*, II
Band III: 1845 bis 1846	*MEW*, III
Band XVI: 1846 bis 1870	*MEW*, XVI
Band XXVII: Briefe	*MEW*, XXVII
Ergänzungsband: Schriften-Manuskripte-Briefe bis 1844	*E*, I
Marx, Karl. *Karl Marx–Friedrich Engels Gesamtausgabe*	
(MEGA). Ed. Günter Heyden and Anatoli Jegarow.	
Berlin: Dietz Verlag, 1975.	
Erste Abteilung: Band I	*MEGA*, I^1
Novalis. *Schriften: Die Werke Friedrich von Hardenbergs.*	
Ed. Paul Kluckhohn and Richard Samuel. 4 vols. Stutt-	
gart: W. Kohlhammer Verlag, 1960ff.	
Band I: Das Dichterische Werk	*S*, I
Hymnen an die Nacht I, 130–58	
Geistliche Lieder I, 159–82	
Heinrich von Ofterdingen I, 183–372	
Band II: Das philosophische Werk I	*S*, II
Band III: Das philosophische Werk II	*S*, III

Novalis. *Novalis Schriften*. Ed. J. Minor. 4 vols. Jena:
Eugen Diedrichs, 1923.
Schlegel, Friedrich. *Kritische Friedrich-Schlegel-Ausgabe*.
Ed. Jean-Jacques Anstett, Ernst Behler, and Hans
Eichner. 19 vols. to date. Munich / Paderborn / Wien:
Verlag Ferdinand Schöningh, 1967ff.
    Band II: Charakteristiken und Kritiken I (1796–1801)   *KA*, II
      Über Goethes Meister   II, 126–46
      Lyceums-Fragmente   II, 147–63
      Athenäums-Fragmente   II, 165–256
      Ideen II, 256–72
      Gespräch über die Poesie   II, 284–351
    Band X: Philosophie des Lebens (1827) *und Philosophische*
      Vorlesungen insbesondre über Philosophie der Sprache und
      des Wortes (1828–1829)   *KA*, X
      Philosophie der Sprache und des Wortes   X, 309–554
    Band XII: Philosophische Vorlesungen (1800–1807)   *KA*, XII
      Transzendentalphilosophie (1800–1801)   XII, 1–106
      Die Entwicklung der Philosophie in zwölf Büchern
        (1804–1805), *Bücher I–V*   XII, 107–480
    Band XIII: Philosophische Vorlesungen (1800–1807),
      Zweiter Teil   *KA*, XIII
      Die Entwicklung der Philosophie in zwölf Büchern,
        Bücher VI–XII   XIII, 3–176
      Propädeutik und Logik   XIII, 177–384
    Band XVIII: Philosophische Lehrjahre (1796–1806) *nebst*
      philosophischen Manuskripten aus den Jahren 1796–1828,
      Erster Teil   *KA*, XVIII
    Band XIX: Philosophische Lehrjahre (1796–1806),
      Zweiter Teil   *KA*, XIX

BIBLIOGRAPHY

Abrams, M. H. *Natural Supernaturalism: Tradition and Revolution in Romantic Literature*. New York: Norton and Co., 1973.

Allemann, Beda. *Ironie und Dichtung*. N.p.: Verlag Günther Neske Pfullingen, 1956.

Arendt, Dieter. *Der poetische Nihilismus in der Romantik: Studien zum Verhältnis von Dichtung und Wirklicheit in der Frühromantik*. 2 vols. Tübingen: Niemeyer Verlag, 1972.

Ash, William. *Marxism and Moral Concepts*. New York: Monthly Review Press, 1964.

Balthasar, Hans Urs von. *Prometheus: Studien zur geschichte des deutschen Idealismus*. Heidelberg: Kerle Verlag, 1947.

Becker, Ernest. *Angel in Armor: A Post-Freudian Perspective on the Nature of Man*. New York: Free Press, 1969.

———. *Escape from Evil*. New York: The Free Press, 1969.

———. *The Denial of Death*. New York: The Free Press, 1974.

———. *The Structure of Evil: An Essay on the Unification of the Science of Man*. New York: Free Press, 1968.

Behler, Ernst. "Introduction" to *Friedrich Schlegel: Dialogue on Poetry and Literary Aphorisms*. Trans. Ernst Behler and Roman Struc. University Park: Pennsylvania State University Press, 1968.

———. *Klassische Ironie, Romantische Ironie, Tragische Ironie: Zum Ursprung dieser Begriffe*. Darmstadt: Wissenschaftliche Buchgesellschaft, 1972.

Berger, Peter. *The Sacred Canopy: Elements of a Sociological Theory of Religion*. Garden City: Anchor Books, 1969.

Berger, Peter, and Thomas Luckmann. *The Social Construction of Reality: A Treatise in the Sociology of Knowledge*. Garden City: Anchor Books, 1967.

Bloch, Ernst. "Epikur und Karl Marx oder ein subjektiver Faktor im Falle der Atome," in *Über Karl Marx*. Frankfurt: Suhrkamp, 1968.

———. *Subjekt-Objekt: Erläuterungen zu Hegel*. Frankfurt: Suhrkamp, 1971.

Brazill, William J. *The Young Hegelians*. New Haven: Yale University Press, 1970.

Brinkmann, Richard. *Wirklichkeit und Illusion: Studien über Gehalt und Grenzen des Begriffs Realismus für die erzählende Dichtung des Neunzehnten Jahrhunderts*. Tübingen: Niemeyer Verlag, 1966.

Brown, Norman O. *Life Against Death: The Psychoanalytical Meaning of History*. New York: Vintage Books, 1959.

Bruford, W. H. *Germany in the Eighteenth Century: The Social Background of the Literary Revival*. Cambridge: Cambridge University Press, 1968.

Büchner, Georg. *Werke und Briefe*. 2nd ed. Ed. Fritz Bergmann. Munich: Deutscher Taschenbuch Verlag, 1967.

Butcher, S. H., trans. *Aristotle's Theory of Poetry and Fine Art with a Critical Text and Translation of the Poetics*. 4th edition. New York: Dover, 1951.

Campbell, Joseph. *The Hero with a Thousand Faces*. 2nd ed. Princeton: Princeton University Press, 1973.

Camus, Albert. *The Myth of Sisyphus and Other Essays*. Trans. Justin O'Brien. New York: Vintage Books, 1961.

Collins, James. *God in Modern Philosophy*. Chicago: Gateway, 1967.

Cornu, August. *Karl Marx: L'homme et l'oeuvre*. Paris: Libraire Felix Alcan, 1934.

Delgaauw, Bernard. *The Young Marx*. Trans. F. Schütz and M. Redfern. London: Sheed and Ward, 1967.

Demetz, Peter. *Marx, Engels und die Dichter*. Stuttgart: Deutsche Verlags-Anstalt, 1959.

Dupré, Louis. *The Philosophical Foundations of Marxism*. New York: Harcourt, Brace & World, 1966.

Eichendorff, Josef Freiherr von. *Eichendorffs Werke*. Vol. I. Ed. Richard Doetze. Leipzig and Vienna: Bibliographisches Institut, n.d.

Eliade, Mircea. *Cosmos and History: The Myth of the Eternal Return*. Trans. Willard R. Trask. New York: Harper Torchbooks, 1959.

————. *Myths, Dreams, and Mysteries: The Encounter Between Contemporary Faiths and Archaic Realities*. Trans. Philip Moiret. New York: Harper Torchbooks, 1960.

————. *Patterns in Comparative Religion*. Trans. Rosemary Sheed. New York: Meridian, 1963.

————. *The Sacred and the Profane: The Nature of Religion*. Trans. Willard R. Trask. New York: Harper and Row, 1961.

Ermatinger, Emil. *Die deutsche Lyrik seit Herder*. Bd. II. *Die Romantik*. 2nd ed. Leipzig and Berlin: B. G. Teubner, 1925.

Eucken, Rudolf. *Die Träger des deutschen Idealismus.* Berlin: Ullstein, 1915.

Fackenheim, Emil L. *The Religious Dimension of Hegel's Thought.* Boston: Beacon Press, 1967.

Fenichel, Otto. *The Psychoanalytical Theory of Neurosis.* New York: W. W. Norton, 1945.

Feuer, Lewis. "The Character and Thought of Karl Marx: The Promethean Complex and Historical Materialism," in *Marx and the Intellectuals: A Set of Post-Ideological Essays.* Garden City: Anchor Books, 1969.

Feuerbach, Ludwig. *The Essence of Christianity.* Trans. George Eliot. New York: Harper and Row, 1957.

———. *Lectures on the Essence of Religion.* Trans. Ralph Mannheim. New York: Harper and Row, 1967.

Frazer, Sir James G. "Sympathetic Magic," reprinted in part from *The Golden Bough* in *Reader in Comparative Religion: An Anthropological Approach.* Ed. William A. Lesser and Evon Z. Vogt. Evanston: Row, Peterson & Co., 1958.

Fromm, Erich. *The Art of Loving.* New York: Harper and Row, 1962.

———. *The Heart of Man: Its Genius for Good and Evil.* New York: Harper and Row, 1964.

———. *Marx's Concept of Man.* New York: Ungar, 1961.

Garaudy, Roger. *Karl Marx: The Evolution of His Thought.* Trans. Nan Aptheker. New York: International Publishers, 1967.

Gebhardt, Jürgen. *Politik und Eschatologie: Studien zur Geschichte der Hegelschen Schule in den Jahren 1830–1840.* Munich: C. H. Beck'sche Verlagsbuchhandlung, 1965.

Glicksberg, Charles I. *The Ironic Vision in Modern Literature.* The Hague: Martinus Myhoff, 1969.

Greene, Murray. *Hegel on the Soul: A Speculative Anthropology.* The Hague: Martinus Myhoff, 1972.

Grimme, A. *Von Wesen der Romantik.* Braunschweig and Berlin: Westermann, 1947.

Guthke, Karl S. "Der Mythos des Bösen in der westeuropäischen Romantik," *Colloquia Germanica,* 1 / 2 (1968), 1–36.

Hartmann, Klaus. *Marxens "Kapital" in transzendentalphilosophischer Sicht.* Bonn: Bouvier Verlag, 1968.

———. *Die Marxische Theorie: Eine philosophische Untersuchung zu den Hauptschriften.* Berlin: Walter de Gruyter & Co., 1970.

Hegel, G. W. F. *Encyclopedia of Philosophy*. Trans. Gustav E. Mueller. New York: Philosophical Library, 1959.

———. *Lectures on the History of Philosophy*. Vols. I and III. Trans. E. S. Haldane. London: Kegan Paul, 1892.

———. *Lectures on the Philosophy of Religion*. Trans. E. B. Speiers and J. Burdon Sanderson. New York: Humanities Press, 1974.

———. *The Phenomenology of Mind*. Trans. J. B. Baille. New York: Harper & Row, 1967.

———. *The Philosophy of Fine Art*. Vol. I. Trans. F. P. B. Osmaston. London: Bell and Sons, 1920.

———. *Philosophy of Mind, Being Part Three of the Encyclopedia of the Philosophical Sciences*. Trans. William Wallace. Oxford: Claredon Press, 1971.

———. *Philosophy of Right*. Trans. T. M. Knox. London and New York: Oxford University Press, 1967.

———. *Reason in History: A General Introduction to the Philosophy of History*. Trans. Robert S. Hartman. Indianapolis and New York: Bobbs-Merrill Co., 1953.

Heller, Agnes. *Hypothese über eine marxistische Theorie der Werte*. Frankfurt: Suhrkamp, 1972.

Heiss, Robert. *Der Gang des Geistes: Eine Geschichte des neuzeitlichen Denkens*. 2nd ed. Bern and Munich: Francke Verlag, 1959.

Henkel, Martin. "Was ist eigentlich romantisch," in *Festschrift für Richard Alewyn*. Ed. Benno von Wiese. Cologne: Böhlau Verlag, 1967.

Hillmann, Günther. *Marx und Hegel: Von der Spekulation zur Dialektik*. Mannheim: Europaische Verlagsanstalt, 1966.

Hillmann, H. "Schläft ein Lied in allen Dingen? Zur Bildlichkeit der deutschen Romantik," in *Deutsche Philologie*. Ed. Hugo Moser and Benno von Wiese. Berlin: Erich Schmidt Verlag, 1970.

Hocart, A. M. *The Life-Giving Myth and Other Essays*. Ed. Lord Reglan. London: Butler & Tanner, 1970.

Hof, Walter. *Pessimistisch-nihilistische Strömungen in der deutschen Literatur vom Sturm und Drang bis zum Jungen Deutschland*. Tübingen: Niemeyer Verlag, 1970.

Hommes, Jakob. *Krise der Freiheit: Hegel-Marx-Heidegger*. Regensburg: Verlag Friedrich Pustet, 1958.

Honecker, Martin. "Die Wesenszüge der deutschen Romantik in Philosophischer Sicht," in *Begriffsbestimmung der Romantik*. Ed. Helmut Prang. Darmstadt: Wissenschaftliche Buchgesellschaft, 1968.

Howard, Dick. *The Development of the Marxian Dialectic*. Carbondale: Southern Illinois University Press, 1972.

Iljin, Iwan. *Die Philosophie Hegels als kontemplative Gotteslehre*. Bern: Francke Verlag, 1946.

Johnston, William M. "Karl Marx's Verse of 1836–1837 as a Foreshadowing of His Early Philosophy," in *Journal of the History of Ideas*, XXVIII (1967), 259–68.

Jung, Carl G. "The Psychology of the Child-Archetype," in *Essays on a Science of Mythology*. Trans. R. F. C. Hull. New York: Bollingen Foundation, 1949.

Kägi, Paul. *Genesis des historischen Materialismus*. Vienna: Europa Verlag, 1965.

Kamenka, Eugene. *The Ethical Foundations of Marxism*. London: Routledge and Kegan Paul, 1962.

Kant, Immanuel. *Critique of Practical Reason*. Trans. Lewis White Black. Indianapolis and New York: Bobbs-Merrill, 1956.

Karoli, Christa. *Ideal und Krise enthusiastischen Künstlertums in der deutschen Romantik*. Bonn: Bouvier, 1968.

Kerenyi, C. *Prometheus: Archetypal Image of Human Existence*. Trans. Ralph Mannheim. New York: Bollingen Foundation, 1963.

Kierkegaard, Søren. *The Concept of Irony with Constant Reference to Socrates*. Trans. Lee M. Capel. New York: Harper & Row, 1965.

Kohlschmidt, Werner. "Nihilismus der Romantik," in *Form und Innerlichkeit: Beiträge zur Geschichte und Wirkung der deutschen Klassik und Romantik*. Bern: Francke Verlag, 1955.

Kojève, Alexandre. *Introduction to the Reading of Hegel*. Trans. Allan Bloom. New York and London: Basic Books, 1969.

Korff, H. A. *Geist der Goethezeit*. Vols. III and IV. 6th ed. Leipzig: Koehler u. Amelang, 1964.

Kronenberg, M. *Geschichte des Deutschen Idealismus*. Vol. II. Munich: Beck'sche Verlagsbuchhandlung, 1909.

Kuhn, Thomas. *The Structure of Scientific Revolutions*. 2nd ed. enlarged. Chicago: University of Chicago Press, 1970.

Kuuisinen, O. V., *et al*. *Fundamentals of Marxism-Leninism*. Moscow: Foreign Languages Pub. House, 1963.

Kux, Ernst. *Karl Marx: Die revolutionäre Konfession*. Erlenbach-Zurich and Stuttgart: Eugen Rentsch Verlag, 1967.

Lafargue, Paul. "Reminiscences of Marx," printed in Erich Fromm's *Marx's Concept of Man*. New York: Ungar, 1961.

Langer, Susanne. *Feeling and Form*. New York: Scribner's Sons, 1953.

Leeuwen, Arend van. *Critique of Heaven*. London: Lutterworth Press, 1972.

Lifschitz, Michail. *Karl Marx und die Ästhetik*. Dresden: Verlag der Kunst, n.d.

Lifton, Robert Jay, and Eric Olson. *Living and Dying*. New York: Bantam Books, 1975.

Lobkowicz, Nicolas. *Theory and Practice: History of a Concept from Aristotle to Marx*. Notre Dame: University of Notre Dame Press, 1967.

Lovejoy, Arthur O. *The Reason, the Understanding, and Time*. Baltimore: Johns Hopkins Press, 1961.

Löwith, Karl. *From Hegel to Nietzsche: The Revolution in Nineteenth-Century Thought*. Trans. David E. Green. Garden City: Anchor Books, 1967.

Lukács, Georg. *History and Class Consciousness: Studies in Marxist Dialectics*. Trans. Rodney Livingstone. Cambridge: MIT Press, 1971.

———. *Der junge Marx: Seine philosophische Entwicklung von 1840–1844*. Pfullingen: Neske, 1965.

McLellan, David. *Marx Before Marxism*. New York: Harper & Row, 1970.

Marcuse, Herbert. *An Essay on Liberation*. Boston: Beacon Press, 1969.

———. *Reason and Revolution: Hegel and the Rise of Social Theory*. Boston: Beacon Press, 1968.

Marx, Karl. *The Eighteenth Brumaire of Louis Bonaparte*. New York: International Publishers, 1963.

———. *Value, Price and Profit*. Ed. Eleanor Marx Aveling. New York: International Publishers, 1969.

———. *Karl Marx–Friedrich Engels: Collected Works*. Edited by Institute of Marxism-Leninism, Moscow. New York: International Publishers, 1975.

———. *Karl Marx-Friedrich Engels: Historisch-kritische Gesamtasugabe. Erste Abtheilung: Band I, Zweiter Halbband*. Ed. D. Rjaznov. Berlin: Marx-Engels Verlag, 1929.

Mehring, Franz. "Einleitung," in *Aus dem literarischen Nachlass von Karl Marx und Friedrich Engels 1841–1850*. Vol. I. Ed. Friedrich Mehring. 3rd ed. Stuttgart: Dietz, 1920.

———. *Karl Marx: The Story of His Life*. Trans. Edward Fitzgerald. London: George Allen and Unwin, 1956.

Meszaros, I. *Marx's Theory of Alienation*. London: Merlin Press, 1970.

Monnerot, Juleş. *Sociology and Psychology of Communism.* Trans. Jane Degras and Richard Rees. Boston: Beacon Press, 1953.

Müller, Andreas. "Die Auseinandersetzung der Romantik mit den Ideen der Revolution," in *Romantik-Forschungen.* Halle and Salle: Niemeyer, 1929.

Muthesius, Ehrenfried. *Ursprünge des modernen Krisenbewußtseins.* Munich: Beck, 1963.

Nicolaievsky, Boris, and Otto Maenchen-Helfen. *Karl Marx: Man and Fighter.* Trans. G. David and E. Mosbacker. London: Penguin, 1973.

Olssen, E. A. "Marx and Resurrection," *Journal of the History of Ideas,* XXIX (1968), 131–40.

Ostow, Mortimer, and Ben-Ami Scharfstein. *The Need to Believe: The Psychology of Religion.* New York: International Universities Press, 1969.

Payne, Robert. *Marx.* New York: Simon & Schuster, 1968.

Petersen, Julius. *Die Wesensbestimmung der deutschen Romantik.* Leipzig: Verlag Quell und Meyer, 1926.

Pöggler, Otto. *Hegels Kritik der Romantik.* Bonn: Rheinische Fr. Wilhelms-Universität, 1956.

Popitz, Heinrich. *Der entfremdete Mensch: Zeitkritik und Geschichtsphilosophie des jungen Marx.* Frankfurt: Europäische Verlagsanstalt, 1967.

Popper, Karl. *The Logic of Scientific Discovery.* New York: Harper & Row, 1965.

Prang, Helmut. *Die romantische Ironie.* Darmstadt: Wissenschaftliche Buchgesellschaft, 1972.

Prawer, S. S. *Karl Marx and World Literature.* Oxford: Clarendon Press, 1976.

Prosch, Harry. *The Genesis of Twentieth Century Philosophy: The Evolution of Thought from Copernicus to the Present.* Garden City: Anchor Books, 1966.

Raddatz, Fritz J. *Karl Marx: Eine politische Biographie.* Hamburg: Hoffmann und Campe, 1975.

Rank, Otto. *Beyond Psychology.* New York: Dover Publications, 1958.

———. *Psychology and the Soul.* Trans. William D. Turner. New York: A. S. Barnes, 1961.

Remak, Henry H. H. "A Key to West European Romanticism," *Colloquia Germanica* (1968), 1 / 2, pp. 37–46.

Ricoeur, Paul. *Prometheus Bound.* Boston: Beacon Press, 1967.

———. *The Symbolism of Evil.* Trans. Emerson Buchanan. Boston: Beacon Press, 1969.

Rodger, Gillian. "The Lyric," in *The Romantic Period in Germany*. Ed. Siegbert Prawer. New York: Schocken Books, 1970.

Rony, Jerome-Antoine. *A History of Magic*. Trans. Bernard Denvir. New York: Tower Publications, 1962.

Royce, Josiah. *Lecture on Modern Idealism*. New Haven: Yale University Press, 1964.

Ruf, Gaudenz. *Wege der Spätromantik: Dichterische Verhaltensweisen in der Krise des Lyrischen*. Bonn: Bouvier, 1969.

Runge, Philipp Otto. *Hinterlassene Schriften*. Volume I. Hamburg: Verlag von Friedrich Perthes, 1840.

Santayana, George. *The German Mind: A Philosophical Diagnosis* [originally entitled *Egotism in German Philosophy*]. New York: Thomas Y. Crowell Co., 1968.

Schacht, Richard L. "Hegel on Freedom," in *Hegel: A Collection of Critical Essays*. Ed. Alasdair MacIntyre. Garden City: Anchor Books, 1972.

Schenk, H. C. *The Mind of the European Romantics*. Garden City: Anchor Books, 1969.

Schleiermacher, Friedrich. *On Religion: Speeches to Its Cultural Despisers (1799)*. Trans. John Oman. New York: Ungar, 1955.

————. *Soliloquies*. Trans. Horace L. Friess. Chicago: Open Court, 1926.

Schiller, Friedrich. *The Works of Frederick Schiller*. Vol. IV. *Poems and Essays*. New York: Lovell Co., n.d.

Schopenhauer, Arthur. *The Will to Live: Selected Writings of Arthur Schopenhauer*. Ed. Richard Taylor. Garden City: Anchor Books, 1962.

Schwartzchild, Leopold. *Karl Marx: The Red Prussian*. New York: Grosset and Dunlap, 1947.

Simon, W. M. "The Historical and Social Background," in *The Romantic Period in Germany*. Ed. Siegbert Prawer. New York: Schoecken Books, 1970.

Smulkstys, Julius. *Karl Marx*. New York: Twayne Publishers, 1974.

Solger, K. W. F. *Vorlesungen über Aesthetik*. Ed. K. W. L. Heyse. Leipzig: n.p., 1829.

Sorokin, Pitirim A. *Social and Cultural Dynamics. Vol. IV. Basic Problems, Principles, and Methods*. New York: The Bedminster Press, 1962.

Staiger, Emil. *Grundbegriffe der Poetik*. 2nd ed. Munich: Deutscher Taschenbuch Verlag, 1972.

Strich, Fritz. *Deutsche Klassik und Romantik*. 5th ed. Bern and Munich: Francke Verlag, 1952.

Strohschneider-Kohrs, Ingrid. *Die romantische Ironie in Theorie und Gestaltung*. Tübingen: Max Niemeyer, 1960.

Sullivan, J. W. N. *The Limitations of Science.* New York: Mentor Books, 1959.

Thalmann, Marianne. *Romantiker als Poetologen.* Heidelberg: Lothar Stein Verlag, 1970.

Thier, Erich. *Das Menschenbild des jungen Marx.* 2nd ed. Göttingen: Vandenhoeck & Ruprecht, 1961.

Topitsch, Ernst. *Vom Ursprung und Ende der Metaphysik.* Munich: Deutscher Taschenbuch Verlag, 1972.

————. "Marxismus und Gnosis," in *Sozialphilosophie zwischen Ideologie und Wissenschaft.* Neuwied: Luchterhand Verlag, 1961.

————. "Seelenvorstellungen in Mythos und Metaphysik," in *Mythos, Philosophie, Politik, Zur Naturgeschichte der Illusion.* Freiburg: Rombach, 1969.

Trotsky, Leon. *Literature and Revolution.* Trans. Rose Strunsky. Ann Arbor: University of Michigan Press, 1971.

Tucker, Robert. *Philosophy and Myth in Karl Marx.* Cambridge: Cambridge University Press, 1964.

Van der Leeuw, G. *Religion in Essence and Manifestation.* Vol. I. Trans. J. E. Turner. New York: Harper & Row, 1963.

Vásquez, Adolfo Sánchez. *Art and Society: Essays in Marxist Aesthetics.* Trans. Maro Riofrancos. New York and London: Monthly Review Press, 1973.

Veit, Otto. *Die Flucht vor der Freiheit.* Frankfurt: Klostermann, 1947.

Voegelin, Eric. *Wissenschaft, Politik und Gnosis.* Munich: Kösel Verlag, 1959.

Weiss, Walter. *Enttäuschter Pantheismus: Zur Weltgestaltung der Dichtung in der Restaurationszeit.* Dornbirn: Vorarberger Verlagsantalt, 1962.

Wessell, Leonard, Jr. "Eighteenth-Century Theodicy and the Death of God in Büchner's *Dantons Tod,*" *Seminar,* VIII (1972), 198–218.

————. "Novalis' Revolutionary Religion of Death," *Studies in Romanticism,* XIV (1975), 425–52.

————. "The Antinomic Structure of Friedrich Schlegel's 'Romanticism,'" *Studies in Romanticism,* XII (1973), 648–69.

Whitehead, Alfred North. *Science and the Modern World.* New York: Mentor Books, 1960.

Wiese, Benno von. *Festschrift für Richard Alewyn.* Cologne: Bohlau Verlag, 1967.

INDEX

Abrams, M. H., 207–208

Bauer, Bruno, 168–69
Becker, Ernest, 2, 17, 86, 183, 211, 213
Behler, Ernst, 3, 15, 43
Berger, Peter, 2, 18
Brentano, Clemenz, 49
Brown, Norman, 87
Büchner, Georg, 61

Camus, Albert, 211–12, 213
Causa sui project, 85–86, 97, 104, 106, 114, 115, 120, 125, 126, 149, 150, 175, 176, 203, 214, 215, 216, 219, 224

Eliade, Mircea, 18, 94, 142, 189, 195, 199, 201
Evil: as fluidity, chaos, 85–86; creation as violent overcoming of evil, 87; Apollonian overcoming of evil, 88–89; Oedipus project as solution to evil, 85–86

Fackenheim, Emil, 124
Feuer, Lewis, 101, 184
Feuerbach, Ludwig, 175–76
Fichte, Johann, 21, 24–25, 26, 36–38, 132
Frazer, Sir James, 195
Friedrich, Casper David, 49
Fromm, Erich, 100

Garaudy, Roger: "key" to Marx's thought, 99–100, 149, 150; Marxist theory as "science fiction," 222–24
God as man, 39

Hartmann, Klaus, 151, 206
Hegel, G. W. F.: concept of philosophy as Promethean power, 108–15; Hegelian vs.

romantic philosophy, 107–108, 111–12; Marx's opposition to, 125–30, 164–66, 175 ff.; ideal vs. real, 129; Hegel's non-dialectical concept of philosophy, 127–28; philosophy as the reflection of completed movement, 127; concept of the soul, 188–89; mentioned, 3, 62, 69–70
Heller, Agnes: Marxism as a faith commitment, 210
Henkel, Martin: definition of Romanticism, 16
Hocart, A. M.: the meaning of myth, 211
Hugo, Gustav, 157–58

Irony: as dialectics, 37, 43, 44; as the romanticization of objectivity, 42; product of man's structure as a unity of finitude and infinitude, 42–43; as urge to obtain higher levels, 43; as the power of magic, 44; as the power to become a god, 45; as the dynamics of history, 45–46; as (religious) war, 47; as fluidity symbolism in Marx's poems, 70–71; as "compulsive wandering," 86; as philosophically guided praxis, 137; Schlegel's concept of, 130–38; and Marx, 146–55; Socrates as irony for Marx, 138–46; Marx's critique of Socratic irony, 143–46; as "will to murder," 179; as pathos, 179–80, 187; and magic in Marx, 195–97; as the material force (viz. the proletariat), 180–83

Jung, Carl, 200

Kant, Immanuel, 68, 184
Kerner, Justinus, 59–69, 62–63
Kierkegaard, Søren, 62
Kojève, Alexandre, 127

295